Music, Art & Politic
a history of the St Pa.
& Camden Festivals,
1954-1987

Helen Lawrence

© Camden History Society 2004
ISBN 0 904491 60 9

Joan Sutherland in Handel's *Alcina* at the 1957 St Pancras Festival

Music, Art & Politics:

a history of the St Pancras & Camden Festivals,

1954-1987

Helen Lawrence

Edited by F Peter Woodford
Designed by Ivor Kamlish

Samulnori from Korea, 1979 Festival

Performers from the London Contemporary Dance Group, 1972 Festival

Contents

	List of illustrations	6
	Introduction	7
1	Genesis (1947–1953)	8
	Notes for Chapter 1	13
2	The St Pancras years (1954–1964) from glory unto glory	14
	Notes for Chapter 2	38
3	Three into one (1965–1968) the Camden Festival emerges	39
	Notes for Chapter 3	54
4	A Festival with a Fringe on top (1969–1972)	55
	Notes for Chapter 4	74
5	Triumph over adversity (1973–1980)	75
	Notes for Chapter 5	92
6	Decline and fall (1981–1987)	95
	Notes for Chapter 6	109

Appendices

1	Operas and operettas produced at the Festivals	110
2	Opera casts, companies and costs	111
3	Musicians and dancers performing in the Festivals	119
4	Jazz, folk music and pop	122
5	Drama groups, plays, actors, poets and writers	124
6	Exhibitions and lectures	125
7	Annual gross and net expenditure on the Festival	126
	Index	127

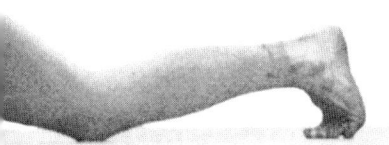

Illustrations

Unless otherwise noted in the caption to an illustration, the source was the Camden Local Studies and Archives Centre, whose help is gratefully acknowledged.

Chapter 1
Krishna Menon	8
Leonard Marcus, "Mr Festival"	8

Chapter 2
St Pancras Arts Festival programme 1954	14
Winners of first Drama Festival	14
Glenda Jackson as Eliza Dolittle in 1956	17
Charles Farncombe (Handel Opera Society)	18
Joan Sutherland as *Alcina* (1957 Festival)	19
April Cantelo, Monica Sinclair in *Theodora* (1958 Festival) (Handel Opera Society)	21
Blacher's *The Tide*, 1960 (*Opera*)	25
Marcello Cortis, Lauri Sarti in Haydn's *Il Mondo della Luna*, 1960 (*Opera*)	26
Festival brochure design, early 1960s	27
Verdi's *Un Giorno di Regno*, 1961	28
Pauline Tinsley in Verdi's *I Masnadieri*, 1962 (*Opera*)	30
Heather Harper, Johanna Peters in Arne's *Artaxerses*, 1962	30
Verdi's *Ernani*, 1963	32
Finchley Children's Music Group in *Noyes Fludde*, 1963	33
First British performance of Verdi's *Aroldo*, 1964	34
Gluck's *Iphigenia in Aulis*, 1964	35
Haydn's *L'Infedeltà Delusa*, 1964	35
Il Turco in Italia (Rossini) in 1965	36
Conductor and composer Joseph Horovitz	37
John Williams (Festivals 1965-1979)	37

Chapter 3
Logo of Music and Arts (Hampstead)	40
Heather Harper (1955 et seq)	44
John Dankworth and Cleo Laine, 1966 et seq.	44
Christopher Bowers-Broadbent, organ recitals 1966-1987	44
Henze's *The End of a World* (1954), 1966 Festival	45
Logos of the St Pancras and Camden Festivals	46
Cartoon on Finnish theme, 1967	47
Paulo Silveri in *Marino Faliero*, 1967	48
Massenet's *Sapho*, 1967	48
Maconchy's *The Sofa*, 1967	49

Chapter 4
'Advert' for first Fringe Festival, 1969	57
Fringe brochure, 1969	58
Contemporary Dance Trust, 1972	59
Kiri te Kanawa in *La Donna del Lago*, 1969	60
Queue for pop concert, 1970	64
Ballet Rambert in *Opus 5* (1970) (Rambert Dance Company Archive)	65
Valerie Masterson in Rossini's *Tancredi*, 1971	69
Logo of Music and Arts in Camden	71
Festival brochure 1972	71
Design for Delius's *Koanga* (1971)	72
Donizetti's comic opera *Le Convenienze Teatrali*, 1972	73

Chapter 5
Sandra Browne as Man Friday (1973)	77
Helen Lawrence, Francis Egerton in Storace's *The Comedy of Errors*, 1974	78
Christian du Plessis, Margareta Elkins in Donizetti's *Torquato Tasso*, 1974	79
Janet Price, Bonaventura Bottone in Meyerbeer's *L'Etoile du Nord*, 1975	80
Donizetti's *Il Castello di Kenilworth*, 1977	82
Costume design, *Francesca di Foix* (Donizetti) 1982	82
Cimarosa's *Gli Orazi ed I Curiazi*, 1977	83
Stravinsky's *Mavra*, 1979	84
Costume design for Wolf-Ferrari's *School for Fathers*, 1983	84
The Nereid Monument, backdrop for *Oedipus Rex* in 1983	85
Jazz musicians Dexter Gordon, Gil Evans, Johnny Griffin,	86
Ian Carr, Trevor Watts	86
Art Ensemble of Chicago (1979 Festival)	86
Keith Tippett, founder of Ark (1977 Festival)	87
Los Awatinas from Bolivia (1979 Festival)	88
Samulnori from Korea, 1979	88
Tabla player, 1983	89
Morris dancers (1984 Festival)	89
Conductors Brian Wright, Julian Williamson, Martindale Sidwell	90
Milein Cosman's drawing of Stravinsky in 1982 exhibition	91
Wally Fawkes, aka "Trogview"	92

Chapter 6
Inside and outside the Shaw Theatre in 1971	93
Elisabeth Schwarzkopf in the 1972 Festival brochure	95
Calman cartoon, 1986	101
Art Blakey (1986 Festival)	103
Calman cartoon on front of 1986 Festival brochure	104
Designs for *Silverlake* (1987)	105
Ornette Coleman, Charlie Haden, Carla Bley (1987 Festival)	107

Introduction

I was surprised, when preparing a recital of music connected with Camden some years ago, to find that there was no history of the Camden Festival (the St Pancras Festival until 1965) other than a brief entry in Grove's Dictionary of Music. I resolved that as soon as time permitted I would try to provide one.

This remarkable celebration of the arts, which gave encouragement to generations of performers and creative artists, some of them now international stars, is fondly remembered by many and deserves to be recorded. I am grateful to the Camden History Society for agreeing to publish this account and particularly to Peter Woodford, editor of the Society's publications, for his perceptive work in preparing the book for publication. Ivor Kamlish, book designer for the Society, has contributed his skill, as usual, brilliantly.

It has proved to be a fascinating and challenging project in which I have been greatly helped by many friends and colleagues who participated in the Festival over the years.

I would like to thank in particular Michael Johnson of the Handel Opera Society, Keith Martin, erstwhile treasurer of Music and Arts in Camden, Patric Schmidt of Opera Rara, Paul Collett of Camden Council Leisure Services, Mary Hill of Abbey Opera, Oliver Davies of the Royal College of Music and John Allison, Editor of *Opera* magazine, for their kindness and generosity in lending me valuable archival material and photographs.

I am also most grateful to Charles Farncombe, Joseph Horovitz, Denby Richards, Ivor Walker, Roy Shaw, Gerry Isaaman, John Richardson, Dan Shaw, Jim Miles, Christopher Gordon, Frank Cole, Christine Nickson, Dick Witts, Tom Hawkes, and Douglas Craig for sparing the time to answer questions and talk about their involvement in various Festivals.

I would like to record my deep appreciation of the help, interest and encouragement I received from Malcolm Holmes, Borough Archivist, and Richard Knight and all the staff at Camden's Local Studies and Archives Centre at Holborn Library, ever willing to haul out heavy tomes of Council minutes and old newspapers for me and to make helpful suggestions as to new sources of information. We are fortunate indeed in Camden to have such an excellent resource.

Last but not least I must thank my husband, Bram Marcus, for his encouragement and patience during the last year or so of my obsession with the subject, unfailingly willing to discuss it with me, and reading through various drafts of the text with ever helpful suggestions.

1   Genesis (1947-1953)

[Notes for chapter 1 are on p 13]

1 Krishna Menon, St Pancras Borough Councillor 1934–46

2 Leonard Marcus, 1904–1994, "Mr. Festival", photographed in 1971 –"the impresario who appeared in the guise of a deputy borough librarian."

Two men of vision

The Camden Festival had its origin in the coming together of two men of remarkable vision. The story starts in the Borough of St Pancras after the Second World War in 1946. It is an extraordinary story, not only of artistic achievement, but as an example of what could be achieved by local government.

At that time, the Borough was lucky enough to have amongst its councillors the distinguished Indian barrister Krishna Menon [1], who had come to England in 1924 to further his studies at the London School of Economics. He was a teacher, journalist, barrister and, almost incidentally, the first editor of Pelican Books. Dedicated to the cause of Indian independence, he was secretary of the India League, High Commissioner for India in 1947, and after independence, Indian representative to the United Nations. While living in London he was intensely active in British local politics, being elected to St Pancras Borough Council in 1934. He had served on all the major committees of the Council when he became Chairman of the Education and Public Libraries Committee in 1945. He had a vision of a Library Service at the centre of the cultural life of the Borough, catering for all tastes and all ages, giving help to existing cultural activities, and inaugurating new ones. It should be a people's university and a medium through which "to encourage local citizens to take an interest in the arts and thus widen their mental horizons".[1]

His vision was undoubtedly shared by all the leading officers of the St Pancras Library Service, headed by the Borough Librarian Frederick Sinclair and his deputy, William Taylor. Sinclair was a highly cultivated man with a great knowledge of literature and of the borough's history, who worked hard to improve the Library Service.

But it is another remarkable figure, the unsung hero whose name is today all but forgotten, who, almost by accident, was to become the driving spirit behind the development of the borough's arts programme and of the Festival. Leonard Marcus [2] was born in 1904 in East Ham and began his career as a librarian in Bethnal Green Library in 1923. He joined the St Pancras Library Service a year later and by 1939 he was Second Assistant librarian. During the War he was Acting Deputy Librarian. As he admitted himself in an interview published in *Musical Events* in October 1965, he had no expert knowledge of the arts and music: "At the beginning I knew nothing about running festivals, indeed I didn't know how one got critics to these things. I thought they saw an advertisement somewhere and they just toddled along." The interviewer added "He knows different now!". But he loved the arts and believed in their value; he had a feel for the flavour of a programme and how the works of different composers would mix.

Those who remember him describe him as friendly and humorous, a "civil servant with a smile" as one put it, while *Musical Events* gives us a picture of a man with "an urbane and civilised outlook…smiling sanity and cool logic". Under this quiet exterior was a man with great entrepreneurial skill, a clear view of what he thought should happen, and a determination to see it done. He was a good listener, encouraging and facilitating, and had the knack of drawing information from people on which he could then build. His view as told to *Musical Events* was simple: "Let plays, operas, concerts be available, see that they are there and let the public decide and choose for themselves". Crucially, he understood the local authority system, how money worked in it and how to seize the right moment in Council meetings to get his plans through.

Changes in attitude to the arts after World War II

The other crucial factor in the story is the extraordinary transformation in attitudes towards arts provision in Britain as a result of events in World War II. Before 1945, State support for the performing arts did not exist in Britain as it did in other European countries; even provision for libraries and museums had been made only grudgingly. It took St Pancras councillors more than 50 years to take advantage of their powers under the 1850 Act even to provide libraries! Typical of the prevailing attitude, as late as the 1930s, was that the libraries were "fools' enterprises" which "might be useful, but they were not vital and were more of a luxury for people".[2]

Ramsay Macdonald's administration of 1924 had proposed giving powers to local authorities to spend the product of a penny rate on the provision of entertainment facilities, but the Lords amended the Bill to confine it to sport and recreation. Politicians continued to ignore this area of education, but people made great efforts to educate themselves and also to provide themselves with performances of music and drama. In the absence of professional provision, amateur choral, orchestral and concert societies were started in all parts of the country to provide music, using professional soloists whenever possible.

Organisations such as South Place Ethical Society in Holborn, Toynbee Hall in London's East End, the Birmingham Musical Association and the Working Men's Concerts in Manchester were set up to provide concerts. As these organisations were supported by voluntary contributions, the seats were very cheap and often free, and there was huge demand for tickets. St Pancras had its own Working Men's College in Crowndale Road, which offered classes in arts and music. The Mornington Music Club was based there and had been very successful before the War. The Mary Ward Settlement in Tavistock Place, founded in 1890, was home to the St Pancras Players and the Working Class Dramatic Club; Gustav Holst was in charge of music there in 1904.

Ordinary working people, given the opportunities to hear great music or drama for the first time through these efforts felt a sense of liberation and elation: "After most recitals I came away with my head in a whirl, and my emotions and feelings in a state of tumultuous rebellion."[3] At the Mary Ward Settlement "music proved to be a main draw among the local population, who came in droves to the Settlement concerts".[4] One of the most revealing comments in the St Pancras Library Reports from pre-war days is how the growth of audiences for the BBC broadcasts influenced demand for books, music scores and drama. Whenever a play or an opera was broadcast or if books were read or recommended on a programme, borrowers wanted to get them from the Library. Before World War II in St Pancras there were also the North London Music Festival (a competitive event to which the Borough contributed by giving concessionary rates on the hall hire), a St Pancras Schools Music Association, and the St Pancras People's Theatre at Charrington Hall.

The British Drama League, founded in 1919 with private finance to encourage theatre at all levels, both amateur and professional, was also based in St Pancras.

At their premises in Fitzroy Square they created a 70-seat practice theatre which was opened in 1943 by Peggy Ashcroft. They organised competitive drama festivals and summer schools throughout the country for amateur groups, and lobbied government on behalf of professional theatre. They were involved in the pre-war campaign to persuade government to provide money for a national theatre, which led Stafford Cripps to allocate a million pounds to the project.

However, "it took Britain's trials and dangers in World War II to open the eyes of politicians, the civil servants and the public to what the nation could and should do about the arts."[5] The story of ENSA and CEMA is well known. The Entertainments National Service Association, started in WWI to entertain the troops, was revived in 1938, while the Council for the Encouragement of Music and the Arts was formed in 1940 to provide entertainment to the hard-pressed civilian population. Orchestras, the Sadler's Wells Ballet, the Old Vic Company, art exhibitions and dozens of artists and performers visited every corner of the country, and performances for working-class audiences were given at factories, mining villages, hostels, churches and air-raid shelters – bringing the arts to people who had never experienced them before. Concerts were not only well received but passionately demanded by a large public. Myra Hess's recital series at the National Gallery, remembered with affection and gratitude, were packed out, often with over 1,000 people who had queued round Trafalgar Square to get in. In 1944 more than 1.5 million people attended a total of 6,140 CEMA concerts.

After the War CEMA became the Arts Council, and a new era dawned for the arts. As Maynard Keynes said on BBC radio in 1945: "At the start, our aim was to replace what the war had taken away, but we soon found that we were providing what had never existed, even in peacetime." It was estimated that of the factory and hostel audiences, only about 2% had ever seen a play before.[6]

These experiences had brought home just how backward Britain was in such matters. The land of Shakespeare still had no national theatre, much less a national opera, and there was little understanding of the importance of a flourishing arts sector to a successful economy. Before 1948 local authorities not only had no powers to fund promotion of the arts directly, they were actually prohibited from promoting stage plays or anything requiring scenery or costumes. In London, the by-laws were even more restrictive, barring any variety entertainment such as music hall. The only thing they could do was fund bands or orchestras in parks and open spaces, and it required an Act of Parliament in the form of a Private Member's Bill to allow boroughs to set up municipal orchestras like those formed in Bournemouth in 1893 and in Birmingham in 1920.

As the *Municipal Journal* reported[7] in November 1946: "one of the signs of the times is increased demand for serious music". It was recognised that "art, literature and music having been accepted as essential civic amenities", more would need to be done in future as leisure time increased. At first progress was slow, but the subject had now been raised and put firmly on the agenda. A Gallup poll in 1954 found that the preference for symphony concerts over other forms of entertainment had risen from 15% before the war to 31% afterwards.[8] Even the political parties eventually realised that there had been an important change, and by 1959 they issued manifestos and discussion papers such as *Leisure for Living* (Labour) and *The Challenge of Leisure* (Conservative). Local authorities began working to get the law changed, and both the LCC and the Association of Municipal Corporations launched campaigns to that end. In the meantime they looked for ways round the legislation, setting up Entertainments Committees or Arts Councils.

The St Pancras Arts and Civic Council

In London, St Pancras led the way. In 1946 Krishna Menon set up the St Pancras Arts and Civic Council as a device to overcome the limitations of local government law. Krishna Menon wanted the public libraries to take their place in the forefront of the arts. He wanted concerts, art exhibitions, plays, debating societies, ballet clubs, youth parliaments, etc.[8] Leonard Marcus was invited by Menon to become the first secretary of the St Pancras Arts and Civic Council in 1946. Thus, Marcus was involved in the borough's plans for the arts from the beginning and found himself in charge of all the administrative arrangements. The Council was to be a democratic organisation, controlled, guided and financed by the public and supported by grants from the General Rate Fund. Wide consultation took place within the borough, with a series of conferences involving teachers, cultural, voluntary, educational and artistic organisations such as the Workers' Music Association, the London Philharmonic Orchestra, Unity Theatre, The British Drama League, The Salvation Army and the Highgate Literary and Scientific Institute. With Menon as chairman, its membership consisted of representatives of the Borough Council, cultural organisations and individuals interested in the arts. Its offices were in the Council's hall in Thanet Street.

It was officially inaugurated on 2 June 1946 by Dame Sybil Thorndyke and proudly reported in the local press as being the first of its kind in London. Dame Sybil spoke stirringly of the role of the arts in giving us a broader, higher, vision: "Without the imaginative and wider outlook on life which come from cultural interests, a nation perishes." Tom Russell of the London Philharmonic Orchestra, remembering the work of CEMA, ENSA and the National Gallery recitals, said that "one of the good things resulting from the War was that people realised that culture was not only for a few who had benefited from higher education, but for everyone. Culture is a thing we all want and it should not be left to a few rich enthusiasts".[9] The inaugural concert included performances by the pianist Leonard Cassini, a choir of St Pancras school children and a string orchestra.

A scheme of Associate membership was set up, with a small annual subscription, open to all members of the Libraries and anyone else who was interested. The borough began promoting an extraordinary range of events with a full programme throughout the year. A winter season of music was provided with regular concerts by the London Philharmonic Orchestra and Sunday evening concerts by individual artists in the St Pancras Assembly Hall. The first season included the London String Orchestra conducted by Alan Bush, and a concert of "Swing" music.

There were regular talks and discussion clubs for children, young people and adults; provision of gramophone record and art lending facilities; film shows; a centre to foster public interest in art, music and drama, and dances at the Prince of Wales Road Baths. Later on there were opera performances. The public was urged to contact the Arts and Civic Council if there were other activities they wanted to suggest, and these were organised through small section committees such as Music and Drama clubs, a children's section, and a horticultural section. During the first two years direct grants from the borough amounted to £541. By 1948 the Ballet Circle was already setting the tone that was later to become a characteristic of the Festivals: "Thinking internationally, the Circle has had illustrated lectures on Indian, Spanish and Greek dance, and we hope in the near future to have a lecture on "Dance in the Chinese Theatre".[10]

A *Library Journal* – an idea first mooted in 1937 – was begun in 1947, edited and published by the librarians themselves. It kept Library members up to date on policy, book stocks and new publications and contained many interesting articles about the history of the borough and its residents. Later, when the Festival became more and more successful the February/March issues were devoted to wide coverage of the programmes. No other authority published a Journal of the same size or scope. By 1956 1000 copies were being printed at a cost of £51 and sold monthly through the libraries at 2d each.

Krishna Menon, with the enthusiastic help of Leonard Marcus, Frederick Sinclair and William Taylor, certainly saw to it that St Pancras "fulfils this vital role of a modern patron of the arts, and that the Public Libraries of today should be the focal point of the artistic and cultural life of the community they serve".[11] By May 1947 Alderman Miss W E C Gode proudly claimed in the *Library Journal* that "Some people are already making the Town Hall their 'Sunday rendezvous', knowing that they can get first-class musical entertainment at the lowest prices, whether they prefer the classics played by the Jaques String Orchestra or more popular works played on the accordion by Tollefsen".[12]

Although it was slow taking off, the Council was not going to be deterred, as Miss Gode made clear: "It can be rightly claimed that in the St Pancras Arts and Civic Council we have a "great invention", but its successful growth depends upon the…support given to its activities by the people. It is a democratic organisation designed to bring the appreciation of art and culture within the reach of all citizens of the Borough: it was created expressly for their benefit. This venture is the first of its kind amongst Metropolitan Boroughs and is unique in the country generally. The way has not been easy. Lack of funds, due to limitations placed upon the Borough Council in regard to spending money for this purpose, lack of staff to carry out the considerable amount of work involved, lack of that degree of public support which would have ensured the Arts and Civic Council being at least financially self-supporting, these and various technical difficulties had to be overcome. They made the first year uphill work. But it is a job which is infinitely worth doing, and the experience and support gained augurs well for future developments. Like all good things, we cannot keep it to ourselves; nor do we want to. Other London Boroughs are now busy forming their own arts and cultural organisations, and we wish them every success in their efforts, Let us remember, however, that the torch was lit in St Pancras, and it is our communal responsibility to hold it high and keep it in the forefront." [12]

The first Festival

In the summer of 1947, the Arts and Civic Council announced its first "Festival of Leisure", an "Arts and Civic Week" to be held throughout the Borough in September, demonstrating all the various activities run by the Arts and Civic Council. It was officially opened by Sir Ralph Richardson, and the "full range of the cultural life of the Borough" was to be "brought into the spotlight of publicity".[13] There was an exhibition showing the Borough's work "for our citizens" which included a section on the history of the borough, plans for the future, and paintings and handicraft work by local artists. A flower and vegetable show was held at Parliament Hill Fields followed by open-air dancing, while in the evenings at the Assembly Hall local dramatic societies presented plays. There were concerts by local choirs and other "artistes". There was also a full programme for schoolchildren with sporting fixtures, visits to the exhibition and a Borough Youth Parliament, which, said the *St Pancras Journal*, would be open so that "members of the public will be able to see how the younger generation might behave if they become Members of Parliament". Nearly 70 organisations participated, with a grand finale at Parliament Hill, and "a splendid Procession of Industry – a fitting climax to a memorable week". All the events were free except for the Grand Carnival Dance in 1948, for which 4s 6d was charged.

It was a great success, and The *Evening News* devoted a leading article to it, calling it "a vigorous challenge to the attitude of 'No, it isn't any use.' Of course it's of use," the article declared, "it's of use in battered and grimy streets, to care for the things of the spirit; it's of use in the many wastes of greyness which lie between Camden Town and King's Cross to lift your eyes to the green heights of Parliament Hill and Ken Wood". This successful experiment was repeated again in 1948, and these were the precursors of the Camden Festival.

In 1948 the much-needed new Local Government Act was passed. Its famous Section 132, the so-called "Entertainments Clause", was one of the most significant political developments for the arts. At last local authorities were empowered to use the product of a sixpenny rate to make direct expenditure on the arts. Although most were slow to use this right, as they had been to provide public libraries a century earlier, the Public Libraries Committee at St Pancras was able to forge ahead. Alongside the Arts and Civic Council work, it had already developed a programme of what was called Extension Activities – the Book weeks, lectures and so on – all part of Leonard Marcus' responsibility. By July 1947 he found himself so busy with the administrative work for these activities that he asked to be relieved of his role as the Arts and Civic Council Secretary in order to devote himself to Extension Activities full time. Frederick Sinclair himself took over as Secretary.

Once Section 132 was in place, Marcus's department was able to sponsor all these activities directly, and the need for the Arts and Civic Council began to decline. By September 1949 Extension Activities had its own Sub-Committee, and Marcus was producing an increasing programme of lectures, concerts, and summer entertainments. Orchestral concerts were the most popular – it was noted in 1948 that seats for the LPO concerts were selling out well in advance. Audiences for solo and chamber music were more limited.

There were two great national celebrations in the early 1950s: the Festival of Britain in 1951 and the Coronation celebrations of 1953. St Pancras did its bit for both events, directly organising and funding them through the Public Libraries Department. For the Festival of Britain an Art Exhibition was added to the Drama

Festival, Book Week and Spring Flower Show, and the London Philharmonic Orchestra's May concert, conducted by Basil Cameron with pianist Cyril Smith, was designated a Festival Concert. For the Coronation Festivities a Committee was set up with a budget of around £10,000. In addition to the Drama Festival, a Flower Show and an Art Exhibition entitled *Yesterday and Today*, there were programmes for children and for "the old folk", an industrial procession, a grand finale with a Tattoo at Parliament Hill Fields and a firework display arranged in conjunction with Hampstead Borough Council. £3000 was earmarked for street decorations with flags and floodlighting for the main roads and the Town Hall, with "double bannerets to each lighting column with strings of bunting streamers hanging between the columns." [14]

Frederick Sinclair, the Borough Librarian, died in 1953 and was succeeded by his deputy William Taylor, who had worked closely with Marcus on all these projects. Marcus was now promoted to Deputy Borough Librarian.

The groundwork laid in these immediate post-war years was about to come to fruition; the festival idea had taken hold and the stage was now set for the St Pancras Festival proper. As Councillor John Richardson remarked, "St Pancras has always seemed an unlikely place for an Arts Festival. This particular saint has been too closely linked with railways, dirt and arches for the mental image to change quickly", but that image was about to be challenged.

Notes for chapter 1

1 Annual Library Report 1961, p 12.
2 *The end of one story – A souvenir of the Borough of St Pancras* St Pancras Library Department, 1965.
3 Jonathan Rose *The intellectual life of the British Working Classes* Yale University Press 2001 p 199.
4 John Sutherland *The Mary Ward Centre* The Centre.
5 Harold Baldry (Chairman of the Arts Council Regional Committee 1975–8 and Founder member of Southern Arts) *The Case for the Arts* Secker & Warburg 1981 p 12.
6 Hugh Jenkins (Minister for the Arts 1974–6) *The Culture Gap: An experience of government and the arts.* Marion Boyars 1979, p 40.
7 *Municipal Journal*, February 1946.
8 Article by Leonard Marcus in the Municipal Review, Vol 37, May 1966.
9 *St Pancras Chronicle* 7.6.46.
10 *St Pancras Library Journal* March 1948 Vol 2 p 161.
11 Recalled in the Annual Library Report 1955–6, p 3.
12 *St Pancras Library Journal* May 1947 Vol 1 p 5.
13 Note 11, p 18.
14 St Pancras Borough Council Minutes Vol 69. Report of Coronation Committee, 8.10.52, p 411.

2 The St Pancras years (1954–1964): from glory unto glory

[Notes for chapter 2 are on p 38]

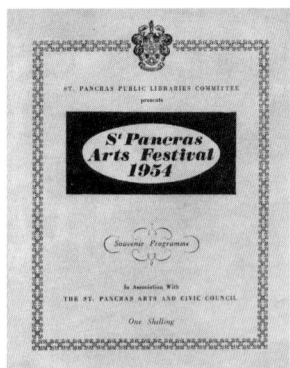

3 Cover of the first St Pancras Arts Festival programme (1954)

After the success of the Coronation celebrations in 1953, Leonard Marcus suggested to the Committee that the festival should be repeated the following year. A few other events would be added and it should be called the St Pancras Arts Festival. It took place in November 1954 [3], starting with little fanfare, on a tiny budget – about £650. Thus the Drama Festival, Book Week and Art Exhibition, established the previous year, plus two events with professional performers, began the Festival. "Amateur of course – in many ways Utopian, and certainly not the sort of stuff to bring in the critics or audiences"[1] – or so they thought.

The Drama Festival was a competition for local amateur drama groups, in the theatre at the Stanhope Institute. It was adjudicated by Martin Browne of the British Drama League, with prizes for one-act and full-length plays. The performances were well attended. Ticket prices were 2s 6d and the receipts exceeded £100. It was won by the Alexandra Repertory Company [4].

The Art Exhibition, entitled *Looking at London*, was also competitive, with 130 works selected from 207 submissions by local artists. Although they were mostly amateur, the show was run along professional lines, with submission and hanging fees, and catalogue sales which brought in £25. Approximately 1000 visitors came to see the pictures, and art films were shown three times a day in the Council Chamber.

The third week of the Festival was Book Week, with capacity audiences throughout. There was a competitive section for children, which attracted more than 300 entries, and a programme of talks attended by 3000 children. Among the speakers were Margaret Rawlings, Max Adrian, Huw Wheldon and Hammond Innes, while Wynford Vaughan Thomas was quizmaster at a book quiz at Highgate Library. For adults there were two Literary evenings at the Assembly Rooms: one featured Peggy Ashcroft and Stephen Murray with pianist Nina Milkina in an evening of Poetry and Music, while the other was a celebration of George Bernard Shaw with a discussion led by Margaret Rawlings, a performance of his short play *Overruled*, and readings of scenes from *Pygmalion*. It had also been hoped that at least one of the regular LPO concerts might be included in the Festival, but this could not be arranged.

A report in the *Manchester Guardian*

4 The Alexandra Repertory Company, winners of the first Drama Festival, 1954 with *Rose Without a Thorn*

saying that "with its busy railway termini and drab lines of back streets, St Pancras is an unlikely place to find an Arts Festival" drew indignant comment in St Pancras's *Library Journal*, reminding everyone of the Borough's notable artistic heritage, a source of pride to those who worked in the Library Department. As the editor pointed out, the Bancrofts and Ellen Terry had been at the Prince of Wales Theatre in Charlotte Street (rebuilt in 1905 as the Scala); the Regent Theatre, opposite St Pancras Station, was home to a successful repertory company in the inter-war years, while the Bedford Theatre in Camden High Street staged everything from Shakespeare to music hall. Sickert and the Camden Town Group, the Euston Road School and the Pre-Raphaelites all began, and flourished, in the area. The Slade School was located in St Pancras; George Bernard Shaw had been a member of the St Pancras Vestry earlier in the century.

Second St Pancras Festival

Before the second Festival took place in 1955 a constitutional change was made. Since the 1948 Act the Arts and Civic Council had become superfluous and was now replaced by an Arts Sub-Committee of the Public Libraries Committee, with the power to co-opt members with expert knowledge of the arts from outside the Council to help and advise with the ever-growing annual programme. The intention was to "preserve the most valuable element of the Arts and Civic Council: the voluntary participation of local citizens in the cultural work of the borough".[2] The first to be co-opted were E Martin Browne, Director of the British Drama League, Ivor Fox, Director of Art Studies at the Working Men's College, Roger Levy who advised on music, Miss W M Hicks who had been vice-chairman of the Arts and Civic Council, and Mr A Tomlinson, headmaster of the Richard Cobden School and chairman of the former Arts and Civic Council Teachers' Committee. The chairman of the Public Libraries Committee in 1955–6 was Councillor Mrs G F Lee.

The official policy promulgated was "to assist local authorities and individuals practising the arts by providing opportunities for them to show the work they are doing, and to foster an interest in the arts among the people of St Pancras by presenting high-quality drama, music and art, at reasonable prices, within the borough boundaries."[3]

From now on full, illustrated, annual library reports were published with detailed information of the year's activities and departmental budgets. In the first of these in 1955-6, the opportunity was taken by William Taylor, the new chief librarian, to enlarge on the policy – although one suspects that it might have been Marcus who actually wrote this section of the report:

"The arts, and those who practise them, have always needed support of two kinds – the stimulus of those who admire their work, and financial aid to enable them to continue working. For centuries the latter was provided by wealthy patrons, but in recent times these have become few in number, particularly in Britain. Their place has been taken, in part, by State aid, through such agencies as the Arts Council of Great Britain; but these agencies are remote and their work needs to be reinforced by the local authorities, who are in closer contact with the artistic life of the area they serve.

"The local authority should act as patron of the arts in its own area, and should also endeavour to stimulate local knowledge of the arts, so that their practitioners will not lack the public interest and admiration which is the only other aid they need. It is my firm belief that the Public Libraries Committee should be the agency whereby the local authority fulfils this vital role of a modern patron of the arts, and that the Public Libraries of today should be the focal point of the artistic and cultural life of the community they serve.

"One of the pleasures of working in St Pancras is the knowledge that my views are fully shared by the Committee. For these reasons my report is entitled *The Arts in St Pancras* and many of the pages which follow deal with activities far removed from the functions of a public library as conceived by the sponsors of the Act of one hundred years ago."[4]

Such an approach is in stark contrast to today's attitude towards art and culture with its dread words "élitist" and "inaccessible", which appear rather to encourage people to narrow their mental horizons and look no further than what they already know or like. Equally notable is the difference in attitude of the media in those early years, which praised and encouraged every effort rather than, as today, disparaging the arts and questioning expenditure of tax-payers' money on them. The Festival organisers fearlessly produced programmes whose chief aim was to encourage the public to explore the unknown and provide them with the most challenging and stimulating works. The public, not having been told that these were élitist or inaccessible, lapped them up insatiably over the years. The St Pancras, later the Camden, Festival became one of the most adventurous, significant and admired events in the UK artistic calendar, attracting both national and international attention. Moreover, in addition to the Festival, the Department maintained a lively year-round programme which included opera performances, concerts and many other events.

It is clear that there was cross-party support in the Council for these activities, although there was certainly some dissent behind the scenes – and on occasion more publicly – since the *Library Journal* felt it necessary to justify these activities in introducing the second Festival:

> "It has sometimes been asked why a London borough should need to stage any kind of arts festival, for is there not a perpetual festival of the arts in progress in this great intellectual and artistic centre? The most hungry play- or filmgoer, the greediest viewer of pictures and sculpture, the most ardent concertgoer, could find daily satisfaction, were he to need it, in London's theatres, galleries and concert halls. So let us make it clear that our aim in St Pancras is not to compete with these institutions, an attempt which would be doomed to certain failure, but to organise a festival which will combine artistic events of an unusual kind, which have been found to be particularly suitable to our "native soil", with competitive events, which have a wider currency up and down the land – briefly, to marry a miniature Edinburgh Festival and a miniature Welsh National Eisteddfod. Although our Festival is only in its second year, it has not been thrust administratively on the borough, for its constituent parts have been in existence for a number of years. Their bringing together into one Arts Festival last year, the focusing, as it were, of the various artistic interests in the borough into one picture, was successful enough to warrant a repetition of the venture in the autumn of 1955." [5]

The Drama Competition, Art Exhibition and Book Week again provided the main fare of the second Festival, but the professional music and drama side of the programme began to expand. Two of the London Philharmonic Orchestra's usual concerts with conductor Hugo Rignold were included and there was also a concert by the MacNaughton String Quartet as part of the Book Week. The actor Victor Rietti, with the International Theatre Company, offered the first British performance of Pirandello's comedy, *Think it over, Giacomino*, and RADA made their first contribution to the Festival, starting a collaboration which went on for several seasons. They presented a Literary Evening featuring the work of playwright Charles Morgan, with a performance by RADA students of the second act of his play *The River Line* in the presence of the author, followed by a discussion between Clemence Dane, Martin Browne and Michael MacOwan, who had directed the original West End production.

The Opera arrives (1955)

The major innovation in the second Festival, establishing the hallmark of the future, was the first performance in Britain of an unknown opera by Haydn. A concert performance of his *L'anima del filosofo*, based on the story of Orpheus and Eurydice, was presented by the Impresario Society with Heather Harper and Derek Hammond-Stroud in the leading roles. It was Haydn's last opera, composed during his 1791 stay in London for the old King's Theatre in the Haymarket, but never performed there because of various operatic and political intrigues. The Impresario Society had been founded in 1951 by Dr Hans Ucko "to increase public knowledge and appreciation of the art of music by giving operatic and other performances of musical works which are of artistic value but rarely performed."[6] Its first productions were Mozart's *La finta giardiniera*, produced at Chelsea Town Hall in 1953, and *Il rè pastore* at St George's Hall in 1954. After the company's appearance at the Festival all its performances took place in St Pancras Town Hall.

The Apollo Society gave an Evening of American Poetry with Constance Cummings, Sam Wanamaker and Guy Kingsley-Poynter. The Society was formed in 1943 by Dame Peggy Ashcroft together with a group of actors, musicians and poets, among them Edith Evans, Natasha Litvin, Cecil Day Lewis and Stephen Spender, to put on recitals of poetry and music for a war-weary population. They performed in canteens, camps and colleges as well as in theatres and concert halls. These performances were such a success that they decided to continue after the war, going to schools and universities as well as other festivals. They became regulars in the first few years of the Festival.

Costs of the different elements of the Festival were £163 for the Book Week, £301 for the Drama Festival, and £132 for the Art Exhibition. The financial arrangements for the opera and the Pirandello play established a *modus operandi* which enabled the Borough to bring in professional productions at minimal cost. The Hall was provided free of charge and all the other costs were met by the producing company in return for keeping the box office receipts. An income of £230 was generated from sales of tickets, which cost between 2s 6d and 12s 6d, while the Literary evenings were free. It was the play, rather than the opera or the orchestral concert, that had the highest ticket prices. The souvenir programme cost a shilling and sales of the catalogue for the Art Exhibition, together with submission and hanging fees, produced £42 4s 6d. By now Marcus had a small team of helpers within the department, and stewarding for the exhibition was done by fifteen volunteers.

The Council minutes noted with satisfaction: "On this occasion the Festival included events which were not purely local in their origin or their appeal and there is no doubt that this added to its attraction. At all events, publicity given in the national and local press, and widespread comments from all quarters, indicate that the Festival was an outstanding success." [7]

1956

With the Third Festival, major changes occurred. It was moved from autumn to spring in order to ease the workload on the staff, which meant that it skipped a year and there was no Festival in 1956. The Book Week, an event of long standing in the borough, which had been included in the first two festivals, was detached from it, staying in its usual November slot.

However, even without the Festival, 1956 was full of activities including several opera performances. The Impresario Society persuaded St Pancras to promote a Mozart Festival jointly with them to commemorate the bicentenary of the composer's birth. With an Arts Council grant supplemented by £92 from the Borough, *La finta giardiniera* was

5   Glenda Jackson as Eliza Dolittle in the RADA performance of *Pygmalion*, 1956. Wendy Hiller commented (quoted in The *North London Press* 30.11.56) "This actress has considerable ability and should go far in her profession"

put on in June with Lord Harewood amongst a distinguished audience, and later in the year they performed Mozart's *The Impresario*. The Handel Opera Society, which had started the previous year, with the encouragement of Leonard Marcus, mounted a production of Handel's *Hercules* which drew high praise from the critics. Andrew Porter wrote in *Opera*: "Handel is a dramatic composer long overdue for recognition in the country of his adoption.... The Handel Opera Society put us in their debt by staging this musical drama". [8]

Shaw's centenary was also marked by performances of *Pygmalion* given by students of RADA, one of whom was Glenda Jackson [5] in the role of Eliza Dolittle.

The Handel Opera Society

The founding of The Handel Opera Society was a notable event in British operatic history, launching it on an extraordinary journey which put Handel's forgotten operas back in the repertory. It might not have happened but for the direct support and encouragement that

6 Charles Farncombe, founder and artistic director of the Handel Opera Society

Charles Farncombe [6], its founder, received from St Pancras Arts and Libraries Department and Leonard Marcus. Handel's operas and dramatic oratorios had scarcely been performed for 200 years. They required singers proficient in the style and technique of *opera seria*, and it was debatable whether a modern audience, unaccustomed to its conventions, would accept Handel for the consummate musical dramatist he is.

Following a performance of *The Beggars' Opera* in Westminster, Farncombe received a visit from an old gentleman who complimented him on his flair for such music and urged him to turn his attention to the works of Handel. He said that if Farncombe would put on a performance of Handel's last opera *Deidamia*, a wonderful comic piece, he himself would make him a translation. The old gentleman was none other than the great Edward J Dent, the doyen of English musicologists, translator, teacher and scholar of international standing.

A short time later a note arrived informing Farncombe that the translation was ready and inviting him to come to dinner to pick up the score. Over a superb meal, waited on, as Farncombe recalls, by a flunkey in 18th-century costume, Dent handed him a beautifully bound score with the promised translation, but Farncombe left Dent's flat with absolutely no idea of how he was to get it performed. He confided the story to Gwyneth McCleary, secretary of the Board of Trade Choir, of which he was the conductor, and this proved to be the beginning of a famous partnership. The obvious person to approach was Leonard Marcus, for whom he had already done some Christmas concerts. Marcus showed immediate interest in the project. "The first production could not have taken place without the goodwill and understanding of the then St Pancras Borough Council, already achieving fame for its enlightened encouragement of the arts." Farncombe ploughed his own war gratuity into the project, and Professor Dent put in a good word with the Arts Council, which made a grant of £35 while "St Pancras generously overlooked some outstanding items due for payment".[9]

The orchestral parts had to be copied from the original manuscripts in the British Museum – 4 months of solitary toil at night, after a day's work. Artists were prepared to sing for tiny expense fees because it was an interesting project, a first performance and in London, where it would be likely to be noticed by critics. Marion Studholme and Norman Walker were thus persuaded to sing the leading parts.

Bits of props and scenery were begged and borrowed from everywhere, including a vital broken column which was ferried over from Covent Garden in a taxi. The taxi driver, curious at such an unusual 'passenger' asked what it was for. When told it was for a performance of an opera that had not been seen for 200 years, his apt response was: "Well, at least they can't say in the press that it was done better last time they saw it!"

The show was fraught with last-minute disasters which seemed calculated to prevent it from ever getting on. With all the posters and leaflets already printed, a general election was unexpectedly called on the date of the opening night, and the Assembly Hall was requisitioned as a polling station. Fortunately the performances could be rearranged for other dates, but all the advance leaflets had to be altered by hand. Norman Walker fell ill and had to cancel, and another singer had to learn the role at short notice. Then by the time the first night arrived a rail strike had been called.

Still, an audience turned up and the opera went ahead. Somewhat to Farncombe's amazement it was successful; the shows were full, the press reports were favourable and the Handel Opera Society was launched. The Camden Festival programmes in later years list these performances of *Deidamia*, which took place in June, as having been part of the 1955 St Pancras Festival, but they were not. It was only with their third production in 1957 that Handel Opera appeared in the Festival for the first time and it was to be a seminal event both for them and for the world of opera.

1957: "Eviva St Pancras"

Many opera productions were now taking place at the Assembly Rooms during the year, and in 1957 the number in the Festival increased to three. The Handel Opera Society's contribution, their first in the festival, was the first performance for more than two centuries of Handel's *Alcina*, which played to capacity audiences who gave the cast a tremendous ovation. With Joan Sutherland in the title role [7] it was a landmark not only in the Handel revival but in Sutherland's career, as she recalled in her autobiography[10]:

"....two momentous performances of *Alcina* for the Handel Opera Society at St Pancras Town Hall. I say 'momentous' as it was probably my singing of the role of the sorceress which finally convinced the Garden [Covent Garden] that my future lay away from the dramatic works of Strauss, Wagner and late Verdi and most definitely in the grand and varied *bel canto* repertoire. The performances were done on a shoestring and the costumes were borrowed from old Sadler's Wells stock. I had jewellery made from chandelier drops wired together and a beautiful Brazilian topaz and pearl ring given me by Richard [Bonynge], which he found in Portobello Market; I prize it to this day."

Andrew Porter wrote "Now that in Miss Sutherland we have a first-rate Handelian soprano, who phrases, flourishes, trills and embellishes with lovely tone and exquisite art, we must have Handel added to the national repertory."[11]

The Handel Opera Society's cash books record that Miss Sutherland was paid £21 (20 guineas in old money) for her two performances.

Desmond Shawe-Taylor, the eminent music critic, headed an article in *The New Statesman and Nation* on 30 March 1957 "**Eviva St Pancras**":

"Local authorities are always being badgered to do something for the arts: so let us raise a cheer when one of them takes positive action. The Borough of St Pancras has just concluded an Arts Festival which lasted a month and was nothing if not comprehensive, ranging from Drama and Films through the spirited jazz of Mr. Humphrey Lyttelton to the exalted heights of *opera seria*. It is quite an achievement to have presented within three weeks professional performances of both Mozart's *La Clemenza di Tito* and Handel's *Alcina*; Edinburgh can show nothing comparable."

The Mozart opera, given by the Impresario Society, was also immensely successful. The third offering was a musical play called *Love from Judy* written by Hugh Martin and Jack Gray and based on a book by Eric Maschwitz and Jean Webster. It was one of a series of such pieces, specially written for amateurs, that could be hired from Emile Littler's Musical Play Department, which catered for a then flourishing amateur sector. Billed as the "first London amateur performance" it was given by the Baltic Operatic Society at the Scala Theatre in Charlotte Street, which had become a base for amateur companies. The Baltic Amateur Dramatic and Operatic Society, founded by members of the Baltic Exchange in the City, dated back to 1893 and its distinguished membership at one time included Herbert Beerbohm Tree.

Other musical content also increased with two lunch-time chamber music concerts for which tickets were one shilling, and an evening concert by the Dolmetsch Ensemble at the Working Men's College. One of the London Philharmonic Orchestra's regular concerts was again included, and the Apollo Society returned with Margretta Scott, Julian Bream and Michael Hordern. Ticket prices for the operas ranged from 2s 6d to 15s; the top price for the orchestral concert was 5s, while the Dolmetsch and the Apollo were free.

7 Joan Sutherland in the title role of Handel's *Alcina* at the St Pancras Festival in 1957 (courtesy of *Opera* magazine).

The Festival was launched with a Civic Service at St Pancras Parish Church, Euston Road and film was introduced into the Festival with the first showing in England of the epic Czech film, *Jan Hus*. Humphrey Lyttelton provided traditional jazz, attracting a very large audience, and the Festival ended with "a grand Arts Ball" attended by 350 people which the *Library Journal* advertised as "not yet quite so well known as its more hectic Chelsea counterpart, but nevertheless an enjoyable social evening". Interestingly, the jazz concert was more expensive than the orchestral concert, with top-price tickets at 7s 6d.

The Art Exhibition at the Town Hall featured works by the Slade School, the Working Men's College and professional and amateur artists at work in the borough, although it was judged somewhat less successful than the previous year.

The Drama Competition was reorganised so that the participating companies performed at their own premises, instead of travelling to the Stanhope, and the adjudicator travelled to them. Each society was responsible for its own costs, while the Council paid for the adjudicator, the publicity and the trophy. The offerings ranged from Beaumont and Fletcher's *A King and no King*, performed by The Birkbeck Players, to Mabel and Denis Constanduros' *Acacia Avenue* given by the S. K. Amateur Players. RADA presented the first British performance of an American play set in Korea with an all-female cast (including Sian Phillips), *Cry Havoc*, by Allan Kenward.

1958

By the Fourth Festival in 1958 it was clear that the borough had a real success on its hands. It had attracted more than 200 press reviews and editorial comments. The one singled out for special mention in all the Council records that reflects the flavour of the general comment was part of a leading article in the London *Star*:

"The Arts Festival which began today in St Pancras should be encouraged by anyone who believes that it is better to be active than passive. It lasts a month. It presents opera and plays, pictures and poetry, chamber music and jazz, the enriching by-products of man's genius that sweeten our ordinary mundane lives. But it competes with the growing and insidious idea that the arts are something to be enjoyed spinelessly from the depths of an armchair. Bravo St Pancras, for bravely supporting the idea that enjoyment of art demands effort. Where are the other London Boroughs that will make hearts dance and sing at their festivals?"

An attractive brochure was produced and 7,000 copies were distributed. In a very full month there were 22 events, still mixing amateur and professional: the Drama Festival for local amateur groups along with two art exhibitions – 'St Pancras Artists' and 'The Lost Theatres of St Pancras' – provided the backbone of the Festival. RADA returned with Shaw's *Candida* and Unity Theatre presented Arthur Miller's *The Crucible*. The Company of Nine presented Barbara Jefford and Christopher Hassall at the Working Men's College in a programme entitled *Poets of St Pancras*.

Music of all kinds was becoming the dominant element of the Festival, ranging from Chris Barber and his Band and a skiffle competition to the London Mozart Players with Nina Milkina as soloist. The recently formed Wind Music Society gave the first performance in England of Rimsky-Korsakov's Clarinet Concerto with Jack Brymer. The Mornington Music Club, which was based at the Working Men's College, contributed a concert of 20th-century music. The English Folk Song and Dance Society, with headquarters in Primrose Hill (then part of the Borough of St Pancras), gave a concert of British and American folk songs and dances.

Three operas were staged, all new to London. The Handel Opera Society put on *Theodora*, the first performance in London [8], which according to the Council minutes "opened during a blizzard." Directed by Anthony Besch, the cast included April Cantelo, Monica Sinclair and Geraint Evans and it was broadcast by the BBC Third Programme. Monica Sinclair became such an established favourite with St Pancras audiences "that a Festival without her would be almost unthinkable" (*Annual Library Report* 1960, p 12). The Impresario Society staged Mozart's *Idomeneo* with Adele Leigh, Nancy Evans and Alexander Young. Douglas Craig, who directed, remembers a moment of near disaster. The company had gone through elaborate negotiations with the Musicians' Union to be allowed to use a recording of an off-stage chorus as a simpler and more manageable way of producing the required distant effect. Alas, they did not expect to have a technician who pressed *erase* instead of *play* at the crucial moment. Some quick thinking and superb musicianship by Derek Hammond-Stroud saved the day, as he hid himself behind a pillar and sang the passage from memory as an unaccompanied solo.

The third piece was an opera based on the *Ballad of Lord Bateman*, presented by the New English Opera Workshop for the jubilee of the founding of the Folk Song Society. At least forty versions are known of this very old ballad, thought to date back to the Crusades. On this occasion the lyrics were adapted by Joan Sharp, the daughter of Cecil Sharp, and set to folk tunes and orchestrated by Arnold Foster. The Workshop was an offshoot of the New Opera Company, founded to give young singers more experience of professional work. The producer was Colin Graham and among the cast were Kenneth Bowen, Peter Hemmings and Noelle Barker.

There was also a showing of the Russian film of the Moscow State Opera Company's production of Mussorgsky's *Boris Godunov*.

The festival was widely reviewed in the national press and extensively featured by the BBC including the *Today* programme, attracted more than 12,500 people and ended with a most successful Festival Ball. The box office was in the capable hands of two members of staff from the Borough treasurer's office. The *Library Report* for 1958 notes that the council spent a total of £7,664 on its year-round programme of arts and entertainments, which was a fraction of the sixpence in the pound rate that was permitted.

A pattern was now becoming established which differentiated St Pancras from Festivals elsewhere and gave it its unique flavour and appeal. There was never an artistic director – Leonard Marcus was the driving spirit, but he remained firmly a librarian and stayed in the background. For that reason references to his achievement are hard to find; Library Reports are assumed to come from the Department and it is the Department which takes the credit. Press releases for many years were issued in the name of the Borough Librarians, and it was William Taylor who was quoted in the many press stories about the Festival and the borough's other artistic promotions. It is only when one talks to those who were involved in these early years that Marcus's role as the real impresario is revealed.

Being so close to the theatres and concerts halls of central London, Marcus had understood early on that there was no point in duplicating what was already on offer there. He developed a clear aim to present rarely performed as well as new music; to encourage little-known artists as well as already celebrated ones, and to establish a proper balance of visual and

8 *Theodora* (1958). Centre: April Cantelo and Monica Sinclair (Trans World Photographic Co.; Handel Opera Society archive)

dramatic arts. Councillor John Richardson tells the story:

"The Festival, thank heaven, refused, in those early days, to be patronising. It steered away from the more obvious programmes that can be heard any evening in London. There was no talking down to people, no tender, music-by-numbers enticement to serious art. They went feet first into productions never seen in this country, giving professional groups their heads, and we all kept our fingers crossed on the night. It could have petered out, like most of the good intentions engendered by the Festival of Britain. Two factors, however, got the St Pancras Arts Festival over the 'amateur' hump. One was the enthusiasm of Council, staff and performers and the second was the urge, seemingly inherent in that borough, to try new things: new operas, new orchestral works and new plays have been staged and dozens of premières were notched up.

There have been many difficulties – mainly due to the accommodation available. The architect of the Assembly Rooms had not visualised having Verdi on his stage nor a massed chorus changing costumes behind it. The companies taking part have to use more ingenuity than usual and produce expansiveness in a nutshell." [12]

Marcus also unashamedly declared on more than one occasion that the Festival was "quite deliberately highbrow". The *Hampstead & Highgate Express*, always known locally as the *Ham & High*, as indeed it will be in the rest of this book, chose to headline this in 1958:

"Highbrow" Festival a great success

"When the programme for St Pancras's fourth Arts Festival was drawn up many thought it too highbrow to be successful. But so great has been the response to the Festival that even the organisers have been surprised at its enormous success." [13]

The Festival's *modus operandi* evolved more or less by accident in response to what was possible and what was available. It was to give "other organisations...and local groups actively engaged in making music or drama or practising the visual arts...that measure of financial assistance or guarantee which enables them to bridge the gap between income and expenditure and to embark with confidence on the promotion of artistic projects which might otherwise be impossible". [14] The operas were facilitated through very small 'pump-priming' grants in a highly cost-effective way.

It owed something to a memorandum issued by the Association of Metropolitan Chief Librarians in November 1948 in connection with the new Act and its Section 132. They were worried that resources might be diverted away from the core library service, and suggested that the aim should be to encourage and help the development of other independent agencies as the prime movers. The St Pancras Committee did not agree with this, but clearly their librarians took it on board. [15]

It also owed much to the tradition that had developed over centuries in a Britain devoid of the great aristocratic patrons of the Continent. While other European countries took over the old aristocratic theatres and provided State subsidy for permanent, fully professional companies in every major town, the provision in Britain, particularly of opera, remained intermittent and unplanned, often left to the musicians themselves or enthusiastic impresarios: *inter alios* Handel, Thomas Beecham, Carl Rosa, D'Oyly Carte. The great flowering of interest in opera in the post-war years encouraged a new generation of enthusiasts such as Hans Ucko, Charles Farncombe and Gerald Gover, resulting in numerous small companies many of which found a home at St Pancras.

As it became known that the authorities in St Pancras welcomed new and unknown works and artists, were open to suggestions from them, and were willing to help fund interesting ideas, the Borough became a magnet for enterprising artists of every discipline, not only throughout London, but occasionally from further afield. Many groups were helped into existence with performances at the Festival and also at the borough's many other promotions throughout the year.

The Handel Opera Society was typical of the way some of these companies operated: "Our Committee has always been a working Committee...here were no salaried employees and all this work was entirely voluntary." [16] Financing was by a mixture of small grants and box office receipts. All the effort was directed at producing the highest possible professional standards on stage. Costs were kept to a minimum but so too was risk, so that companies could afford to be adventurous.

Financial constraints shaped events, the obvious one being the limit on what the Council could afford to spend, but also the ticket prices were kept low so that all would be encouraged to come, thus remaining true to the original aims of encouraging local audiences as well as artists.

Many young singers and musicians trying to make their way could not afford the hire of venues like the Wigmore Hall. Leonard Marcus made the borough venues available for a minimal or zero fee, and the Festival provided a means through which generations of young artists gained experience and got themselves noticed. The degree to which artists and performers themselves subsidise the arts in Britain, often being prepared to perform for almost nothing, is little understood by the wider public or by politicians.

Thus, in contrast to the trend at most other festivals, which tended to be part of a 'circuit' using the same well-established artists often playing the same programme at each festival, St Pancras created its own programmes and, as time went on, even its own 'stars'. The success of Joan Sutherland began a new sport: that of spotting the next potential 'star' at a St Pancras Festival performance. Many like John Williams, Janet Baker, Heather Harper, Cleo Laine and John Dankwd remained loyal to the Festival for many years. There was then, and still is now, no career path or structure for would-be opera singers in Britain, and St Pancras provided much-needed opportunities in every department – for singers, conductors, producers, orchestral players, designers, costume designers, lighting experts and administrators, to develop professional skills. A community of artists developed, many of whom lived locally, supported by local audiences who all regarded the Festival as their own.

It was a high-risk strategy in political terms: always presenting new artists and untried works, which could well turn out to be failures, and eschewing the well-tried favourites. The risks were that audiences would stay away, compromising financial viability, and that the programming would attract adverse comment in the press, which would have given rise to legitimate questions about the Council's use of taxpayers' money.

In fact, the opposite happened. In that post-war period, audiences still had an appetite for new work and would go to concerts expecting to hear something new. The long-held assumption that there was no audience for opera in the UK, that it was too exotic an activity to gain widespread popularity, was proved wrong. Those early efforts to present opera by whatever means revealed that an enthusiastic audience would flock to these novel performances, encouraged by the critics who constantly heaped praise on the Council for their enterprise in promoting such unusual repertoire, even when they criticised the quality of some of the works presented.

It is hard to imagine now, but many operas by Mozart, Verdi, Rossini, Handel and Mahler that are now standard repertoire were then scarcely known in Britain. It was the Festival's pioneering work that made many of them part of the mainstream repertoire.

Moreover it was all done under the most difficult circumstances. The Assembly Hall, built in 1937 with seating for 1000, was totally unsuitable for operatic performances. Tom Hawkes, director of many Festival opera productions, wrote in the *Camden Library Journal* in 1966: "At St Pancras we have a shallow platform incapable of flying scenery and with no alternative wing space. If the stage had to accommodate a chorus demanded by Verdi it would need to be completely bereft of anything else." In these early years there was not even any lighting or rigging; it all had to be hired and set up specially for the performances, with the crew working through the night to get it ready; each group using the hall had to start from scratch.

Accommodation for artists backstage was pretty inadequate as well. There were no proper dressing rooms or other facilities and no possibility of proper technical rehearsals or musical preparation: there would be one piano dress rehearsal, one orchestral stage dress rehearsal if you were lucky, then on with the show. The problems did not end there: the acoustics were terrible, and shows were often spoiled by noise from other parts of the building, as Felix Aprahamian commented in *The Sunday Times* many years later: "The quiet final scene was marred by a high-pitched bell ringing somewhere in the Town Hall. It joins the Shaw Theatre's drone as something municipal bureaucracy must see to." Indeed, the facilities did not really suit anything, whether theatre, exhibitions or film, as regular references in the Council records show.

On one occasion, amusingly recounted

by Charles Farncombe in *Music and Musicians* (February 1958), the Handel Opera arrived for rehearsal to find a circus act featuring a small dog already *in situ*. The dog's *pièce de resistance* was to ring a loud bell and play the accordion. Its master obligingly assured the opera singers that their noise would not affect the dog and for two hours the circus and the opera worked amicably, if not harmoniously, side by side.

Nevertheless, over the years the Festival came to be held in the highest regard and affection by every section of the community, including the critics and certainly by the audiences who benefited from it all.

1959

Sir Arthur Bliss, Master of the Queen's Musick, opened the Fifth Festival in February 1959 at the inaugural concert given by the London Symphony Orchestra, conducted by David Littaur. So great was the demand for tickets that it was necessary to employ a temporary box office clerk, and this became a regular procedure every year from then on. A new departure for the Festival was a matinée programme of ballet excerpts given by dancers of the Ballet Rambert and the Royal Ballet, for a large and enthusiastic audience of St Pancras schoolchildren. The St Pancras Municipal Choir had been formed at the suggestion of J Pinches, one of Marcus's team, and was joined by dancers from the Sigurd Leeder School of Drama, assisted by a full orchestra for an unusual concert. The Glasgow Phoenix Choir also appeared.

Two new orchestras gave concerts. The Philomusica of London had been formed by players from the Boyd Neel Orchestra when Neel returned to Canada in 1957. Its first two Artistic Directors were Thurston Dart and George Malcolm, both distinguished harpsichordists specialising in baroque music. The other was the Kensington Symphony Orchestra, founded in 1956 by Leslie Head, to provide orchestral training for amateur and student musicians who played for nothing. Again the emphasis was on rare and unusual works.

Surprisingly, the Festival Ball and the jazz concert, given by Humphrey Lyttelton and his Band, were not as well supported as in previous years: the smaller numbers were attributed to a 'flu epidemic.

The annual St Pancras Artists' exhibition attracted 2000 visitors, and the drama competition was won by Unity Theatre with their production *Puerto Franco*. RADA presented Shaw's *Heartbreak House* and the Tavistock Repertory Company, which had begun life at the Mary Ward Settlement in 1932, gave Vanbrugh's *The Relapse*. Film had its place with Chaplin's *A King in New York* and the Bolshoi production of Prokofiev's ballet *Romeo and Juliet*.

Opera was less prominent. Handel Opera was preoccupied with preparations for a Purcell–Handel Festival and therefore presented only a concert version of *Alcina* with a new cast – Joan Sutherland had been billed to appear, but was indisposed and was replaced by Heather Harper. The Impresario Society staged Cimarosa's *The Secret Marriage* conducted by Dr Hans Ucko.

Press comment in national and local newspapers was again glowing:

"The artistic enterprise of the Borough of St Pancras was proved again in the Town Hall on Saturday night when Sir Arthur Bliss opened their fifth Arts Festival." (*The Times*)

"The single performance of *Alcina* last week in the course of the excellent St Pancras Arts Festival was the most exciting musical occasion in London for many weeks." (*Observer*)

"The Fifth St Pancras Arts Festival should be a model to other Metropolitan Boroughs." (*The Strad*)

The 1959 Annual Library Report itself attracted press comment. *The Guardian* observed that "It is greatly to the credit of the Librarian and to the good sense of the citizens that St Pancras has established a distinguished reputation in the arts without even having a central library." The *New Statesman* commented that "The St Pancras Borough Council spends just under £10,000 a year [on cultural work] but it has promoted an impressive range of activities through its Library Committee...These functions serve a wider audience than the ratepayers of St Pancras. But London's cultural life would be much richer if all the Metropolitan Boroughs were as generous."

1960: "There comes a Festival season"
(the 1960 *Library Journal*)

In 1960 another major change was made to the original Festival formula: the competitive element of the Drama Festival was dropped so as to give all the amateur companies and groups in the borough the opportunity to take part.

The Handel Opera Society gave the opening concert, with soloists Monica Sinclair and Owen Brannigan in a mixed programme of Handel, Bach and Haydn.

The Art Exhibition of work by St Pancras artists, professional as well as amateur, continued. "Each year we show some two hundred examples of the art currently being produced in the borough; paintings of professional and 'Sunday' painters hang side by side, having passed the scrutiny of a representative and expert selection committee. In addition, an 'invited' section demonstrates the work of established professional artists who are intimately associated with St Pancras." [17] Space was also devoted to a small one-man show of work by young local artist Peter Luther, a laboratory technician at a local hospital and "part-time" painter whom the selection committee felt to be worthy of special encouragement. Most of the paintings shown were for sale, and the Borough Council itself bought some half-dozen or so pictures every year for the St Pancras Municipal Collection. Many of these were later to be sold off.

The Annual Report[18] remarks on the problems of success:

"One advantage of a regular, annual event like the Arts Festival is that it is possible to learn from, and improve upon, previous Festivals, so that each successive programme should be better than the last. In the 1959 Festival there was a marked decline in interest in the Jazz Concert and the Festival Ball, and both these items were omitted from the 1960 programme. On the other hand, in the 1959 Festival there seemed to be too little opera, always popular in St Pancras, so the operatic content of the 1960 programme was increased. Running an Arts Festival is always costly, but its results cannot be measured in monetary terms."

Indian dance was included in the Festival for the first time, with the appearance of the famous dancer Ram Gopal, supported by a talented company. This was presented in association with the Asian Music Circle, which had been founded in 1953 to foster the appreciation and study of music and dance of all Asian countries and create greater understanding of Asian peoples and cultures. The programme included classical and modern Indian dances, and Gopal explained the technique and meaning of some of them as part of his performance – "a fascinating insight into an art so beautiful and yet usually so mysterious".[19]

A new opera company made its first appearance; its curious name, Group Eight, was adopted simply because a group of eight people based in Hampstead founded it in 1959. Peter Harwood and Rowland Holt Wilson, an architect by training, who had both worked on events at previous festivals, were the director and designer and the conductor Myer Fredman was asked to be Musical Director. Sir William Walton became its patron. Other members of the team were the architect Christopher Gotch, who for many years wrote for the *Ham & High*, and Patrick Gilbert, who was connected with 'Music and Arts' in Hampstead. Encouraged by Leonard Marcus and nurtured by St Pancras, they also received funding from the Arts Council, the London County Council and private sponsors. Their aim was to bring small-scale opera to the public.

They mounted two productions for the Festival. The first was a double bill of modern operas, which played to somewhat sparse audiences. *Opera* thought Boris Blacher's *The Tide* [9] "a dry and

9 Emily Maire, Shirley Minty and Denis Wicks in Group Eight's production of Blacher's *The Tide*, 1960 (photo Michael Boys; *Opera*)

10 Marcello Cortis and Laura Sarti in Haydn's *Il Mondo della Luna*, 1960 (photo Don Jarvis; *Opera*)

uninteresting little piece", but enthused over *The Sorrows of Orpheus* by Darius Milhaud, and generally gave the new company a guarded welcome.

The second production was Haydn's *Il Mondo della Luna*, with the well-known Italian singer Marcello Cortis [10], in a production first seen at the 1959 Holland Festival. The Library Report described it as
> "an outstanding event in every way... this wonderful production was a fitting climax to what was possibly the most exciting Arts Festival yet."

However, the editor of *Opera* was rather more circumspect:
> "one does not generally have to look very far for the reason for the neglect of certain operas...it might be that the work just cannot come to life dramatically. This is surely why Haydn's stage works have seldom been performed....This I fear is the case with *Il Mondo della Luna*."

Nevertheless, he certainly concurred with the author of the Library Report about the performance, finding that "all the enjoyment came from the timing, acting and singing of that master of buffo, Marcello Cortis". A mark of the Festival's growing reputation was that both the Gulbenkian Foundation and the Arts Council were now prepared to help organisations associated with the Festival. The Gulbenkian's £500 towards the cost of the Haydn production was described in the Annual Library Report as "another generous gesture, of great moral as well as financial encouragement." [19]

The Impresario Society repeated Mozart's *Idomeneo* in a concert performance, with a cast including Ilse Wolf and Nancy Evans.

Other musical events were a piano recital by the Greek pianist Maria Kalogridou at the Working Men's College; a concert of 17th- and 18th-century music in the fine concert room of the Mary Ward Settlement, then in Tavistock Place, and Haydn's oratorio *The Seasons* given by the Board of Trade Choir, conducted by Charles Farncombe.

The Evening of Poetry and Music presented by the Apollo Society drew a large audience for Dame Edith Evans and Christopher Hassall, as did the films of Mozart's *Don Giovanni* in the Vienna State Opera's Salzburg production conducted by Wilhelm Fürtwängler, and *The Burmese Harp* by the Japanese director Kon Ichikawa.

The *Evening Standard* declared "if every borough council were prepared to follow the enterprising example of St Pancras, the state of music in this country would be much healthier."

1961: "First signs of Spring in St Pancras"

The *Library Journal* heralded the 1961 Festival with this title, announcing the month-long Arts Festival in March. "Our Festival has come to have a predominantly operatic flavour and year by year, the programme has included some of the most novel and well produced operas of the London year." [20] That year saw the third major change to the format, completing its evolution from amateur to fully professional status. The Drama Festival was dropped altogether in favour of two professional productions. RADA brought Shaw's *Major Barbara*, and the performance began with a recording of the speech made by GBS himself when he was given the Freedom of the Borough. In-Stage, a professional company founded in 1958 with the encouragement of the British Drama League, gave the first British performance of William Saroyan's play *The Cave Dwellers*, specially written for the Festival and directed by Charles Marowitz. It attracted only modest audiences and was not liked by the critics.

From now on, it was noted in the Council report, not only was the Festival treated by the critics as equal in standing to the great international festivals, but for the first time full houses became the rule rather than the exception; "and it is this, after all, which justifies our work".[21] Its budget had reached £10,000, with the emphasis now very much on professional performances of music and opera at reasonable prices. It was praised in an Arts Council report as "a notable example of imaginative policy and planning in its aims to provide London with opportunities to hear many new and unfamiliar programmes".[22]

The opening concert, Mahler's 3rd Symphony, played by the Polyphonia Symphony Orchestra, conducted by Bryan Fairfax, was a major coup for the Festival. Interest in the works of Mahler was only just beginning and this performance, the British première, attracted nationwide attention. Nearly two hundred people had to be turned away at the box office. *The Times* commented in a preview article: "...though one might wish that the belated première could be undertaken by Dr Bruno Walter and one of the major symphony orchestras, the societies that should have presented it have been put to shame by a London Borough's Public Libraries Committee." In similar vein *The Scotsman* wrote: "The enterprising St Pancras Festival of the Arts (run by a public library, be it noted)...This performance might nudge the guiding hand of another festival. After all, you can travel to Edinburgh from St Pancras".

However, the most astonishing event of the 1961 Festival was the first performance for many years, and the third only in Britain, of Schönberg's *Gurrelieder* conducted by the redoubtable Leslie Head, with an augmented Kensington Symphony Orchestra plus no fewer than five choirs and six soloists, including Monica Sinclair and Robert Thomas. The Town Hall being too small to accommodate these forces, the performance was given in the hall of the Friends' House in Euston Road. As Leslie Head wrote in the St Pancras Journal "Among the whole output of post-Wagnerian music it is doubtful whether there is any work so much talked about and yet so little heard as this. It is ironical that the inclusion of iron chains among its array of percussion instruments is often given more prominence than the splendours which are to be discovered in the vast, opulent and lavishly orchestrated work".[23] The performance was hailed as a triumph by the press. The *Sunday Times* commented that "the Borough Fathers of St Pancras have led the way, followed at a respectful distance by those of Vienna and Edinburgh".

Opera, too, was an unqualified success. Group Eight offered a full-length classical opera and a modern double bill. Rossini's *Italian Girl in Algiers* with the English Chamber Orchestra conducted by Peter Gellhorn was very well received, especially the singing of Jean Allister and Derek Hammond-Stroud. The double bill consisted of Menotti's powerful melodrama *The Medium* and Chabrier's light and very Gallic *A Lesson in Love*. In the former, Monica Sinclair, the St Pancras favourite, scored a tremendous personal success.

The Impresario Society gave the first British performance of Verdi's early comic opera *Un Giorno di Regno* [12], which played to two near-capacity houses. It was the first of a series of such Verdi rediscoveries at the Festival, which with the encouragement of Lionel Dunlop, critic and Verdi enthusiast, who had joined the Arts-Subcommittee, played almost as important a role in the renaissance of interest in that composer in Britain as the Handel Opera Society's performances were doing for Handel. That Society staged three Carissimi oratorios. *Opera* praised the Festival in its May editorial, noting that with the dearth of opera in the provinces, other boroughs should be following St Pancras's example.

The London Bach Society, conducted by Paul Steinitz, participated for the first time with a programme of Bach, Mozart and Lennox Berkeley with Janet Baker, then at the beginning of her career, as soloist. The Apollo Society returned with Sybil Thorndike and Lewis Casson.

Cecil Sharp House celebrated the Golden Jubilee of its Folk Dance section

11 Festival brochure 1961 – the design used for several years in the early 1960s

12 Verdi's *Un Giorno di Regno*, Festival 1961

with an exhibition and four concerts of folk music, billed as The Folk Variety Theatre, the first of which opened the Festival.

The Festival ended with an evening of excerpts from classical ballet with Doreen Wells and Alexander Bennett from the Royal Ballet. It was judged not entirely successful: "If ballet is to have a place in the Festival it will require as much money as is spent on the operas, which are still the centrepiece of the Festival." [24]

Amongst the many press cuttings about the Festival praising the work of the borough the following from a *Music and Musicians* editorial is typical: "The broad vision of the Borough Public Libraries Committee is a shining light and an example for others. The least it can do is to shame them into doing likewise".

With the greatly expanded programme came ever higher expectations. "The festival is now established as a national event. But if this brings a larger audience it also brings higher standards of criticism".[25] It began to be noted that the large Assembly Hall was unsuitable for some of the smaller concerts and reference is made to the Central Library which was being planned, and which was to have its own small theatre-cum-concert hall where more specialised programmes could be given. New civic premises were in the planning stages; these were eventually to become the Shaw Theatre and the Swiss Cottage Library and Baths, but it was some years before they were opened.

1962

St Pancras' *Library Journal* had now become a useful medium through which to publicise the Festival, with many pages in its February and March issues on the forthcoming programmes and informative articles about the works and performers. Only in 1962 did Leonard Marcus come out from the shadows and write a rare article for it under his own name, introducing the Festival, in which he reiterated the policy:

"The paramount reason for the Festival is firstly to give the citizens of St Pancras an opportunity to see, in their own area, performances of opera, concerts and plays performed by professionals of very high standard and produced by the best possible producers, and secondly to give an opportunity for the Borough's own amateur and professional painters and actors to exhibit their capabilities." [26]

"The fame and popularity of the Arts Festival continues to increase from year to year and we are very grateful for the support we receive from the critics, who almost invariably praise our enterprise, if not always its results, as well as from the public, the only real justification for the work we do." [27]

Indeed, not all the critics were able to praise the choice of works for the opening concert of 1962, again given by the Polyphonia Symphony Orchestra conducted by Bryan Fairfax. Concentrating as it did on 20th-century work, the Busoni piano concerto was thought over-long and dull, and few found the first performance of Havergal Brian's 18th symphony a very exciting occasion. Arthur Jacobs in the *Financial Times* was representative: "Having made the customary salaams to the municipal enterprise behind the annual St Pancras Arts Festival, I must be frank in describing last night's opening concert: two of the dullest works I have ever heard." [28]

The Chanticleer Orchestra conducted by Ruth Gipps (who paid most of the costs of her concert herself) and the Francis Chagrin Ensemble both appeared at the Festival for the first time with interesting programmes which also concentrated on new music. The composer Francis Chagrin had founded the Society for the Promotion of New Music in 1943 and now saw a need for an ensemble to explore the repertoire of works that lie between chamber music and orchestral music and require a conductor. The original group of eminent musicians who became the Chagrin Ensemble in 1952 had all at some time been soloists with the London Symphony Orchestra.

The Chanticleer played Elgar's cello concerto and Bliss's concerto for two pianos, while the Chagrin Ensemble's enterprising programme mixed work by contemporary composers – Malcolm Arnold, John Addison and the Danish composer Niels Viggo-Bentzon – with concertos by Bach and Vivaldi, and rounded off with Saint-Saens' "Carnival of the Animals". However, these programmes failed to draw the public. As the Annual Library report commented: "Unfortunately, audiences seem prepared to listen to concerts consisting entirely of 18th-century or even 20th-century music, but not to mixed programmes like this one."

Venues other than the unsatisfactory Assembly Hall were tried out. The Finchley Choral Society performed Honegger's *King David* with Sir Donald Wolfit as narrator at Friends' House in Euston Road, and St Pancras Church on Upper Woburn Place proved more congenial for The London Bach Society than the Assembly Rooms. Very successful was the concert of baroque music given by the Mary Ward Cantata Choir with their conductor Dr Walter Bergmann, and Ilse Wolf, Alfred Deller and Carl Dolmetsch among the soloists. *The Times* described it as "good planning" and *Musical Events* called it "among the most pleasing events" of the Festival. The Apollo Society's Evening of Poetry and Music featured Jill Balcon with C Day Lewis and harpist Osian Ellis.

The drama contribution followed the same pattern as in 1961, with RADA students in Oscar Wilde's then little-known play *An Ideal Husband* and a presentation by Theatre Group Productions of Peter Albery's play *Anne Boleyn*. Again it was the RADA production which was a success while the fully professional company was a disappointment. Of Sylvia Read's playing of the name part the *Guardian* said "If this is what the woman was really like, small wonder that Henry's passion cooled so pretty damn quick."

"Perhaps the Assembly Rooms are unsatisfactory for drama, perhaps the overcrowded programme of the Festival did not allow the company enough time for rehearsal, but, whatever the cause, the play was not a success. This is the second time that the Festival has included a professional production of a new play, and the second time that the production has not been a success. The way that actors tend to work for long seasons while singers only work for a few nights at a time makes it difficult to produce plays in the same way as the operas, though if the Festival is to retain any sort of balance some solution to the problem must be found". [28]

The most successful opera production of the season continued the Festival's Verdi revival with *I Masnadieri* [13] presented by yet another new company, Philopera Circle. It also gave an early platform to the soprano Pauline Tinsley, who was to become another Festival "star". Philopera had started as an amateur company in 1950, giving regular annual performances of neglected operas such as Glinka's *Ruslan and Ludmilla*, Gounod's *Romeo and Juliet*, *Lucrezia Borgia* by Donizetti and Auber's comic opera *Fra Diavolo*. In 1960 the Public Libraries

13 Pauline Tinsley in Verdi's *I Masnadieri*. "By any standards she sounds to me one of our best sopranos" (photo Stewart L Galloway; *Opera*, May 1962)

14 Heather Harper, Johanna Peters in Arne's *Artaxerses*, 1962 (photo Reg Wilson; Handel Opera Society archive)

Committee offered to increase its grant to them if they would in future employ professional soloists. After some highly successful performances of Rossini's *Otello* in the 1961–2 season, with Pauline Tinsley as Desdemona, they were invited to appear at the Festival. The name, as their founder conductor, Franz Manton explained in an article in the *Library Journal*, "is a Greek–Latin construction meaning a 'love of opera'. It is this love of opera which St Pancras, in association with societies such as this, has done so much to sponsor and which has enabled so many fine works to be enjoyed by music lovers who could not have seen them on the stage in any other place." The applause for *I Masnadieri* from a capacity audience was tumultuous, and box-office receipts broke all records for St Pancras Festivals. The *Opera* critic wrote: "The opera proved heady, exhilarating, full of life and energy" and although "the faults of the libretto are plain enough" it was "the sheer impact of the music" which made its mark.

Group Eight's double bill – the first British production of *Crane Feathers* by the Swedish composer Sven-Erik Back, who himself conducted the performances, and Bizet's *Doctor Miracle*, in Anthony Besch's production, was considered "one of the Group's most valuable undertakings to date" by *The Times* and was also very popular with the public.

The third opera in the 1962 Festival, Thomas Arne's *Artaxerxes*, performed by the Handel Opera Society [14], had a more mixed press. The *Daily Mail* headed its review "Dr Arne won't be best remembered for this" while *The Stage* thought it "hard going". *The Times* and the *Daily Worker*, however, agreed that its resurrection was well worth while, and the box-office receipts and the prolonged applause suggested that the public agreed.

In addition to the annual exhibition of

St Pancras Artists there was an exhibition of Swedish design, arranged by the Swedish Cultural Institute to complement the performance of *Crane Feathers*, a new idea for the Festival. However, it put pressure on the space available. There was also a Civic Exhibition arranged by the Highgate Literary and Scientific Institute in association with the St Pancras and Hornsey Borough Councils.

1963: "Music? St Pancras is the place"

By 1963 the size and popularity of the Festival was such that staff had difficulty in coping with the extra work. Demand for tickets almost overwhelmed the box-office. Costs rose to £12,898, but so did income to £1,938. The cost estimates for 1963 had been £11,420, of which only £9000 was available. The Committee discussed the possibility of reducing costs but found themselves "quite unable to agree to the omission of any items which would make a worthwhile reduction". They therefore requested an extra £2,420 from the Finance Committee. This became a regular procedure to get the requisite funds and push the budgetary boundaries each year. The amount asked for at an early stage tended to be based on the previous year's outlay. Later in the year another request would explain that the forecast was now exceeding what had been asked for, and the small extra amount was granted.

Improvements were made to the Assembly Rooms. Over £3,500 was spent on a new stage lighting system with a 36-way dimmer board, long- and short-range mirror spotlights, stage spotlights and battens. There was an attempt to improve the acoustics and £500 was spent on an up-to-date amplifying system.

The Press was as enthusiastic as ever. **"Music? St Pancras is the place"**, ran the headline to Leslie Ayre's article in the *Evening News*, while the *Evening Standard* had "Pennywise St Pancras packs in the culture seekers". David Cairns in the *Spectator* wrote that

> "St Pancras Town Hall has made itself in the past few weeks into a musical centre not inferior in interest to several of the grander institutions and superior in the atmosphere of enterprises boldly planned and brought to deservedly successful conclusions."

The borough's minutes record their appreciation that it was a "subtle compliment" that the press no longer felt the need to praise the enterprise and courage of the Council but simply accepted the Festival as a major event, applying to it the highest critical standards. With such encouragement the Department thought of their Festival from now on as a fully professional enterprise.

For the first time a foreign orchestra, the Hungarian State Symphony, was invited to open the Festival. Yet again the inadequacies of the Assembly Hall and the need for a smaller concert hall were felt. There was the usual eclectic mix of music – the Chagrin Ensemble did a programme ranging from Purcell to the modern American composer Gail Kubik. The London Bach Society sang Mozart, Nicholas Maw and Bruckner; Brian Fairfax conducted Mahler's Seventh Symphony and the French organist André Marchal gave a recital at St Pancras Church.

The Park Lane Group presented some of their young recitalists, so beginning a collaboration with the Festival that continued until the penultimate year. "It was perhaps inevitable" wrote the Borough Librarian "that the Committee should eventually be associated with the Park Lane Group whose objects – the presentation of new artists and new music – are so close to our own".[29] The PLG was started in 1956 by music students from the Guildhall School of Music to provide a central London platform for young artists that did not involve them in the relatively high cost of the usual public recital, and to provide an opportunity for rarely played works to be heard. It was originally called the Music Section of the Related Arts Centre, and concerts were given at Park Lane House, once the home of Philip Sassoon, which had its own small theatre. It was made available free of charge through the generosity of the company that owned it and was organised on a basis of trust, with the students having their own key.

When Park Lane House was demolished in 1961, the Arts Council allowed the concerts to be held in the beautiful Great Drawing Room of their headquarters at 4 St James's Square and it was decided to adopt the name Park Lane Group to maintain the link with past activities. Amongst the many distinguished artists given a platform at the beginning of

15 Philopera Circle's production of Verdi's *Ernani*, 1963 (photo Crispian Woodgate)

their careers were Gwyneth Jones and John Ogden. Their first association with St Pancras, a concert performance of Britten's *The Rape of Lucretia* in May 1962 as part of the Council's regular annual concert season, led to their first invitation to appear at the Festival.

There were two poetry evenings, one entitled Poetry of St Pancras, Past and Present, at Hamilton House, organised by the Highgate Poetry Circle, the other a programme of Poetry and Jazz presented by Jeremy Robson at the festival for the first time. Robson had first staged a Poetry and Jazz evening at Hampstead Town Hall in 1961 that was an astonishing success – 500 people had to be turned away and a follow-up reading was arranged at the Festival Hall. He wrote

> "At that time the format of our programme was very rough indeed. Nobody knew exactly what was needed and as a result those early days really were 'experimental.' Since then we have given a number of performances up and down the country, steering clear of London until a programme had evolved that was more definite in shape and more even in the standard of performance." [30]

This performance too attracted a capacity audience.

The St Pancras Artists' exhibition was opened by Arnold Wesker, with the one-man show devoted to the work of the Camden Town artist Peter Peri.

The drama production by Centre Stage, Muriel Spark's *The Ballad of Peckham Rye*, adapted from her novel, was not entirely successful. But it was felt that by using the stage extension in front of the proscenium arch the company had solved the problem of the shape and size of the Assembly Hall, which had always bedevilled drama presented there.

The highlights of the Festival were, as ever, the operas. Philopera Circle's performances of Verdi's *Ernani* [15] were a complete sell-out. David Cairns reported that "the house was packed and piteous tales were going round of distinguished musicians vainly combing London for a seat". The critic of the *Evening Standard* was fulsome in his praise:

> "But for real operatic novelty last week I was diverted to St Pancras Town Hall, where the St Pancras Borough Council shames other municipalities with its annual Arts Festival. Here the Philopera Circle, under the baton of Franz Manton, revived a little-known, early opera of Verdi's, *Ernani*. The St Pancras fans – who, I should say, form the most sophisticated opera audience in London – cheered it mightily."

One of the performances coincided with a *Meistersinger* at Covent Garden, and according to one press report some of the chorus managed to combine both, appearing in *Ernani* at St Pancras Town Hall and rushing to the Opera House for the last act of the Wagner as soon as *Ernani* ended.

This success was equalled by the performance of Britten's 1957 children's opera *Noye's Fludde* [16]. It was given by the then newly formed Finchley Children's Music Group and the London Boy Singers conducted by John Andrewes, with Owen Brannigan as Noye and Edith Coates as his wife. The audience filled the large St Pancras Church to overflowing.

The third opera, Rossini's *La Pietra del Paragone*, was another interesting première given by Group Eight, of which Desmond Shawe-Taylor wrote in the *Sunday Times*:

"Everyone who has read Stendhal's *Life of Rossini* must have felt some curiosity about the composer's first big success, *La Pietra del Paragone* or *The Touchstone*; and now St Pancras, great allayers of curiosity, have enabled us to see it in a lively and successful production by Group Eight."

The translation by Arthur Jacobs included witty references to St Pancras which delighted the audience.

There were two disappointments. The Mahler performance was not well attended and the performance of the opera *Ulysses* by John Christopher Smith, Handel's assistant, by the Handel Opera Society's Chandos Chorus was not a success. Apart from *Opera*, whose critic thought the music very enjoyable, few of the critics thought the work worth reviving. But of course for the Festival promoters the justification for presenting it remained the same – that such works must be heard at least once so that their worth can be truly measured.

1964

This year marked the 40th anniversary of Leonard Marcus's period of service in the Libraries Department. Councillor John Richardson, Chairman of the Libraries Committee, offered congratulations on his long and distinguished career.

The Festival programme contained some of the most interesting opera revivals so far as well as two of the biggest names in British music. It is an indication of how far the Festival had come that they were able to secure Peter Pears and Benjamin Britten to give a recital, presented in conjunction with *Youth and Music*. Founded in 1954 by Sir Robert Mayer, *Youth and Music* began its association with St Pancras in 1962 when the borough helped fund two new series: *Your Concert Nights*, featuring performances of chamber music, and *Your Discussion Nights*. The Pears–Britten recital was one of these Concert Nights and the tickets were gone within days, leaving many people disappointed.

Ringing endorsement of the Festival was demonstrated by the larger than ever audiences, with full houses for many events, and by the press comment. *The Times* felt that "One of the most significant contributions of the St Pancras Arts Festival to London's musical life lies in the opportunities it provides for hearing unfamiliar works" while Desmond Shawe-Taylor, long a firm fan of the Festival, made his usual tribute in the *Sunday Times*: "St Pancras, thou art of boroughs *a per se*...The operatic annals of St Pancras are both various and glorious; all the off-beat Mozart and Verdi and Rossini that we despair of hearing anywhere else turn up sooner or later in the Euston Road."

The staff situation was improved by employing an additional assistant in the box office and a temporary copy-typist. The music critic Denby Richards, then writing for the *Ham and High*, was co-opted onto the Advisory committee.

16 Finchley Children's Music Group in Britten's *Noye's Fludde* in St Pancras Church, 1963 (photo Mason Bryar Studios)

17 Opera Concert's production of Verdi's *Aroldo* (photo Crispian Woodgate). "The demand for Verdi is insatiable, and the exhumation of his less successful operas goes on apace to meet it. Last night's specimen was having its English première 107 years late. It proved quite a lively corpse." (*Daily Mail*, 26.2.64)

The programme was settling into a pattern, with a group of performers who were the mainstay of the Festival but also introducing many newcomers: the New London Wind Ensemble, yet another group of chamber music players, formed in 1962, and the Schoenberg Wind Quintet, and a new venue, Camden School for Girls. The Bournemouth Symphony Orchestra gave the opening concert conducted by James Loughran with soloist Tessa Robbins, and the final concert given in conjunction with *Youth and Music* was devoted mainly to the works of Stravinsky. The London Bach Society returned with an interesting programme which included Dallapiccola's *Canti di Prigionia*. Other return visits were the Finchley Children's Music Group at Friends' House, organ recitals at St Pancras Church, the Francis Chagrin Ensemble with its usual adventurous programme and Dr Walter Bergmann's concert of 17th- and 18th-century music, which attracted a large and appreciative audience.

There was lengthy consideration of jazz programmes, taking into account the advent of the new movements in jazz emerging in America. The committee would have liked to expand the programmes by forming a band from various jazz groups specially for the Festival. But nothing came of this and the Poetry and Jazz evening was repeated.

Drama was provided by Unity Theatre with performances of Brecht's *The Good Woman of Szechuan*, but these were not considered up to the usual Festival standard. *The Times* conceded that the production might be more successful in its home theatre, but "at present...it is not clear whether one is watching an opera or a circus."

The Annual Art Exhibition, opened by David Kossoff, attracted a record 1,281 visitors, who came to admire and also to buy the varied paintings and sculptures on display.

Yet another new opera company appeared with another British première of a Verdi opera, *Aroldo* [17]. Opera Concerts was set up in 1962 by the conductor and composer Gerald Gover to give concert performances of rare operas, in particular those whose stage presentation was beyond the resources of a small company. It had already presented excerpts of Verdi's *Giovanna d'Arco* in Hampstead, where Gover lived, but now launched into a fully staged effort with producer John Cox.

Harold Rosenthal in *Opera* was, as ever, demanding:

"Verdi's *Aroldo*, one of the very few Verdi operas till now never staged in London, was enthusiastically received by a capacity audience largely made up of 'opera aficionados' – for how else could one explain the cheers and bravos for an opera whose libretto is almost hysterically funny, and for a performance that was hardly distinguished musically? Unless of course this was the usual British audience reaction to a 'jolly good shot' by a shoestring group, an attitude which may at times make us forget our sense of proportion."

The cast was led by Anne Edwards and Michael Maurel.

Philopera Circle mounted a production of *Iphigenia in Aulis* [18] by Gluck, which found marginally more favour with Rosenthal:

18 Philopera Circle's *Iphigenia in Aulis*, 1964: "Martin Lawrence, immense in stature and voice, was a commanding Calchas." (Photo Crispian Woodgate; *Opera*, May 1964)

"A welcome production of Glück's first Iphigénie opera, which is performed far less frequently than *Iphigénie en Tauride*. Indeed, these were only the second series of performances in London...even a rough and ready performance, such as this was, gives more than an adequate idea of its dramatic and musical power...."

Cherubini's *Pygmalion*, given in a concert performance, was another of those rediscoveries which the critics felt had remained unknown for a very good reason. As *The Times* put it:

"That not every neglected composer is a neglected master, nor every neglected work a neglected masterpiece, are commonplace discoveries. Yet we have a right, perhaps even a duty, to make these discoveries for ourselves from time to time...."

It was conducted by Joseph Horovitz, his first appearance at the Festival, and he received high praise for its polished performance, as did the stylish singing of Maureen Lehane, although Donald Mitchell of the *Daily Telegraph* commented that "When Pygmalion, according to the stage directions, falls asleep, I was consumed with envy."

The major success was the Handel Opera Society's beautifully presented light-hearted performance [19] of *L'Infedeltà Delusa* by Haydn, which was sold out. The critics were unanimous in their praise.

The Financial Times said "the performance should not be missed", although *Opera* was again more circumspect: "Considered as music, the whole of *L'Infedeltà Delusa* is well worth hearing for its liveliness and charm; but as a comic opera it scarcely gets going until the second of its two acts." Patricia Clark, Eric Shilling, Adrian de Peyer and Kenneth Bowen were in the fine cast, directed by Colin Graham.

The Council minutes recorded with satisfaction that: "Box-office reaction seemed to indicate that people were more and more prepared to sample anything that St Pancras had to offer, with the knowledge that it would certainly be unusual and probably stimulating.[30]

1965

Preparations for the eleventh Festival in 1965 proceeded against the background of the imminent amalgamation of St Pancras with Hampstead and much of Holborn. The elections for the new London Borough of Camden had already taken place, and the Festival took

19 Haydn's *L'Infedeltà Delusa* (Handel Opera Society, 1964) (photo Crispian Woodgate)

advantage of the enlarged borough to spread into new areas.

Jennie Lee, the recently appointed Under Secretary of State for Education and Science with special responsibility for the Arts, opened the proceedings at the Exhibition of St Pancras Artists, with a eulogy for the borough's achievements: "If every Council had the same regard for the arts as you have, we would be leading the world. We have to break through both political and class barriers – and the latter will be more difficult. But courage, we are already on the way, as by your presence here you testify."[31] That exhibition concentrated on work by the Art Department of the Working Men's College and there was also a St Pancras Exhibition at Maple's, the well-known furniture store, then on Tottenham Court Road.

There were more operas than ever: the "first authentic revival" of Debussy's *Pelléas et Mélisande*, *The Lodger* by Phyllis Tate, and a repeat of Britten's *Noye's Fludde*. Monteverdi's *Il Ritorno d'Ulisse in Patria* played to a full house with enthusiastic applause and drew gratitude from the *Opera* critic for bringing it back to the stage. However, the Handel Opera Society's unusual production of Rossini's *Il Turco in Italia* by Michael Geliot, in which the singers remained hidden behind cardboard cut-out figures with only their faces showing during the whole evening [20], was a disaster, panned by the critics and calling forth a particularly elaborate curse from Harold Rosenthal in *Opera*: "If murdering or attempting to murder operas was a criminal offence I think I would sentence them both [Geliot and the designer, Jennifer Agnew] for the next five years to attend a series of performances of operas by Rauzzini, Mayr and Marschner by superannuated singers, produced by failed students of the Max Reinhardt and Stanislavsky schools in Eastern European opera houses…" and much more in the same vein.[32] Opera-Concerts, Finchley Children's Music Group, and Group Eight all returned, and a new name, Basilica Productions, appears – also run by the Group Eight team.

The performance of new music was more prominent than ever. The opening concert was given by the Macnaughton Concerts, playing in the Festival for the first time. One of the most significant organisations in the country for the promotion of new music, it was founded in 1931 by Elisabeth Lutyens, Iris Lemare and Anne Macnaughton to improve performance opportunities for young composers. Benjamin Britten was one of the early beneficiaries. They presented four challenging 20th-century works: Peter Maxwell Davies's Five Motets and Chamber Music No.4 by Hindemith received their British premières, while Lennox Berkeley's *Stabat Mater* and Stravinsky's *Canticum Sacrum* were given second hearings. Norman del Mar conducted the English Chamber Orchestra and the Ambrosian Singers.

Composer Joseph Horovitz [21] returned with a programme featuring concertos, including the first performance of his own Trumpet Concerto, played by Philip Jones with the New Philharmonia Orchestra.

"As listener as well as composer I find the concerto form more exciting than any

20 *Il Turco in Italia* (Rossini) in 1965, with cardboard cutout figures on stage.

other, and I applaud the imagination and generosity of the St Pancras Arts Festival in making it possible to arrange this 'Concerto Concert'. Although we shall be performing six concertos, I like to think that this seeming marathon will be an enjoyable 'sprint'." [34]

The other works were the Tuba Concerto by Ralph Vaughan Williams and Gordon Jacobs' Trombone Concerto.

Poetry and Music was provided by the Barrow Poets and Jazz by the Mike Westbrook Jazz Band. The New London Wind Ensemble, the London Bach Society with Heather Harper and Janet Baker, and Youth and Music with the Camden Wind Quintet, returned.

The guitarist John Williams [22] gave a recital that began a long association with the Festival. He played every year until 1979. An innovation was a 'Celebrity Concert' with Jacqueline du Pré and Stephen Kovacevich (then known as Stephen Bishop) – no doubt due to the help of Jack Henderson, who was then working for Youth and Music and was shortly to join the Festival team.

James Roose-Evans' Hampstead Theatre Club appeared in the Festival for the first time with a new translation of *Hippolytus* by Euripides.

The Festival had cost around £13,000; about 12,000 people attended the various events and many performances were sold out. For the first time, some of the concerts were broadcast by the BBC.

An end and a beginning

By the time the Festival ended, the various transitional stages of amalgamation had been completed, and St Pancras Borough Council was no more.

Leonard Marcus, Acting Borough Librarian for a short period during the interregnum, was responsible for the 1964-5 Annual Report, and heralded the change with the hope that the success of the last Festival would augur well for the new Borough of Camden:

"In this report on the work of the St Pancras Public Libraries to be presented to the last meeting of the Libraries and Arts Committee of the St Pancras Borough Council, and as the Committee's longest-serving senior officer, I would like to express my sincere thanks to the members of the Committee for their kindness, understanding and patience in furthering and enhancing the value of the work of the Public Libraries of the Borough, and to me personally.

"I would also like to express my thanks publicly to all members of the staff – officers and employees – for their conscientious work and for their willingness to undertake all kinds of duties which have furthered the value of the libraries and made them of greater use to the people of St Pancras.

"Since 1924 I have seen the Public Libraries of the Borough grow from one old-fashioned purpose-built library at Highgate and a temporary conversion in Camden Street with a staff of 16 and an issue of about 350,000 [volumes] a year, to a system of seven branch libraries – five opened in the past three years, and two separate junior libraries, with a staff of 80 and an annual issue of more than 1,300,000 items.

"With regard to the St Pancras Arts Festival and its allied cultural activities, it is certain that the Committee has established a reputation for artistic patronage that is second to none in the whole country and I am sure that the Committee is aware that the Festival is now looked forward to eagerly by people from all parts of England and even from America and Europe."

An article in *The Times* in August 1965 concurred; comparing the Festival with Glyndebourne, Salzburg and Edinburgh, the writer concluded that "St Pancras does [the less familiar Mozart] much more justice and the singing is more

21 Joseph Horovitz (Allegro Photographic Studios).
"[The St Pancras Festival] was a major stepping stone in my musical life; it gave me a chance not only as a conductor but as a composer." [33]

22 John Williams, who played at the Festival from 1965 to 1979

agreeable. The tickets are much cheaper as well."

Christopher Grier, in an interview with Marcus for *The Scotsman* in 1966, throws more light on the man and his views:

"Listening to Mr Marcus's saga, one soon realised that his enthusiasm was backed by a very shrewd sense of timing and a certain relish in the disciplines of local government. Furthermore, while he made no claims for expertise on artistic matters and avoided any such title as artistic director it was quite obvious that his was the voice that was listened to by the programme committee.

"I fancy that the present course as well as the past survival of the festival is very much his doing. But leagued with him is his chairman, a highly intelligent youngish executive in J Walter Thompson, Councillor J C Richardson, and a Head of Arts Services in the person of Jack Henderson, formerly with Harold Holt Ltd. It is a formidable team.

I began to see why people come from all over the country and foreign parts to see how St Pancras–Camden does it."

The Festival had completed nine years of astonishing achievement which had transformed the reputation of the borough. Now a turning point loomed.

Notes for chapter 2

1. *St Pancras Library Journal* Dec 1953 (vol 8) p 128.
2. St Pancras Borough Council Minutes (StPBCM) 27.4.55 (vol 72) Report of General Purposes Committee, p 218.
3. Annual Library Report 1956–7, p16.
4. Annual Library Report 1955–6, pp 2–3, *The Arts in St Pancras*
5. *St Pancras Library Journal* Oct–Nov 1955 (vol 9) p 84.
6. Camden Festival Press release, 29.2.68.
7. StPBCM 3.1.56 (vol 73) Report of the Public Libraries Committee, p 3.
8. *Opera* May 1957 (vol 7) p 385.
9. *The Story of the Handel Opera Society* Handel Opera Society.
10. *Autobiography of Joan Sutherland* Weidenfeld & Nicholson, 1997, pp 56–7.
11. Andrew Porter, *Financial Times*, 20 March 1957.
12. John Richardson. Introduction to Festival Programme 1966.
13. *Ham & High* 14.3.58.
14. Annual Library Report 1958–9, p 13.
15. Education and Libraries Committee Report 23.11.48.
16. See note 9.
17. *St Pancras Library Journal* Feb 1960 (vol 13), p 81.
18. Annual Library Report 1959–60 pp 12, 14.
19. Annual Library Report 1960, p 12
20. *St Pancras Library Journal* Feb 1961 (vol 14) p 159.
21. Libraries and Arts Sub-Committee, 6.9.61 Agenda Item 2a: Seventh St Pancras Arts Festival.
22. Public Libraries Committee Minutes 17.10.61 Agenda item 11.
23. *St Pancras Library Journal* Feb 1961 (vol 14) p 166.
24. Annual Libraries report 1960–1 p.14
25. Public Libraries Committee minutes 27.3.62, Agenda item 9.
26. *St Pancras Library Journal* Feb 1962 (vol 15) p159. "Omnes artes....
27. Annual Library report 1961-2 p 15.
28. *The Financial Times* 27.2.62.
29. Report to Library Committee 29.5.62.
30. StPBCM 29.4.64, Libraries and Arts Committee Report, p 195.
31. *North London Press* 12.3.65
32. *Opera* May 1965 (vol 16) p 382.
33. Joseph Horovitz interviewed, 2002.
34. *St Pancras Library Journal* Feb 1965 (vol 18) p 171.

3   Three into one (1965–1968): the Camden Festival emerges

[Notes for chapter 3 are on p 54]

The upheavals caused by the Local Government Act of 1963, when the borough of St Pancras was merged with that of Hampstead and much of Holborn to become the new 'superborough' of Camden, could have posed a serious threat to the continuation of the Festival. However, the Festival was by now so well regarded that there was no real doubt that it would continue, but some people were fearful for the future of the St Pancras Arts Festival in the context of a new London Borough.[1] In his interview with Christopher Grier in *The Scotsman* in January 1966, Leonard Marcus reveals that continuing the Festival was by no means plain sailing. Grier began by asking

> Why should Camden, even if it is the second richest borough in London (way after Westminster but ahead of Kensington & Chelsea) be spending about £75,000 on the arts during the current financial year? To find out, I went up to Basil Spence's new library at Swiss Cottage to talk to Mr Leonard Marcus, first deputy borough librarian, a twinkling bonhomous veteran of St Pancras enterprises…Mr Marcus was in on St Pancras's art promotion and patronage from the beginning. "My best achievement," he declared, "was to keep the Council spending money on this sort of thing. It wasn't easy at first. Some councillors thought it money down the drain. We wondered what would happen when the Tories got control, but fortunately the new chairman of the libraries committee turned out to have a passion for opera, especially early Verdi. But now they realise the value of the Festival."

Many of the councillors had their own vision of the Council as a promoter of the good life, and for the councillors who did not share their artistic views, there was always the pleasure of the success and publicity which came to the Borough to compensate.[2]

Nevertheless, it was fortunate that under the new Labour administration the newly formed Camden Libraries Committee had as its first chairman Councillor John Richardson, whose enthusiastic interest not only saw the Festival safely through this transitional period, but turned the change to advantage by seizing the opportunities of increased funding to greatly expand it. Camden adopted the clear and generous policy of support for the arts begun by St Pancras, and the following decade saw further growth, and enhancement of the Festival's reputation.

There were, in addition, important developments in the wider context of national government and its relationship to the arts. Under Harold Wilson's premiership in 1964, Britain had for the first time a Minister for the Arts, Jennie Lee. She immediately set about drawing up a White Paper on the subject. It was a revolutionary document, the most farseeing and significant statement of Government policy on the arts ever issued in Britain,[3] in striking contrast to the negative attitudes of the pre-war years. It gave the arts world an unprecedented sense of optimism and hope for the future, calling upon local authorities to spend money on the arts and declaring that:

> "If a high level of artistic achievement is to be sustained and the best in the arts made more widely available, more generous and discriminating help is urgently needed, locally, regionally, and nationally. In some parts of the country professional companies are non-existent. Even amateurs find it hard to keep going. And lack of suitable buildings makes it impossible to bring any of the leading national companies, orchestral, operatic, ballet, or theatre, into those areas.... Too many working people have been conditioned by their education and environment to consider the best in music, painting, sculpture and literature outside their reach."[4]

Even the Trades Union Movement had come out with a rare pronouncement on the arts, with Resolution 42 passed by Congress in 1960 which recognised "the importance of the arts in the life of the community.... [Congress] notes that the trade union movement has participated to only a small extent in the direct promotion of plays, films, music, literature and other forms of expression....Congress considers that much more could be done" (p 43 of ref. 5, p 13). This was to be significant for the Festival later on when Arnold Wesker, encouraged by Resolution 42, established Centre 42 at the Round House in Chalk Farm, giving the Festival an important new venue.

Against this background the new Camden councillors could not but feel that they were already on the right path. Compared with anything before or since, these were halcyon days for the funding of the arts and Camden played its part in full.

Borough differences

Although they were neighbours geographically, the history and political style of the three Councils had been very different, with little contact between them. Hampstead and Holborn were dominated by the Conservatives and retained a sedate quiet image. St Pancras had a long history of radical and unconventional councillors[5]: for instance, in the late 1950s the borough hit the national news when some of its councillors were surcharged by the government for refusing to raise rents. Hampstead and Holborn had also funded arts activities such as local drama, art and music societies, but on a far smaller scale than St Pancras.

As at St Pancras, Holborn's annual programme of arts activities was organised directly by the Borough and took place during the winter months. It included concerts organised in conjunction with the music department at the City Literary Institute: recitals of recorded music, lectures and student drama productions. Its lively film club, showing many art house films as well as more mainstream fare, had been in existence since 1947. It had also pioneered a picture lending scheme.

In Hampstead, arts activity developed independently of local government, promoted by two organisations set up and run by local people: the Hampstead Artists' Council (HAC), which covered the field of visual arts and started the Hampstead Festival in 1951, and Music and Arts in Hampstead (M & A), which looked after music, drama, literature, photography and other activities, and later took over responsibility for the Festival. Although both organisations received some backing and financial help from Hampstead Council, they remained independent.

M & A, which was rather similar in structure to the old St Pancras Arts and Civic Council, saw its main role as a co-ordinating body for the activities of its member societies, of which there were about ten, all based in Hampstead; they included the Hampstead Choral Society, Hampstead Music Club and Hampstead Photographic Society and all paid M & A a membership fee. Its chairman and guiding spirit was Noel Woolf, who represented the Hampstead Drama Guild, and who ran the theatrical publishers Samuel French. Although a wide range of professionals and amateurs contributed their services, all their work was voluntary. Their enthusiasm created a lively arts scene with a great variety of programmes, mostly using local talent to entertain local audiences. In addition to the biennial summer Hampstead Arts Festival, which included outdoor events such as Morris dancing, jousting on Hampstead Heath, visits to the studios of Hampstead painters and sculptors, and guided tours of the district as well as concerts and drama productions, it also arranged three Music and Arts Weeks each year. From 1962 onwards there was an arrangement with the recently created Hampstead Theatre that M & A could stage events there during these weeks as one of the conditions of the Theatre Club's lease from the Council, in return for which £225 of its annual rent was waived.

The HAC was a society of professional artists with some 300 members, which had been established as a regional society of the Artists' International Association by the artist Richard Carline in 1944. It ran art classes at Burgh House (owned by Hampstead Council) and began to mount exhibitions locally, including the annual Open Air Exhibition at the top of Heath Street near Whitestone Pond, first held in 1953. In June 1964 they launched an appeal to raise at least £8000 for a permanent arts centre. Thus, when the new Central Library at Swiss Cottage opened that year, leaving the old building in Arkwright Road vacant, the HAC approached the new Camden Council with a proposal to turn the old library into an Arts Centre. The Council had first thought in terms of a centre for all the arts, but agreed on finding an organisation virtually ready to run the centre to let the HAC have the building to mount exhibitions and run classes in the visual arts. It was to be a joint

23 Logo of Music & Arts in Hampstead

venture between the HAC and the Council.

The Camden Arts Centre opened in 1965 and was an immediate success, with over 1000 applications for places in the arts classes. Its rapid establishment and early success was due to one of those happy conjunctions in time between an active well-organised voluntary society which knew exactly what it wanted, an available empty building, and a Council committee eager and willing to back the arts.[6]

To prepare for the amalgamation of the three boroughs a joint committee of heads of departments for each service was set up in the spring of 1963 to draw up proposals for an integrated service. The borough librarians unanimously agreed that the library service should be vertically integrated, but one important matter, the organisation of arts activities, was left unresolved. Eventually this vital decision – whether to adopt the St Pancras and Holborn arrangement whereby arts activities were run by the libraries departments, or the Hampstead one where they were the responsibility of the Deputy Town Clerk reporting to a separate Entertainments Committee – was resolved without dissent by the Steering Committee of the newly elected Camden Council in favour of the Libraries and Arts arrangement. "The decision had in fact been taken earlier at a meeting of the Labour Group and was no doubt a reflection of the fact that the newly appointed chairman of the Camden Libraries Committee, Councillor Richardson, had held the same post in St Pancras."[7]

The selection of the new chief officer was a close contest between William Taylor of St Pancras and W R Maidment, the Hampstead Librarian, in which Maidment was selected. Taylor was bitterly disappointed, as he told the local press in no uncertain terms. This too could have threatened the future of the Festival. Taylor had worked closely with Marcus and provided full support for him; Maidment had no experience of the arts, partly because they had not been part of the Libraries brief in Hampstead, but also because they were simply not his sphere of interest. However, he was a distinguished librarian who had clear ideas on how the new department should be organised. He "firmly opposed the easy way out of appointing three district librarians and allowing everything to carry on as before. Such a system would be an evasion of the intention of the London Government Act and would make it impossible to offer the public any benefits from the merger of the boroughs".[8] The department was divided into three sections based on function, not area, each with a deputy librarian in charge. One of these was a distinct arts division, and Leonard Marcus was appointed First Deputy Head Librarian in charge of it. Thus the St Pancras tradition of support for the arts was firmly embedded in the new borough and continuity was assured.

Concern to safeguard jobs led to some departments, such as Libraries, with its three deputies, being top-heavy. But these arrangements proved vital in getting the Festival off to a confident start under the new regime. Three extra staff were taken on to cater for the increased workload of dealing with a much larger area and population, and a new post of Head of Arts was specially created, bringing Jack Henderson onto the team to assist Marcus in June 1965. His brief was, as John Richardson told the *Ham & High*, to be a "cross between a civil servant and a theatre manager"[9] and to build up links with all the arts groups in the new borough.

Henderson was a Canadian who had come to London in 1946 to study at the Royal College of Music for two years and never went back. He had already graduated in music from the University of Manitoba. A fine pianist and knowledgeable musician, he gradually moved into the administrative side of music, and had built up considerable expertise and a wide range of contacts. He lived in Hampstead and, with his Afghan hounds – called Boosey and Hawkes after the music publishers where he once worked – he was a well-known figure. He had been music advisor to the American Embassy in London for seven years, responsible for bringing over artists and orchestras to perform in Europe. After that he was associated with *Youth and Music* and it was this which brought him into contact with the Festival. A larger-than-life character who knew everyone in the business, he was a kind and generous man who was well liked and respected. He was also, by all accounts, "the best gossip in the business" possessing a fund of stories, some quite salacious, which added to his popularity.

The Arts Sub-Committee was re-established, but the tradition of co-opting outside arts experts was re-examined. It was decided that such members should not in future have voting rights and should act solely as advisors. E Martin Browne and

Roger Levy, who had been on the Committee since its inception, were joined on this first Camden Arts Sub-Committee by the composer Malcolm Arnold, F Cromwell Cooke, Director of Arts Studies at the Working Men's College, and Miss W M Hicks, a stalwart of the former St Pancras Arts and Civic Council.

The *Library Journal* was continued and renamed the *Camden Library Journal*. By then it had a gratis circulation of 2000, including an overseas mailing of 200. It cost £970 to produce and had a small income of £220 from adverts. It was decided to raise the print run to 5000, but with fewer pages in order to stay within the same budget.

To begin with there was a sense of optimism and great willingness to co-operate. Soon after the election in May 1964 the new Council Leader, Councillor Charles Ratchford, confidently announced a "go-ahead scheme for libraries and arts. We have built up a great name in St Pancras, and Hampstead has also gone far.... I am sure we are going to be one of the leading Boroughs in this field."[10] In October 1965 John Richardson announced that a total of £70,000 would be spent on the arts in the coming year; "other boroughs don't get anywhere near Camden's output of artistic events. If they did we should be only too willing to exchange productions of music, drama and opera events."[11] The HAC Chairman, Jeanette Jackson, reported to its annual general meeting

> "Nothing can dim the fact that we now have an Arts Centre of our own. Our relationship with the Council is now entirely different from that which existed before Camden was formed. In most of our ventures we receive the support of the Libraries and Arts Committee .....working together to make this Borough and our Society trend setters in providing for the visual arts ... It is absolutely amazing what Camden is doing for the arts."[12]

M & A renamed itself *Music and Arts in Camden* (MAC) and began to draw members from all over the new Borough. Its membership of societies had increased to 15 in 1970 and by 1972 had more than doubled to 38, including the Holborn Film Society, the Greek Arts Theatre Group, Unity Theatre, the British Music Hall Society and the English Folk Song and Dance Society. It became an affiliate of the newly formed Greater London Arts Association, set up in 1966 by the GLC and the Arts Council. This consisted of representatives from local authorities and from London arts organisations and served as a central source of information, education and assistance to arts organisations in the London boroughs.

However, as Enid Wistrich had observed[13], more time should have been spent on discussing what the resources and long-term objectives of the new Borough should be. Where the Festival was concerned, this failure soon threw up problems. Discussions had barely begun behind the scenes about how best to co-ordinate and rationalise the myriad arts activities of the three former boroughs. The new Libraries and Arts Committee got as far as acknowledging that concerts and opera were the hallmark of the Festival, but felt that the visual arts, drama and literature needed strengthening and that some more 'light-hearted' events should be introduced.

More serious was the failure to anticipate the frictions which soon emerged between the new Libraries and Arts Department and M & A, the organisers of the Hampstead Festival, as the new borough "took in at one gulp a mixed bag of fresh supporters, including Hampstead's famous intellectual population of *New Statesman* readers, bed-sitter dwellers and politicians, and the businessmen, students, nurses, Italian coffee bar proprietors and lawyers who live and work in the busier streets of Holborn."[14]

The St Pancras Festival had become highly professionalised, with a national reputation, while the Hampstead one was informal, with a large amateur element. The fundamental problem, identified by Noel Woolf later in a letter to the *Ham & High*[15] was that the Council was "not keen on supporting or giving increasing amounts of money for a Festival to be run by an independent body over which they had no direct control". After the demise of the St Pancras Arts and Civic Council, all activities in St Pancras had been run by the borough's Libraries and Arts Department. They were unable to accommodate the devolved way of doing things which still prevailed in Hampstead.

It was clear that whatever happened, the St Pancras Festival would continue. Thus the discussion had to centre on what was to happen in Hampstead: should it continue or could the two festivals be merged? If they were to merge, how would it be done? Nor was it just a simple matter of amateur versus professional – just as important were the individual personalities involved. Noel Woolf was a committed and passionately outspoken advocate of M & A's amateur approach. It was a reflection of a wider national problem: where did amateurs, once the backbone of music performance in Britain, fit in? This became ever more problematic with the post-war expansion of professional provision, and the growth of passive TV entertainment. The original commitment by CEMA to support amateur activity had been dropped when it became the Arts Council.

First shots across the bows were fired in January 1965 when John Richardson, in the press release[9] about the search for a new Head of Arts, unexpectedly announced that the Council, not Music and Arts, would in future run the Hampstead Festival. This brought a sharp reply from Noel Woolf the following week, expressing alarm at not having been consulted in any way: "We are deeply concerned at the bald announcement that M & A will apparently no longer be required to have anything to do with the Festival it has created and run for so many years". Richardson was forced to backtrack and admit that no official talks had taken place, and in May he announced on the front page of the *Ham & High* that the Hampstead Festival would continue, funded by Camden, that discussions were continuing and that the Festival's administration would be a partnership between the Council and M & A. A meeting took place with Christopher Gotch and Noel Woolf in September 1965 about the future of the Hampstead Festival.

Thus, for the moment, both Festivals were to continue. Denby Richards had been critical of the Hampstead Festival in the past, but welcomed the 1965 event as "by and large more professional and less amateur both in spirit and in programmes".[16] It included a performance by Group Eight of Monteverdi's *Il Ballo dell' Ingrate* conducted by David Lloyd Jones in the garden of Fenton House, and concerts by the Royal Philharmonic Orchestra at the Odeon Cinema, Swiss Cottage. These concerts had begun in 1964 when the RPO, faced with severe financial problems following the death of their founder Sir Thomas Beecham and their exclusion from the London Orchestral Board grant scheme at the South Bank, announced that it was to have a new home at Swiss Cottage. The move was backed by the Arts Council, who provided most of the subsidy, and the Rank organisation, while Hampstead Borough Council promised £100 against loss per concert. £3,500 was spent to make the cinema suitable for concerts, including a sound reflector over the stage, and the consensus was that the acoustic was very good. Over 20 concerts were given there each season, the average cost of each being £1,600 and the top price for tickets only 15s (75p), but this later rose to 21s. In the first season the cinema was almost full, with many young people in the audience, although in later years audience figures declined.

The only noticeable change to the next three St Pancras/Camden Festivals was their increased size and scope, as they benefited from the greatly enlarged resources now available. In 1964–65, the combined expenditure on the arts of the three boroughs had been estimated at £21,808, £12,000 of it on the St Pancras Festival. This was immediately increased to £25,500 in 1965–66 and £32,000 in 1967–68. The Festival was moving into a different league. Using locations in parts of the new Borough other than St Pancras, there were more opportunities for visual arts, more operas than ever, and the roster of distinguished artists brought in by Jack Henderson who appeared regularly in the Festival now began to grow every year. On the Arts Sub-Committee Roger Levy, having served for many years, was replaced by Felix Aprahamian, the music critic, and Malcolm Arnold stepped down in favour of the conductor Stanford Robinson.

The last St Pancras Festival (1966)

The 1966 Festival was the first to be arranged by Camden and the last to be called St Pancras. John Richardson set the tone with an upbeat and forthright introduction in the Festival guide:

"St Pancras is now in Camden and to celebrate this we have pleasure in presenting our largest Festival yet. Familiar companies are still with us and others make their debut. There are six unknown operas, one new play, and several first hearings of orchestral and choral works.

"You will notice, as well, that we are spreading out into the whole area of the new Camden borough. Swiss Cottage and Holborn are included, and this is a process which will continue.

"In a recent, rather muddled,

24 Heather Harper, who first appeared at the 1955 Festival

25 John Dankworth and Cleo Laine, who first appeared at the 1966 Festival

26 Christopher Bowers-Broadbent, organist at St Pancras Church, who played in 1966 and then every year until the last Festival

discussion on television about the support of arts by local councils, someone suggested that if an art needed subsidy it ought to die anyway. A good, cold, logical point this. I suppose we could allow opera to disappear completely and gag contemporary music. We would be the first rich country to do this but I doubt if we would enjoy it.

"In Camden we're certainly not going to hold any funerals."

With a budget of over £22,000 there was for the first time a large glossy programme book, which itself was the subject of remark by *The Stage*: "The brochure is of international standard and a credit to its designers, for it is clearly laid out with a page devoted to each event and is full of helpful information, from the obtaining of tickets to how to travel to the various halls by public transport". The Festival also received the financial accolade, as the Council press release put it[17], of the first direct Arts Council grant (£2000). Previously, such grants had been given only to the individual groups performing in the Festival. By 25 February the *Ham & High* reported that there had already been record advance bookings.

The opening concert was a starry occasion held in the presence of the Queen Mother, with the Royal Philharmonic Orchestra conducted by Rudolph Kempe playing at the Swiss Cottage Odeon. Camden had continued the funding arrangement started by Hampstead Council in 1964 and two of the orchestra's other concerts were also included in the Festival, one of them featuring works by composers associated with Camden.

A special concert to mark the 80th anniversary of Liszt's death was given at Friends' House with Rhonda Gillespie, Heather Harper [24], Tessa Robbins and Sian Phillips. The London Wind Soloists with Vladimir Ashkenazy was billed as the Camden Celebrity Concert, while the London Ripieno Society made their first Festival appearance with a programme of Britten, Bach, Vivaldi and Telemann.

Other newcomers to the Festival were the London Soloists Ensemble, and Cleo Laine and John Dankworth [25], who presented a fascinating programme that included Lieder by Schubert and Wolf as well as songs by Gershwin, Ellington, Weill and Dankworth. In her autobiography *Cleo* (Simon & Schuster 1994) Laine describes how Jack Henderson, who was convinced that she could be a great Lieder singer, collaborated in devising the programme especially to suit her voice. The critics raved about her performance, and the programme was then in demand at many music festivals in the British Isles and in Europe, thus helping to launch her international career.

Many old friends returned: guitarist John Williams, the MacNaughton Concerts, the Finchley Children's Music Group, the London Bach Society with Janet Baker and Heather Harper, Francis Chagrin, and the Philomusica of London with Joseph Horovitz. There were organ recitals with Gillian Weir, then at the start of her career, and Christopher Bowers-Broadbent [26], who had recently been appointed organist at St Pancras Church. Youth and Music presented the Dartington and Amici String Quartets.

First performances of contemporary music became an increasingly prominent feature of the Festival, no doubt due to Jack Henderson's influence. The Festival press release drew attention to

"the opportunities to hear the work of modern composers. Particular attention has been paid to British contemporary composers...for instance Richard Stoker's *Ecce Homo*, Gerald Gover's *Songs of Death and Immortality*, Joseph Horovitz's Jazz Harpsichord Concerto, Francis Chagrin's Symphony, Wilfred Josephs' Octet, Richard Arnell's Symphony no.5 and works by Richard Rodney Bennett and Gordon Crosse."

A work commissioned from Harrison Birtwhistle was not available in time and had to be replaced.

The new Arts Centre in Arkwright Road was used for the first time for an exhibition mounted by Hampstead Artists' Council called *The artist at work, from the Renaissance to the present day*. It was a high-powered event with works lent by the National Gallery, the National Portrait Gallery, the Tate and the Victoria and Albert Museum as well as a number of provincial galleries and required a million pounds' worth of insurance. It was opened by Sir Anthony Blunt, then Keeper of the Queen's Pictures. To coincide with the exhibition the HAC held the first National Conference of Artists to take place in this country. At the Swiss Cottage Library there was an exhibition of photographs of 20th-century writers by Mark Gerson. The regular annual exhibition was renamed Camden Artists and was distributed between the three Town Halls: that of St Pancras in Euston Road, which was now Camden Town Hall, and the old Holborn and old Hampstead Town Halls.

The Hampstead Theatre Club staged an adaptation by Andrew Sinclair of Dylan Thomas's only novel, *Adventures in a Dead Man's Skin*. Left incomplete at his death, it was intended as a fantasy autobiography of his first coming to London. Student performances of *The Fire Raisers* by Max Frisch and Ibsen's *The Pretenders* were staged at the Central School of Speech and Drama's Embassy Theatre during the Festival period as "associated events".

The operas had a mixed reception. Opera Concerts under their musical director Gerald Gover produced Donizetti's *Maria Stuarda*, the first time ever performed in England. Basilica Opera gave the first

27 Henze's *The End of the World* (1954), at the 1966 Festival. Left to right: Edmund Bohan (standing), Angela Moran, Dorothy Dorow, Peter Leeming, Geoffrey Chard (photo Patrick Eagar)

performances in Great Britain of three one-act operas by Henze: *The Miracle Theatre*, written in 1948, and the other two dating from 1954: *A Country Doctor*, and *The End of the World* [27], "which required an entire island and palace to sink into an open sea – on the St Pancras Town Hall stage!"[18]

These wonders went unappreciated by the *Opera* critic, who complained that "A more miserable and uncomfortable evening (the St Pancras seats seemed harder and smaller than ever) I have rarely spent". The Handel Opera Society presented Haydn's *L'Incontro Improviso*.

Leslie Head, the indefatigable conductor of the Kensington Symphony Orchestra, had now also launched into opera with a new company called Opera Viva. Their first production for the Festival was another contribution to the Verdi revival, the stage première in this country of *Il Corsaro*, which Head had recently seen in a somewhat disastrous production in Venice. In the *Library Journal* he recounted how the indisposition of the soprano combined with the St Mark's campanile striking midnight "reduced part of the last act to a dumb show, and a final scuffle between orchestra and audience necessitated the hasty arrival of the police complete with whistles."[19] However, his faith in the opera was fully vindicated by the acclaim from the critics for this London performance: *Opera* praised it "not only for the way it illuminates Verdi's progress, not only for its historical interest, but also because, for all the unevenness, it *lives*". The cast included Pauline Tinsley, Donald Smith and Jeanette Sinclair.

Thus, Camden's first year as steward of the Festival was a huge success.

"The St Pancras Festival has its own inimitable flavour for the opera-goer; the atmosphere of excitement never fails before the performance...the amenities are appropriately different. Canvas chairs, legs skewed to avoid the iron bar of the seat in front instead of the comfort of plush, a rush in the interval to the bar across the road – it is these things as well as the rare work revived which give St Pancras its character. It is a world which concentrates everything upon the individual, the human being for whom to live is to feel and to feel is to act; and this essential aesthetic is brought out more clearly by the typical scenic nudity of St Pancras than it is, often, by the elaborate presentations of other institutions."[20]

1967 The first Camden Festival goes Finnish

28 Logos of the St Pancras and Camden Festivals designed by Ken Garland

In his introductory note to the Camden Festival in 1967 John Richardson pointed out: "For those who are superstitious...this would have been the thirteenth St Pancras Festival had it not been for the absorption of that borough into Camden and the consequent change of name." Many expressed their regret at the change. It took place against a background of national financial crisis: the pound had been devalued and all Council departments were directed to look for savings. There were to be severe restrictions on amenity, cultural, leisure and recreational projects. However, these were mostly centred on capital expenditure, and for the time being the Festival was unaffected. It was the most novel and most ambitious so far, with another hugely expanded programme, for which the programme book was divided into three large, glossy sections. Top ticket prices were still under £1 and 14,000 were sold. The Arts Council gave a grant of £3000 and the Greater London Council also contributed.

At the suggestion of Denby Richards, Finnish music was the centrepiece of the programme. On a first visit to Finland in 1964 to prepare himself for the Sibelius Centenary Festival, Richards had been so amazed by the wealth of beautiful music he heard by contemporary composers who were completely unknown outside Finland that on his return home he determined to do something about it. Leonard Marcus was the obvious person to approach:

"I felt that some effort should be made to have some of this music performed publicly outside Scandinavia. Accordingly I suggested to Leonard Marcus, the founder and guiding spirit of past St Pancras Festivals and Councillor John Richardson of the London Borough of Camden that the 1967 Camden Festival should include some Finnish music, and their enthusiasm and help resulted in performances of no fewer than nine contemporary Finnish works, including six premières, four of which were commissioned by Camden and chosen through a competition organised for the purpose and judged by a non-Finnish jury of musicians and critics." [21]

The jury members were Heather Harper, William Mann, Denby Richards, Walter Susskind and Graham Whettam, Arts Officer for Camden. The competition was open only to Finnish composers and the prizes were given by the Finnish Ministry of Culture jointly with Camden; the Royal Philharmonic Orchestra was to play the winning pieces with Walter Susskind conducting, and Phillips agreed to record them.

The orchestral prize was awarded jointly to Tauno Marttinen for his 4th Symphony and Paavo Heininen for his concerto for orchestra. Usko Merilainin's Second Piano Sonata was awarded first prize in the piano section and received its world première, played by Yonty Solomon, in the presence of the composer. Lief Segerstam won the song cycle section with three settings of texts from Walt Whitman's

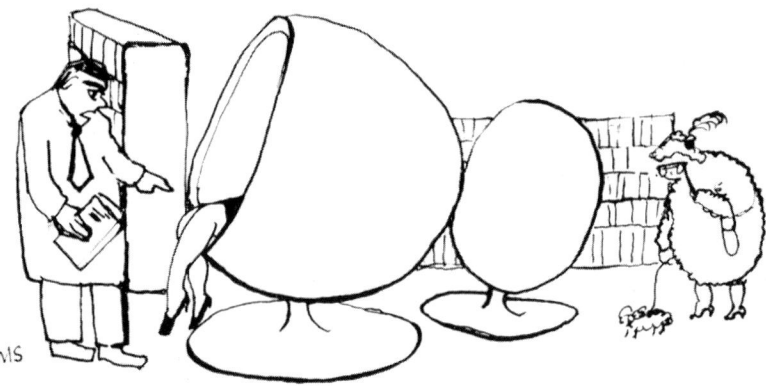

29 Cartoon in the *Camden Library Journal* February 67, p 106. Accompanying comment: "There will be new spherical arm-chairs in fibreglass designed by Eero Aarnio in the Central Library, Swiss Cottage, throughout the Festival. Their womb-like shape enables them to be used out of doors, turned against the wind, and indoors turned against other members of the household. Small round people will find them especially comfortable."

Leaves of Grass. These were sung by Heather Harper, accompanied by Walter Susskind, at a concert at Friends' House which also included the winning piece of the chamber-music section, Aulikki Rautavaara's Third String Quartet, played by the Delmé String Quartet.

The Finnish Government sent top designer Tapio Wirkkala to mount two exhibitions which had already been seen in several European capitals: one of Finnish architecture and design called *Helsinki, Capital of Finland* took place at the Camden Arts Centre and was opened by Anthony Crosland MP, Secretary of State for Education and Science as the official opening of the Festival. The other was *Books from Finland* at the Central Library, Swiss Cottage. The Camden Artists' Exhibition found a new venue at Congress House in Great Russell Street.

Press reviews varied from lukewarm to enthusiastic, but the general impression was summed up by Edward Greenfield in the *Guardian*, when he wrote that "Anyone who may have the vague impression that Finnish music today is like Sibelius watered down will certainly have to think again after Camden." The audiences were impressed, and gave the composers, who had been invited to England for the occasion, a great welcome.[21]

After the Festival Denby Richards wrote to the Council giving details of the successful recording sessions, adding:

"The recordings will pay tribute to the Camden Festival's enterprise in introducing this music to London audiences, and will mark the first occasion when a Festival of this kind has been commemorated by discs issued on the International market. I am sure that your committee should know how grateful the Finnish composers are to Camden for bringing them out of the comparative obscurity which their geographical and political situation had placed them in for so long."[22]

There was a wide variety of other events. With the greatly enlarged area and new venues a new pattern began to emerge under Jack Henderson's guidance. Concerts were presented in series: Lunchtime Jazz at the Cochrane Theatre; Poetry and Jazz at Holborn Library Hall; Lunchtime Recitals at St Pancras Church on Wednesdays and lunchtime Organ Recitals on Mondays – including one with Larry Adler, harmonica. Other innovations were late-night events which included all kinds of music and poetry, and Sunday morning chamber music concerts at the Everyman Cinema where the Allegri opened festivities, followed on the three succeeding Sunday mornings by the Amadeus, the Tel-Aviv and Tatrai String Quartets. There had been fears that these would find no audience at this time of day, but they proved so popular that people had to be turned away.

Four of the Royal Philharmonic Orchestra's regular Sunday evening concerts at Swiss Cottage were included in the Festival, with specially devised programmes. The first concentrated on the Finnish prize winners while the third included the world première of local composer Wilfred Josephs' Piano Concerto, played by Yonty Solomon and conducted by Charles Groves. Last was a concert of English music conducted by Malcolm Arnold, then resident in

30 Paulo Silveri (left) in *Marino Faliero* (photo Patrick Eagar). "His presence, moving around the stage with authority and style, belongs to the great opera houses"(*South Wales Argos* 1.3.67)

31 Massenet's *Sapho* (1967 Festival) with Milla Andrew in the title role (photo Romano Cagnoni). The *Camden Library Journal* wag again: "Let me say at once that Sapho is not a kinky opera about the island of Lesbos and its inhabitants" said Gerald Gover. What he said after that seemed rather a let-down.[24]

Hampstead, which included his overture Tam O'Shanter and his Harmonica Concerto, with Larry Adler as soloist.

The 'Celebrity' concert at Camden School for Girls was a feast for lovers of German Lieder, given by one of the world's great opera singers Irmgard Seefried, with Geoffrey Parsons at the piano. Cleo Laine and John Dankworth returned with another imaginative and unusual programme.

There were five choral concerts, three of them given by choirs new to the Festival. The Hampstead Choral Society was invited for the first time. Founded in 1946 by its conductor Martindale Sidwell, the choir had created an outstanding reputation using top-flight soloists and performing at the Proms, the South Bank and on Radio 3. The Finnish Radio Chamber Choir, visiting especially for the Festival, gave the world première of *Laudatio Domini* by Joonas Kokkonen at Camden Town Hall, with Taru Valjakka as soprano soloist. The Zemel Choir sang at Hampstead Town Hall.

Youth and Music returned with two programmes, one called Composers in Person, at which Malcolm Williamson, Nicholas Maw and Thea Musgrave introduced their works and discussed them with the audience. The other featured the Gabrieli Quartet with Hephzibah Menuhin.

For the first time the operas were staged for three nights each instead of only two, to cater for the demand for tickets. Opera Viva's contribution was Donizetti's *Marino Faliero*, for which they secured the services of one of the great Italian singers of the day, Paulo Silveri [30], "a Camden scoop", as Denby Richards described it in the *Ham & High*. He was keen to sing again in London, having visited with the Scala company in the post-war years when he had sung Boris Godunov at Covent Garden, and could have had no idea of the makeshift conditions he would have to put up with. He brought a touch of Italian operatic *primo uomo* behaviour to the proceedings, warming up loudly and audibly backstage while others were singing their arias and generally trying to upstage anyone he considered a rival. As Arthur Jacobs in *Opera* described it, "his acting out-hammed everyone else's". However, he also brought a very starry audience to the first night, with people like Margot Fonteyn "in Dior mink upstairs in the ten bobs"[23] turning up to hear him, and wild enthusiasm from the audience.

Mozart's *Lucio Silla* was Handel Opera Society's choice, while Opera Concerts unearthed Massenet's *Sapho* [31]. All were first performances in this country.

The Irwell Opera, an offshoot of the Park Lane Group, gave a triple bill of comic operas conducted by Joseph Horovitz: Holst's *The Wandering Scholar*, Hindemith's *There and Back* and the first public

32 Maconchy's comic opera *The Sofa* (1967 Festival). Left to right: Neil Howlett, Joseph Ward ('a prince turned into a sofa'), Joy Evans (photo Patrick Eagar).

performance of Maconchy's *The Sofa* [32]. Stephen Walsh in *The Times* commented "Memory can be an unreliable guide to past productions, but it does seem as though since St Pancras became Camden the standard of opera presentation at its Festival has taken a decisive upward step. Irwell Opera's triple bill last week certainly suggested as much."

He found the Hindemith "a brilliant period piece, hilariously entertaining, not just because of the delicious non-sequiturs of its self-reversing plot, but because of the effervescent style with which the company handled them."

There were two drama productions: *The Rebel*, a show devised by Patrick Garland, at the Hampstead Theatre; and *Oh!* by Sandro Key Aberg presented by the London Traverse Theatre Company at the Cochrane Theatre, directed by Michael Geliot.

After the 1967 Festival, Councillor John Richardson, who had steered the Libraries and Arts Committee so skilfully through the last five years, ensuring the continuity of the Festival, stepped down as chairman, although he remained on the committee until 1973 and then served on the Music Advisory Panel until 1977. His last flourish as Chairman was to issue a press release announcing the amalgamation of the two Festivals.

Critical voices begin to surface

Amongst the three local newspapers, the *North London Press* (later the *Camden New Journal*), the *St Pancras Chronicle* and the *Ham & High*, the last, well known for its large and lively arts section, took the most active interest in the Festival. It had always reviewed Festival events and it now took the amalgamation of the boroughs as a cue to examine the Festival in much closer detail, not always reaching favourable conclusions. It described the proposals for the amalgamated Festival as a "new people's festival" that would have "more popular appeal", provoking Richardson to distance himself from it the following week: "Your reference to a people's festival sounds like a left-wing extravaganza, with marchers bearing pictures of Mao up Hampstead High Street". Nevertheless, the paper repeated this view in an editorial on the Festival's future, welcoming the idea that other parts of the borough might be encouraged to "become more culturally minded". It then went on to make much more controversial statements. The main Festival "swallowed £17,000 from the rates [but] appears to have attracted very little interest among Camden residents", and stated "How far this is due to this type of programme not having much appeal to Camden residents…is debatable."

These comments were based on a survey the paper had asked Camden Council to run jointly with it. What it omitted to mention was that it had approached Camden with the idea halfway through the Festival. Of the 14,000 people who had bought tickets (the paper reported this as 12,000) only 299 filled in the questionnaires, a number so small that, as the Borough Librarian pointed out in his report to Committee on the matter, "it is hardly scientific", and no reliable conclusions could be drawn. Its main finding was that 290 of the 299 found the Festival "excellent" and the only real criticism which emerged was of the "the inadequacies of halls, poor acoustics and lack of comfortable seating, particularly at the St Pancras Assembly Rooms". Nevertheless, using selective and unrepresentative quotes from a handful of respondents, the article implied that the programmes were "too cultural", with "not enough popular music". On the question of how many local people actually went to the Festival, 40% of respondents were Camden residents and most of the rest were from North London boroughs. The paper interpreted this as showing that Camden ratepayers were not interested in the Festival programmes, but the Council analysis drew the opposite conclusion, namely "it seems to show that the audience is local." The paper neglected to report the Borough Librarian's assessment of the survey, which questioned most of its assumptions.

Early in 1967 Noel Woolf, foreseeing problems ahead, had set about securing representation for Music and Arts on Camden's Libraries and Arts Sub-committee. He and his colleague Peter Dean, the M & A Treasurer, attended their first meeting in April and were formally co-opted in June. They also secured an unofficial meeting with Councillor Jack Cooper, a Hampstead man, and the new chairman of the Libraries and Arts Sub-Committee, to discuss ways in which they could "broaden the scope of their contribution to the new borough". They hoped, as they put it, that Cooper had "been indoctrinated with the creed of Music and Arts".

The last Hampstead Festival was staged in 1967 with a budget of £8,000. It was opened by Prime Minister Harold Wilson against a barrage of heckling from anti-Vietnam War demonstrators. Noel Woolf then drew up his own report regarding the 1969 Festival, proposing that M & A should arrange events by their own societies, sponsor experimental work and advise on open-air spectaculars. He also suggested that a small committee should run the Festival, including two members of M & A. He reported that these proposals had been well received by the Committee.

1968

A second round of public skirmishing between M & A and Camden's Arts and Libraries Committee broke out in the columns of the *Ham & High* in January 1968 when Councillor Cooper, having called a press conference to announce that "the whole image of the Camden Festival is going to be changed in 1969", took it upon himself to explain that Music & Arts were unable to carry on the Hampstead Festival because their administrative costs were too high. This immediately drew a riposte from Noel Woolf in the Letters page making it quite clear that on the contrary, the administration costs were exceedingly low; the real reason (as quoted earlier, see p 42) was that Council money would be going to a festival run by an independent body over which they had no direct control. However, he welcomed the amalgamation, pointing out that it made more sense to use the full-time administrative department that Camden was already running and hoped there would be cooperation. The *Ham & High* followed up with more provocative editorial comments: "Too highbrow? Too adventurous?" although they did concede that "it attracts surprisingly good public support." A more ominous sign of things to come was reported in an article on the Festival in *The Scotsman*: "Criticism has come from within the Council itself. Some Labour Councillors have urged a "Pop" approach. Some Conservatives have criticised the amount of money spent by the council." [14]

One such critic was Richard Collins,

Councillor for the Regent's Park Ward, chairman of the Regent's Park Estate Tenants' Association and Editor of their Newsletter, in which he criticised the Festival. On the basis of his own local straw poll he considered it was "debatable whether items not popular entertainment and certainly sparsely attended by local residents should be so heavily favoured". Although he admitted that some people from the estate had attended Festival events he maintained that if highbrows wanted this kind of thing they could pay for it themselves; the Council should lay on more popular events. However, in another disquisition a few weeks later he railed against popular television programmes – "a lot of rot" – because they result in everyone doing the same thing at the same time; and on yet another occasion he "hates fanatics who think that everything they think is right and anything other folk think is wrong. We are all individuals with minds and opinions of our own and nobody is right all the time".[25] His views on the Festival found their way into a report in the *North London Press* in 1966 and presumably also into the discussions which must have gone on in the Council Chamber. Significantly, there were no letters either to the Regent's Park Tenants' Association *Newsletter* or to the *North London Press* in support of his critical remarks.

The 1968 Festival followed a similar pattern to the previous year. Jack Cooper, in his first introduction in the Festival guide, struck a rather apologetic note compared with the confident pride of previous years:

> "We have been gratified to learn that our approach to this annual Camden Festival, which some have thought perhaps a little too highbrow or adventurous, is backed by public appreciation. This was clearly shown in a survey during last year's Festival carried out by the Hampstead and Highgate Express. We like to think our arts policy is one which a local authority should pursue in seeking to satisfy what is becoming known as the "problem of leisure". This in itself means we can never sit back in self-satisfaction. New ideas must be constantly sought and new formulas investigated."[26]

The programme book was again split into sections, though it was not as large or glossy as the previous year: operas and choral concerts; recitals, poetry and talks; symphony concerts and chamber music. The four orchestral concerts with the Royal Philharmonic at the Swiss Cottage Odeon all explored 20th-century repertoire including first performances of works by Roger Sessions and Benjamin Lees. Youth and Music in association with Park Lane Group sponsored a concert by the Morley College Chamber Orchestra, who gave the first performance of *Grandma's Footsteps* by John Tavener, then barely out of college.

The original opera programme had to be changed as late as December 1967 because of the exorbitant performing-right fees for a proposed triple bill of Kurt Weill operas. Park Lane Group stepped in with a double bill of Russian opera: Rimsky-Korsakov's *Mozart and Salieri*, and Tchaikovsky's *Iolanta* with Josephine Barstow in the title role, "another find for Camden" as Denby Richards remarked of her performance in his review in the *Ham & High*. In commemoration of the centenary of Rossini's death, his opera *Elisabetta, Regina d'Inghilterra*, was given its first British performance by Opera-Concerts. An evening of Three Medieval Music Dramas was presented at St Mary's Primrose Hill by the Quem Quaritis Singers.

The Handel Opera Society's presentation of two early Mozart operas, *The First Commandment* (his very first opera written at the age of 10) and *Il sogno di Scipione*, received a financial boost in the unexpected form of a small legacy. Dr Hans Ucko, founder of the Impresario Society, the first group to perform opera at the Festival in 1955, had recently died. The Society decided to disband and give their remaining funds of £480 to the Camden Festival with the stipulation that the money be used for the promotion of 18th-century opera. They paid particular tribute to Leonard Marcus: "The Society was closely associated with the St Pancras Arts Festival since its inception, and indeed with its creation, thanks largely to the interest shown by the Borough Librarian, Mr L A Marcus". The performances received a eulogy in the *Evening Standard*, which must have delighted the Festival Office:

> "Euston Road is one of the more unlikely places to find oneself in a state of euphoria but this was the happy condition I was in last night after the first stage performance in this country of two of Mozart's early works at the Town Hall. There was a time when this festival was known as the St Pancras Festival and it operated amid potted palms and brown paint at the Town Hall. Times change: the festival now calls itself the Camden Festival and the Town Hall has been

brightly painted, although the chairs must be the most uncomfortable outside Bayreuth. And not a trace of a potted palm. The festival remains one of the most enterprising to be found anywhere."

The borough was positively teeming with chamber music and other concerts throughout the month: no fewer than eight different string quartets could be heard either at the Everyman or Conway Hall, there were the usual organ recitals at St Pancras Church, Monday Evenings at Holborn Library included recitals and talks, and Shura Cherkassky, who lived in Camden, was the guest artist in the Camden Celebrity Concert. He also stood in for an indisposed Eileen Joyce at one of the RPO concerts. A new series called Prize-winners' Recitals was started, aimed directly at helping young artists who had recently made their mark by winning one of the various prestigious music prizes, such as the Ferrier or the Haydn-Mozart Prize. Thomas Allen was one of the first, having that year won the Queen's Prize at the Royal College of Music. Six different choirs, from small chamber groups to large traditional oratorio choirs, gave concerts.

John Dankworth, Cleo Laine and the Mike Westbrook Concert Band all returned, as did John Williams. There were evenings of poetry and folksong, poetry and music (with Joan Greenwood) and poetry and jazz. A novelty was an evening with Donald Swann featuring his own settings of a wide range of poetry sung by a trio of opera singers led by Marion Studholme.

There were two special film seasons, one at the Everyman and one at the Highgate Literary and Scientific Institution. Hampstead Theatre contributed two one-act plays under the title *Little Boxes* by John Bowen, which was successful enough to transfer to the West End. The Central School of Speech and Drama put on two productions to coincide with the Festival, and a Camden Festival Poetry Competition was introduced, run by Music & Arts.

There were exhibitions all over the borough; the Camden Artists show, opened by Norman Reid, the Director of the Tate Gallery, was held at the Central Library at Swiss Cottage and included works by Frank Auerbach and Anthony Caro. The Camden Arts Centre in Arkwright Road mounted a special exhibition presenting the works of the *De Stijl Group*; the show set up attendance records there. In the south of the borough the Crafts Centre of Great Britain in Earlham Street had two shows: *Exports:* *Detroit USA*, a collection of arts and crafts by contemporary British artists, prior to exhibition in America, and *Metalwork and Silver*. The Highgate Literary and Scientific Institution mounted an exhibition called *London At Our Feet*.

The Festival received its usual wide coverage in the national and local press and on BBC and ITV programmes, and advance bookings were up yet again. A film of the Festival by the Central Office of Information was issued in several languages and shown all over the world.

William Maidment's triennial Library report was the subject of favourable comment in the *Ham & High*, now under a new editor, Gerald Isaaman: "Camden's standing as a progressive authority owes much to the work of its libraries and the borough's promotion and support for artistic ventures". The paper pointed out that all this was achieved at the cost of a mere £3.2.10 per inhabitant per annum on libraries and arts. The Festival department showed that it was the least costly of all festivals of comparable standard, none of which lasted as long as Camden's 4 weeks at £17,000: Cheltenham's 1 week cost £10,000, Brighton's 2 weeks £32,000; Aldeburgh's 3 weeks £36,000, and the Bath Festival's 10 days £43,000.[27]

The end of an era

Although the decision to merge the festivals had already been formally minuted in October 1967 the Council most unusually called a public meeting to give everyone a chance to put forward ideas. It took place in April 1968 in the Council Chamber. A mixture of arts professionals, local people with a special interest such as members of M & A, representatives from civic and residents' groups and members of the general public attended, and a great many suggestions were produced, some of which did find their way into future festivals. Great enthusiasm was expressed from the floor for the involvement of local communities so that it should be a Festival *of* the people, not just *for* them; several speakers suggested that the immigrant and ethnic communities should also be encouraged to play a larger role. According to the *St Pancras Chronicle* the loudest cheers of the evening were for the suggestions that buses should run later and that drinking hours should be extended! There was a plea from Kenneth van Barthold from the City Literary Institute to use the Cochrane Theatre more and bring the Festival eastwards into Holborn. There were also many suggestions for activities which were already in the Festival and it was made clear by Councillor Cooper that the main professional content would not change.[28]

A working party was set up under the chairmanship of Hampstead Councillor Christine Stewart-Munro to consider fringe events for 1969 in the light of what had emerged from the public meeting.

However, it was not long before strains appeared. At the following meeting of the Arts Sub-Committee Felix Aprahamian expressed concern that the Festival's professional status might be compromised by the introduction of too many amateur events. Noel Woolf felt that he and his colleague from M & A were being sidelined, dealing only with "other events" and "amateur events" while another committee dealt with "professional" operas and concerts. They felt that the Festival administration was not really interested in their ideas; as far as Camden was concerned "Music and Arts should in the main confine themselves to looking after events of their own societies".[29] By June the M & A minutes were recording difficulties over the grant for Hampstead Choral Society, and even a proposal for a performance by the Hampstead-based Group Eight, formerly participants in the main Festival, was turned down by the Camden Arts Sub-Committee.

The end of the 1968 Festival was the end of an era. Local elections had resulted in a change in the political leadership, but more momentous for the Festival was the retirement of Leonard Marcus, "Mr Festival" as he had come to be called.[30] Considering the impact on the prestige of the borough of the Festival and all the other arts activities initiated by him over the years, it is remarkable that his retirement was hardly noted by the Council. It is recorded in a brief paragraph written by William Maidment, the director of the department, in the Annual Library Report:

"The retirement in May 1968 of Leonard Marcus ALA, First Deputy Borough Librarian with special responsibility for the arts, was the most visible change in the face of the Arts Section. He had watched and guided successive Councils as they developed the policy initiated in 1946 in St Pancras by Krishna Menon. As Secretary for the St Pancras Arts and Civic Council he had a budget of £450 for the Arts and Civic Week. Twenty years later the combined budget for the Hampstead and St Pancras Festivals was £38,000. In 1954 the first St Pancras Festival was a competitive amateur drama Festival. By 1968 the programme had broadened to cover many more arts forms presented by professionals wherever possible, and the Festival had acquired an international reputation for its production of rare operas. In those 20 years, under the genial and skilled hand of Leonard Marcus, St Pancras and then Camden became a first-class example of local authority endeavour in the arts." [31]

News of his retirement was widely reported elsewhere. By now his reputation as "Mr Festival" was well known. The *Ham & High* published a letter from Charles Samuel Green, one of the original committee members of the Arts and Civic Council, who declared that Marcus deserved a knighthood or at least the Freedom of the Borough. The borough's "rise to national and world fame has been due mainly to the genius of Leonard Marcus", the "impresario who appeared in the guise of a deputy borough librarian".

He is remembered with enormous affection and gratitude by all those who worked with him. "We owe a great deal to the founders of this municipal feast of good things and to one man in particular, Leonard Marcus" was the verdict of *The Stage* in 1967.

Councillor Jack Cooper had already signalled the changes afoot for the next year in his introduction to the Festival guide in 1968:

"It is intended to widen the scope of the Camden Festival. Since the Hampstead Festival is no more, the idea is to embrace the kind of events which were associated with it. There will be the serious side of the festival, as there is now, but we wish to involve the people of Camden more in a festival atmosphere, so we hope for open-air events, dancing in the streets, gaiety, colour and music. We want to make the festival month in Camden an event in everyone's calendar. You will certainly be hearing more about it."

The 1969 Festival would combine the best of both in a truly 'Camden' Festival:

"The professional productions of the main Festival will, for the first time, be reinforced by warmly spontaneous informal activities which promise to set the borough alight from end to end. The organisers have aimed to include something for everybody".[32]

The more informal and amateur Hampstead activities would become a 'Fringe' Festival, remaining under the general direction of Music and Arts in Camden and complementing the activities of the main Festival. It would have to be moved to May when evenings are lighter and weather good enough to allow the outdoor events which had been a feature of the former Hampstead programmes to take place, although it was realised that this might result in clashes of dates with other British Arts Festivals.

A Festival to remember

"Perhaps the [Camden] Festival owes its reputation to its consistent policy of presenting the less well known, and avoiding nonsense. For its first Festival Brighton had a long, long Fringe of audio-visual-kinetic rot; Camden has none of it." So wrote the *Guardian* in 1967.

Was everything about to change?

Notes for chapter 3

1. *Camden Library Journal* Feb 1966 (vol 1 no.5) p 103.
2. Enid Wistrich *Local Government Reorganisation: The First Years of Camden* London Borough of Camden 1972, p 200.
3. Jennie Lee's *A Policy for the Arts* Feb 1965, Introduction.
4. Ref. 6 (see p 13), p 54.
5. Ref. 2, p 6.
6. Ref. 2, p 198.
7. Ref. 2, p 40.
8. *Camden Journal* June 1965 (vol 1 no.1) *New Ideas for a New Borough*, p 5.
9. *Ham & High* 22.1.65 "Wanted: a culture director for Camden".
10. *Ham & High* 20.5.64.
11. *Ham & High* 22.10.65.
12. *Ham & High* 26.11.65.
13. Ref. 2, p 56.
14. *The Scotsman* 10.2.68.
15. *Ham & High* 26.1.68. Letters page "Festival costs".
16. *Ham & High* 21.5.65.
17. *Ham & High* 21.1.66.
18. *Camden Library Journal* Feb 66 (vol 1 no.5) p 119.
19. Ref. 18, p 120.
20. *Times Educational Supplement* 8.4.66.
21. Denby Richards *The Music of Finland* Hugh Evelyn 1968. Preface, p vi.
22. Camden Council minutes 19 July 1967 (vol 4) p 407. Report of the Libraries and Arts Committee.
23. *Evening Standard* 22.2.67.
24. *Camden Library Journal* Feb 1967.
25. Regent's Park Tenants' Association *Newsletter* Jan 1966.
26. 1968 Festival guide, p 3.
27. Libraries and Arts Committee Minutes 25.5.67, Item F.
28. Libraries and Arts Committee Report of Meeting on 30 April 1968 (LIB/68/22, 10.6.68, Agenda Item 4d).
29. M&A minutes Apr 68 (In the archive of Keith Martin, M&A Representaive on Camden Arts Sub-Committee 1968–72).
30. *Camden Journal* Oct 67 (vol 3, no.3) p 51.
31. Triennial Library Report 1968–71, p 17.
32. *Camden Journal* Apr/May 1969 (vol 4 no.6).

4   A Festival with a Fringe on top (1969–1972)

[Notes for chapter 4 are on p 74]

The Festival grows a Fringe: 1969

The 1969 Festival took off in several different directions, with its newly acquired Fringe; its move from March to May; its new management; and new politicians in charge. The May 1968 local elections had given the Conservative Party a majority. There was a new Chairman of Committee, Councillor Sydney Torrance, and Christine Stewart-Munro now became Vice-Chairman as well as chairing the Fringe Working Party. John Richardson remained a member of the Arts Sub-Committee and Ivor Walker, a newly elected Hampstead Councillor, was co-opted in June. Among the advisory committee members were Benny Green and Harold Rosenthal, editor of *Opera*.

Leonard Marcus's retirement provided Maidment with the opportunity to address the top-heavy staffing structure created by the amalgamation. On his recommendation no-one was appointed to replace Marcus at Deputy Librarian level; the administrative and artistic aspects of his work were separated and allocated to appropriate officers.

Jack Henderson now assumed responsibility for Camden's arts programmes, including the Festival, his post being upgraded to Senior Officer. It was the right moment for a music professional to take over at the helm. With his knowledge of the music business Henderson had the qualities needed to be able to build on Marcus's work. He shared the Festival's long-stated objectives of encouraging young artists and making space for new music. He was open to ideas and suggestions, and to a large degree he was successful in broadening the Festival, with increasingly interesting opera revivals, innovative programming, and the glamour of the Celebrity Recitals with artists such as Elisabeth Schwarzkopf whom he persuaded to perform for little or no fee. He is widely remembered as a worthy successor to Leonard Marcus.

However, he had one weakness: he lacked Marcus's organisational and political skills as an administrator and Local Authority civil servant. Neither his contacts nor his way of doing things fitted into the local government picture. This led to difficulties and friction in the running of arts activities and sometimes within the Department itself. He failed to appreciate the difficulties of integrating the independent and largely amateur set-up in Hampstead. He was not interested in amateur music making and did not get on with Noel Woolf. Many feathers were ruffled. Nevertheless, all the officers in the Department recognised Henderson's extraordinary flair and skill in devising programmes and securing artists, and gave him full support.

Another factor had a bearing on the future development of the Festival. Henderson was not well, which necessitated periods of absence, as for instance in 1970 when Christine Stewart-Munro noted that he had been in hospital for a considerable time. As the team expanded to give Henderson the necessary administrative support, other members had scope to develop their ideas and skills, bringing in new elements to the programme mix. The Festival direction became increasingly the work of a team rather than of one person, each member taking responsibility for different elements. In 1969 Henderson had two assistants, Mary Wolf and Tom Andrewes. By 1973, Andrewes was Senior Arts Assistant and was joined by two more Senior Arts Assistants, Graham Marchant and Roger Bastable, two Arts Assistants, Maurice Charlesworth and Katharine Chasey, and Box Office Manager Mabel Mann. They were later followed by others such as Christopher Gordon, Dan Shaw and James Miles. Tony Hayes, who had been committee clerk in the Hampstead days, became Deputy Head of the Department.

Considering the Department's phenomenal output, which included, in addition to the main Festival, a considerable year-round arts programme, the Junior Arts Festival, various other 'festival weeks', and all the back-up work such as assessment of grants which went with it, this was a small team. Early on it had been recognised that they should be recruited from an arts background rather than a local government one, and many went on to other positions in the arts world as theatre or festival administrators. It was an unusual situation. Few other boroughs ran such an active arts programme directly, and the team did not always fit comfortably within the bureaucratic norms of a local government office.

Opera productions now began to benefit from the groundwork laid in the 1950s and '60s as a pool of talented professionals became available to mount productions of an increasingly high standard. Many of them had learnt their art or craft in the Festival, and had great loyalty to it. As Patric Schmid of *Opera Rara* said: "It was a big adventure – if we didn't know how to do something we made up new ways to deal with things which others would then copy. The opportunity to do our first stage production at the Festival was a dream come true." Almost every name that has been prominent on the British opera scene in the last fifty years started his/her career or participated in the Festival. Many have gone on to brilliant international careers which have brought distinction to Britain's reputation in the arts.

The music critics and journals such as *Opera* played their parts too, often (though by no means always) turning an indulgent eye on obvious defects in performance and production, simply grateful that they were happening at all, as David Cairns remembered in *The Sunday Times* in 1977:

> "The cause has grown...since we first began to flock, tongue in cheek but spirits high, to St Pancras Town Hall to hear one more forgotten opera which the best Verdi authorities could hardly bring themselves to talk about....In the ramshackle heady old days at St Pancras where early Verdi was shovelled on to the stage and the drama left to fend for itself, we asked of such works no more than they were abundantly able to provide."

Such was the praise heaped on these early efforts that, as Dr Stanley Sadie, then editor of *The Musical Times,* commented in 1967:

> "Somebody once said that a foreign reader of the London press might reasonably conclude that our best opera house was St Pancras Town Hall, followed by Sadler's Wells, with Covent Garden last of all. The truth, of course, is that we expect the very highest standards from our royal and international opera house, something less grand at our people's opera and merely respectable standards at the home of forgotten operas." [1]

Andrew Porter had made similar comments, writing in *Opera* in 1962:

> "Often critics are reproached for the differing scales of judgement they seem to bring to events....The critics almost with one voice declared recently that *Alcina* was better done at St Pancras than at Covent Garden – yet that St Pancras performance would not really have passed muster in the big house." [2]

Now, in response to the raised standards of performance, critical demands rose too, and a more realistic note began to sound. The few years following the emergence of the new borough seemed to have been the moment for the national press to take stock. Arthur Jacobs, writing in *Opera* in 1967, was frank about the performance of *Marino Faliero* (see p 48):

> "Isn't it about time that we – I mean both the audiences and the critics – dropped the double standard which praises performances of this sort as though they were something different? To read one or two of my colleagues one would hardly realise that this was not opera as Covent Garden or Sadler's Wells is required to present it. Nor did the audience's vociferous applause for nearly everything give any indication of how much downright unpleasant singing and how much bad orchestral playing had to be endured. Opera at Camden is too often sub-standard – an amateur chorus, insufficiently equipped professionals in leading parts, and an under-rehearsed orchestra. Our traditions in England are so 'sporting', so enthusiastic about amateurs, that we too easily cry 'Good show!'" [3]

The move to May did not take place without comment, as the *Camden Journal* indicates:

> "This year Camden's March Festival has been missed by many. Readers of this Journal will be aware of the arguments for and against the move to May; on the one hand, how the old date filled a gap in London's musical year and on the other, how the move to May has made possible the introduction of a whole range of new and exciting events, many in the open air." [4]

The Fringe Working Party drew up

plans for the new section of the Festival, and there was much discussion as to what to call it. Noel Woolf's suggestion of 'Festival Plus' did not meet with approval, so, although working party members were not particularly happy with "Fringe", they could think of nothing better. The press release promised "the first video-tape experiment in an English Arts Festival, an all-night poetry marathon, playabouts for children, and all-night pop concerts", with the aim of bringing "many more people from a variety of backgrounds who live in the borough, into the festival; to increase the experimental art content; to provide more outlets for creative people in Camden; and to generate a free lively and colourful atmosphere."

M&A's aim was to create a Festival of Camden rather than a Festival for Camden. Noel Woolf also waxed lyrical in the pages of the *Camden Library Journal* [33]:

33 Illustration from *Camden Library Journal* which accompanied Noel Woolf's article about the first Fringe Festival, 1969

"Unlike Caesar's Romans you need no conquests to make you rejoice. You are not 'blocks', or 'stones', or 'worse than senseless things'; and you don't in the least mind admitting to a slight case of mental gluttony that allows you to 'sit the livelong day' and night –'with patient expectation' enjoying the Camden Festival and its Fringe. Of course it depends which side you're on whether you think the Festival or the Fringe the more important. We are unashamedly Fringemen and Fringe-women, and for nearly a year we have enjoyed a love–hate relationship with our Fringe. Fringes tend to become self-generating, and this can be quite infuriating for Fringe Planners. Every time they look at their Fringe they find it a little longer, a little thicker, until it threatens to imperil their vision altogether. Their Plan becomes lop-sided, top-heavy, unrecognisable and unworkable. At which point of course they wisely abandon their planning and themselves to sheer Joie-de-Vivre.

"But as their Fringe becomes thicker and longer it also becomes richer. Those who cling to the Fringe bring with them new ideas (and which Planner ever had a real genuine new idea?), fresh enthusiasm and the involvement of countless other people. This is the very essence of the Camden Fringe. The more people that take part in our Fringe the more it becomes part of a genuine unique Camden Festival! Whether it is the sound of music in a decorated street, or the song of a poet in the small hours in the Round House; whether it is an unselected artist challenging us with his paintings on the railings at Gospel Oak, or amateur or professional drama, or music in the garden of The Hill, or talks in Lincoln's Inn, or walks on Hampstead Heath, it will be representative of the immense fullness of life in Camden. The Camden Fringe Festival (1969 variety) will be more than a Festival to attend, it will be a Festival to take part in".

He was not exaggerating. That first Fringe programme [34] was quite remarkable both for quality and quantity, and by no means all of it amateur. There were several events each day in various different categories: Art Unlimited, Open Studios, Camden Potters, Romance and the Romantic, walks, talks, dance workshops, Morris Dancing at five Hampstead pubs, and a Poetry Marathon. There were also quite ambitious concerts with a Hampstead Chamber Orchestra conducted by Michael Graubert, a Highgate Chamber Orchestra conducted by David Littaur, and a wonderful sounding event called Music in the Streets involving "Bands marching through the Borough, meeting at Whitestone Pond". Almost every possible venue in the Borough

34 Fringe brochure, 1969

was used, from Grange Park in Kilburn to the City Lit in Holborn, by way of the Acland Burghley Youth Centre in Tufnell Park, the Regent's Canal and Fenton House. Drama included a production of *Macbeth* by Charles Marowitz at the Open Space in Tottenham Court Road, *Strike* at Unity Theatre and a hugely successful open day at the Central School of Speech and Drama which drew over 900 visitors including Dame Peggy Ashcroft. There was Old-Time Music Hall, lunchtime jazz, a donkey derby, a water-polo tournament and bands playing in all the borough's parks and open spaces on Sunday afternoons. And of course there was the open-air art exhibition at the top of Heath Street.

The pop concerts on the Heath organised by Michael Alfandary were free and cost the festival less than £300 since all the groups played without fee. They were also a cause of huge complaint because of the noise, attracting front-page headlines in all the local newspapers and causing great upset to the park keepers who had to clear up afterwards. Kentish Town police station was deluged with calls, as the 5-hour session went on till 3 am. As one irate resident wrote to the *Ham & High*: "When Yehudi Menuhin gives a concert he doesn't do it out in the open with amplifiers and force everyone in the area to listen whether they want to or not." [5] The problem was solved the following week by bringing the starting time forward to the afternoon, and the *Ham & High* was able to report that 12,000 people enjoyed the event – nearly as many as attended the whole of the rest of the Festival (13,500) – with no complaints.

The novelty of the main Festival, with a budget of £32,000, was a Swedish theme suggested by the Swedish Cultural Attaché, with exhibitions of Swedish artists, crafts and cinema, and a 4-week season of Swedish films at the Everyman Cinema. The music programme included the Stockholm Philharmonic Wind Quintet, the Musica Nova Group of Stockholm, and the brilliant young organist Karl Erik Welin. The RPO concert also featured Swedish musicians with the distinguished mezzo-soprano Kerstin Meyer, conductor Gunnar Staern, and a work by the contemporary Swedish composer, Ingvar Lidholm, in its first British performance. The theme was continued in three free lectures arranged by the Workers' Educational Association at Swiss Cottage Library about aspects of Swedish culture, which attracted capacity audiences.

The London Contemporary Dance Group [35] made its first appearance in the Festival; promoted by the Contemporary Ballet Trust at no cost to the Festival, it was the beginning a long and fruitful relationship. A large and enthusiastic audience for contemporary dance had been revealed by the ground-breaking visit to Britain of the Martha Graham Company in the mid-1960s, and shortly afterwards Robin Howard established the Trust. In 1967 they found a permanent home in the former Artists' Rifles drill hall in Duke's Road just off the Euston Road, which they renamed The Place. Robert Cohan, one of the leading figures of contemporary dance, was Artistic Director and there were lectures and workshops and a dance school. Arrangements were made for Camden Library members to have associate membership of the Artists' Place Society, which enabled them to attend ballet and drama performances and films.

The Festival spread out into new venues. Hampstead Parish Church proved very successful for organ recitals, while at the other end of the borough the Holborn Film Society presented its first series of films in the Festival at Holborn Library. Concerts at Kenwood in the Orangery and in the open air were included as associated events. The University Collegiate Theatre (later to be called the Bloomsbury) was also used for the first time. However, there was disappointment that the Camden Artists Exhibition had to be cancelled due to lack of accommodation.

Old friends returned: John Williams, the Royal Philharmonic Orchestra at Swiss Cottage, chamber music at the Everyman, poetry and jazz, prize-winners' recitals, choral concerts and drama at Hampstead Theatre. New friends were made: the London Mozart Players, Paco Peña, Cy Grant, the Stan Tracey Quartet and Marian Montgomery. The music on offer ranged from medieval Florence to 20th-century Sweden, taking in flamenco, jazz and grand opera on the way.

Concerns over finance were increasing. Four operas had become the norm in the past few years, and for the first time it was felt that this could not be afforded. However, London Chamber Opera in association with the London Opera Centre was mounting a

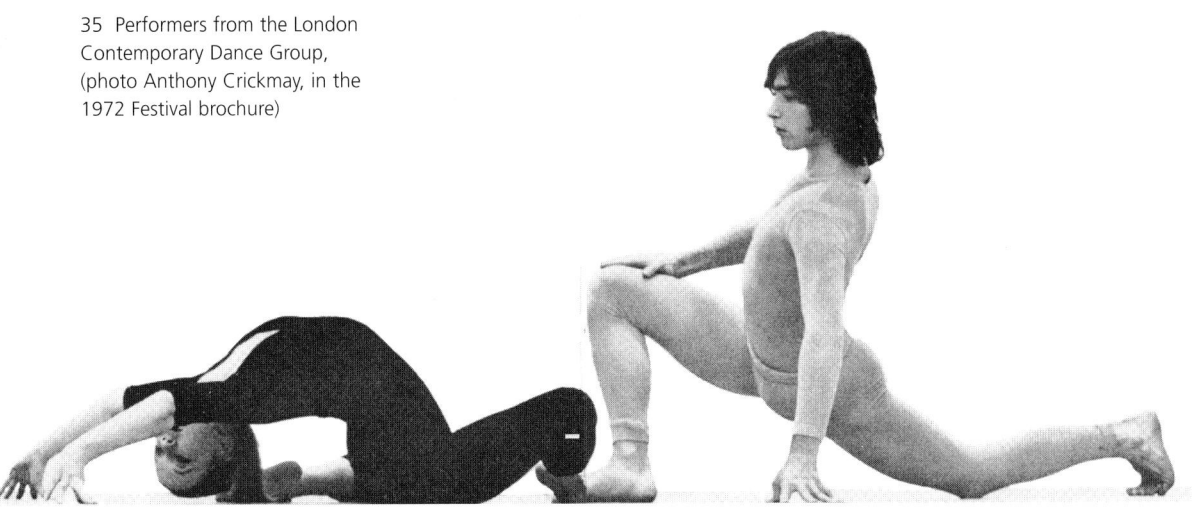

35 Performers from the London Contemporary Dance Group, (photo Anthony Crickmay, in the 1972 Festival brochure)

17th-century double bill by Scarlatti and da Capua during the period of the festival at the Jeanetta Cochrane Theatre, and it was included as an associated event at no cost to the Festival budget. 1969 being the centenary of the death of Berlioz, the Park Lane Group promoted a production of *Beatrice and Benedict*, its first London performance, by the Barber Institute, Birmingham. There was also a world première of a completely new opera: *Under Western Eyes* by John Joubert, completed in 1967. Based on a story by Joseph Conrad, the work was commissioned by the New Opera Company with funding of £1000 from Watney Mann Ltd, one of the first occasions when outside commercial sponsorship was obtained.

But it was Opera Concerts' production of Rossini's *La donna del Lago*, its first performance in Britain since 1851, conducted by Gerald Gover, that is still remembered today, as much for the singer it discovered as for the work itself. Elizabeth Forbes recalled the occasion many years later in *Opera* (July 1981):

"On an evening in May 1969, London opera lovers flocked to Camden Town Hall to hear one of the rarities typical of the Camden Festival, *La donna del Lago*, Rossini's operatic version of the poem by Sir Walter Scott, *The Lady of the Lake*. The curtain rose on the first scene, representing the banks of Loch Katrine at dawn. Morning mist hung heavily over the loch – the smoke machine had been too generously used – and after the opening chorus of huntsmen had gone off in search of prey, a ravishing female voice was heard from an invisible boat on the loch, where Ellen, the Lady of the Lake, waited for the return of her lover. At last the mist dispersed and a girl, whose appearance matched the beauty of her voice, became visible, seated in her boat. For many people in the audience, myself included, that was the first glimpse of Kiri Te Kanawa, the Maori soprano, then 25 years old." [6]

Although her performance was far from flawless, another Camden "star" had arrived [36].

The Borough Librarian gave a measured appreciation of this important transitional Festival: "The first Camden Festival held in the month of May was, in the true tradition of previous St Pancras Festivals, one of experiment" but it had stayed well within budget, with a final gross cost of £28,532, of which the net expenditure by the Council was £17,331. However, he noted that at this later time of year there was more competition with other arts events and festivals and for the first time in 5 years the box office receipts had remained static, with attendances no larger than the previous year at around 13,500. Although the Joubert opera was well received and was recorded by the BBC, it had attracted only small audiences. Similarly, the concerts of avant-garde music, while well reviewed by the press, were not well attended. More surprisingly, the series of jazz concerts at the Collegiate Theatre were also poorly attended, probably because it was an isolated series in a new theatre.[7]

The attempt to broaden the festival, taking account of the communities that were now part of Camden and also of the new

36 Kiri te Kanawa as Rossini's *Lady of the Lake (La Donna del Lago)* in 1969 for Opera Concerts (photo Robert Carpenter-Turner). Left, Maurice Arthur; right, John Serge.

'60s phenomenon of youth culture, was not entirely successful. The *North London Press* was sceptical:

> "What was missing was the much-heralded 'involvement of the public'. The 'promise to set the borough alight during May' did not happen. Probably the people of Camden don't want to be involved, with the possible exception of those living in Hampstead".[8]

Councillor Christine Stewart-Munro bravely claimed that

> "The fringe was a big success....[it] opened up some new ground and I hope some of the things it put on the map will stay. There were many things people said wouldn't work, such as the mammoth poetry and pop events, but they were sell-outs. The fringe is obviously needed and we would like it to go from strength to strength."[8]

However, she also said that the Council had misled the organisers of the fringe about the kind of help they would be given.

> "We only realised our predicament when it was too late to back out. I was promised a lot of help when I agreed to run the festival, but I didn't get it. I was promised use of the main Festival's publicity and administrative machinery, then when the time came it was refused. We couldn't possibly do it again without proper support from the Council."[8]

The report to Committee obliquely acknowledges this complaint:

> "In very difficult circumstances [the Fringe Working Party] succeeded in creating and carrying out a programme which served to spread the name of Camden far and to enhance the Borough's reputation as an adventurous and lively area."[7]

The Festival organisers had failed to understand the character of the Hampstead Festival or to give it the necessary administrative backup. They saw the task as simply tacking the amateur activities on to the professional main Festival. Council reports continually refer to anything produced by M & A as a "free for all, lighter", and "more popular form of entertainment". But not all the events were amateur, as Denby Richards observed in the *Ham & High*:

> "An 'official' fringe, which can include such a fine group as the Richards Piano Quartet...cannot be divorced from the festival proper...If things go on like this, the only difference between the old Camden and Hampstead festivals is that the latter goes under another name, and that there is an uneasy liaison...Future festivals should concentrate more on local artists and composers. A first-rate festival would be possible if 90 per cent of the performers were from Camden...we have several interesting composers living in the borough."[9]

Hampstead Choral Society, which at one time had even considered changing its name to the Camden Choral Society in anticipation of what they hoped would be a regular and fruitful relationship with the festival, were particularly aggrieved. As part of the great British tradition of oratorio performance, using the best professional soloists, they had built a high reputation. Yet Jack Henderson was treating them as if they were a band of inconsequential amateurs. Their programme suggestions were rejected and their grant was halved. They had written to him in June 1968: "It would be really regrettable if the choir's home borough – particularly one which has rightfully gained such a reputation as a generous patron of the arts as Camden – should fail in its own arts festival to support its leading choral society to a comparable extent".[10] They pointed out that it was not possible to maintain their standard of concert on £500, only to be told to get a cheaper orchestra. As it was, the Choir was already resorting to every possible fund-raising effort, including jumble sales. After the Festival, finding their programme suggestions for the following year again vetoed, they wrote to Alderman Luigi Denza (son of the composer Luigi Denza), a former Councillor and the last Mayor of Hampstead, and now on the Camden Arts Sub-Committee, complaining about these and other matters. One of their main problems was that the Council machinery operated from year to year, while they had to plan and book artists a year or more ahead. Another was the view in the Libraries and Arts Department that societies that were already receiving financial help from the Council, such as the Hampstead Choral Society and Hampstead Theatre Club, "could be expected to present an event in the Festival without receiving a further grant from Festival funds."[11]

Noel Woolf took action and in July combined forces with the Hampstead Artists Council to draw up a report for the Council and the Libraries and Arts Committee. It set out their grievances in no uncertain terms:

> "On the creation of Camden, an Arts Department was set up by the new Borough and imposed on the existing Hampstead organisation. This Arts Department ran on the St Pancras pattern and had little or no use for the amateur and voluntary professional workers who had been the backbone of the Arts in Hampstead. The Arts Department preferred in general not to know about them. In the event the purpose of the Hampstead Festival element incorporated in the new festival was entirely misunderstood by the 1967–68 Arts Sub-Committee. They regarded it as supplying little more than a fun element…tacked on as light relief and relegated to a fringe, and not integrated into the serious, 'professional' part of the festival for fear of debasing it…The Arts Department may be doing good work within its own terms of reference, but so far from helping the artists in Camden it is impeding them. The Libraries, Arts and Amenities Committee has no policy for aiding and encouraging the artists and the arts indigenous to Camden".[12]

The grievances also found their way into the *Ham & High*, whose editor Gerald Isaaman was an active member of the Hampstead community. He took up the cause in an editorial:

> "Just how successful was it? And what lessons are there to be learned? For while Camden can – as always – take pride in its artistic achievements, there is no room for smug complacency. As with the merger of the boroughs that now make up Camden, any shotgun wedding creates problems, and any attempt to please all tastes is, in itself, a difficult and dangerous exercise."

He also used the opportunity to question the policy of presenting neglected operas:

> "On the serious side, we have often felt it about time that the tradition of reviving ancient operas was ditched, perhaps not completely, but at least re-examined and lifted out of the rut it is now in. Not that we are against opera. It is simply a case of whether the cost and effort involved produces truly worthwhile results….The pop concerts at Parliament Hill alone proved that the festival has something to offer thousands of teenagers who might otherwise ignore it. Let there be more pop."[13]

The operas were certainly not in a rut, although not all the works revived were judged to be masterpieces. They were the best attended events, got the largest press coverage, recouped a substantial amount of their cost at the box office, and in 1969 brought in a total of £6,500 in grants from outside organisations. Their audience too was numbered in thousands, giving pleasure to people who enjoyed a form of entertainment they had been denied in the past and, unlike pop music, was not available anywhere else. Considering the fame and prestige the opera performances had brought to the borough over the years as none of its other activities had done, and for a minute outlay in terms of the borough's finances, the answer to the question as to whether the results were truly worthwhile was surely yes.

Opera was chiefly what the St Pancras and later the Camden Festival was about – remove it, and an entirely different festival results. Isaaman came to recognise this in later years, and swung the paper firmly behind the Festival; however, underlying the *Ham & High* criticisms in the first few Camden years was a real concern that activities in the old borough of Hampstead were being squashed. The paper continued, in marked contrast to the other two local newspapers, to leave no question unasked. The *North London Press*, by contrast, considered that "The main Festival hardly needs any comment....it has proved to be its usual successful efficient self, with 6,500 tickets sold beforehand".[14]

Working Parties wrestle with the problems

The Council set up a new Working Party under the Chairmanship of Councillor Torrance to re-examine all the options for the future of the Festival. Its other members were Vice-Chairman Christine Stewart-Munro, Noel Woolf, John Richardson and three other Camden Councillors. The *Ham & High* reported this move with another tendentious headline in September 1969: "Festival critics call for change", but this time went much further, accusing the Festival of having "limited appeal" and of not being "popular" enough. Councillor Torrance, the Chairman of the Committee was quoted as saying it was "a success with the critics, but not everyone wants out-of-the-way opera and chamber music." A closer reading of the article, however, reveals that the only "Festival critic" was Mike Alfandary, who had a vested interest as the pop-concert organiser. He was said to have claimed that "80% of the money is going on things which are out of touch with people's needs", although no explanation or evidence was offered to support this claim. There had, in fact, only ever been one letter of complaint about the Festival to the newspaper – about which, more below – although, as has been noted, there was a deluge of complaint about the pop concerts.

The attack drew anguished responses from concerned parties such as Martindale Sidwell and Gerald Gover, who were appalled at the possibility that operas or concerts might be cut. For several weeks the arguments raged on in the Letters column, Councillor Torrance, Noel Woolf and Leonard Marcus all weighing in to defend the Festival but, as Denby Richards pointed out in an article trying to calm matters down, "the apparent fight between the so-called Fringe and the established Festival was more in the mind than anywhere else".[15]

It was indeed a somewhat manufactured controversy. In all the furore, only two people wrote in to criticise the Festival, Bernard Kelly and I D Tomisson, and they turned out to be hardly disinterested critics. Kelly was a self-proclaimed artist who wrote regularly to the paper over a period of several years, signing himself "The Real Camden Arts Festival Forever", and calling for more "experimental art", "a real people's festival, an end to prestige art and a chance for free expression". He disrupted borough council meetings and regularly went in for publicity stunts to attract attention in the local press. On one occasion during a concert given by Yonty Solomon at the 1970 Festival he climbed onto the roof of the Swiss Cottage Odeon and dropped leaflets through the skylights onto the audience. He is quoted in the *Ham & High* on various occasions as condemning Camden in general for a "lack of attention to the arts", and the Festival in particular for its "uselessness... as a platform for easygoing underground experiments and spontaneous entertainment in streets and parks".[16] Tomisson, whose view was that "pop music will replace classical music", adopted a sneering tone towards everyone, including Bernard Kelly and "all so-called arty intellectuals" whose "treasured art forms will become obsolete".[17] He castigated Denby Richards for mentioning Tubby Hayes and Frank Sinatra as examples of great popular artists. Thus, on the basis of this rather partisan criticism an impression was created that the Festival was unpopular, while the real question – how best to adapt the borough's arts funding to its new circumstances – had been all but lost sight of.

It is ironic that the ideas for experimental and community arts and calls for 'pop' culture that were later taken up by radical Camden councillors first emanated from 'conservative' but also so-called "intellectual", bohemian and "arty" Hampstead. Alfandary, Stewart-Munro and Tomisson (who later served on the Council's Leisure Services Committee) were all active members of the local Conservative Party. It was the old working-class, radical St Pancras strand of the new borough that was still the bastion of "high art", a point made some years earlier by one published letter: "St Pancras, a borough written off by the fashionable as a collection of slums and goods yards, puts on a festival...so well supported that hundreds had to be turned away. Hampstead should be ashamed of its Philistinism." [18]

Curiously, another letter in the *North London Press*, which covered the old St Pancras area, took exactly the opposite view: "although the Festival is greatly enjoyed by the professional critics and the cognoscenti it is dedicated to the performance of obscure music and the pleasing of a handful of critics; the response from local residents is less and less. Hampstead Festival with its popular events is much better." [14]

1970

While the Working Party was deliberating, the 1970 Festival went ahead, repeating the 1969 format, with a large Fringe programme. The HAC exhibition *Manufactured Art* at Arkwright Road was chosen for the official opening and immediately sparked a controversy over its posters. Designed by George Cayford in pink and silver they showed three sets of breasts, one of which was human, and were promptly banned by London Transport. Jeanette Jackson, quoted in the *Ham &High*, dismissed the ban, tongue in cheek, as "absolutely tittiful". Yehudi Menuhin was the guest of honour and made a highly complimentary speech about Camden and the Festival, saying that it helped to educate people "with each other's ideas and fantasies, presenting a world of imagination usually so elusive".[19] Bernard Kelly again staged a publicity stunt by trying to make his own speech after the official opening. The Camden Artists' exhibition was also back in the programme at the Swiss Cottage Library.

The Fringe programme was pointedly renamed 'Camden Festival Too', perhaps reflecting the dissatisfaction that it was regarded as peripheral to the Festival. The various problems, especially lack of box office facilities, remained unsolved. The Council made it clear that it was neither practical nor possible for Council Arts staff to take over the administration of the Fringe. Its budget was increased to £5000 to enable them to pay an administrator.

The Fringe staged another rich variety of events, giving many amateur and professional organisations in the borough an opportunity to show their paces. There was particular emphasis on Camden's Cypriot community, with events showing aspects of Cypriot life and culture running throughout the month. There were recitals by the Glenilla Arts Group, a concert by the Hampstead Music Club at Burgh House, and talks and concerts hosted by Fenton House.

The Round House was used extensively, with an evening of Russian dance by the Balalaika Dance Group, a presentation by the Greek Arts Theatre Club and a Poetry 'D-Day'. It was also used for a repeat of the very successful pop concerts of the previous year, attracting a total of 3,826 people. Simon Jenkins in the *Evening Standard* quoted *"How progressive Camden Borough must be to be subsidising such an event! Establishment, boring Camden KNOWS WHERE IT'S AT"* –

"With such endearing deprecation the organisers of the current Camden Rock Festival gave backhanded thanks to their sponsors for a "uniquely mind-expanding experience" at the Round House…three days of rock and soul music complete with psychedelic paraphernalia…I doubt if all that many of the stout rate-payers of Camden were there to see what their bountiful £1000 has unleashed on Chalk Farm. A crowded hall of uniformly way-out people – not all that young either – watched…some superb music…a stripper and fire eater as well as some more mediocre entertainment, all bathed in some truly fantastic lighting effects. Round the back of the hall, amid the scent of joss-sticks, etc., the prevailing sub-culture sold its wares…..it was all a memorable experiment. And Camden deserves all congratulations for taking the unquestionably bold step of making it possible." [20]

The *Ham & High*'s Peter Halstead thought "It was one of the happiest, best-run pop events in my experience" which "drew more fans than could be fitted in. By late Saturday afternoon two long queues [37] had built up for the 8 pm concert, and late-comers had to be turned away".[21]

The *Financial Times* took a novel view of the events: "The Camden Festival has a reputation for reviving obscure operas, so it was a good idea to start this year's culture course with a weekend rock-and-roll revival meeting."

There were performances by students of the Central School of Speech and Drama at the Embassy Theatre, and amateur drama groups including the Dramateurs and Hampstead Drama Guild. There were exhibitions, walks, photographic and poetry

37 The queue for the pop concert at the Round House, 1970

competitions, mixed media events, and street performances by 'Dogg's Troupe Jug Band' and 'Hello Day' put on by Inter-Action.

Rising costs were again a problem, leading to lengthy deliberations as to whether to reduce the number of operas to three and whether symphony concerts at Swiss Cottage were possible. The view was that "the principle of presenting four opera productions has never been abandoned" and "if it was at all possible the operas and symphony concerts should remain", but that "concerts of esoteric chamber music such as the concerts of Swedish music… of May 1969 were more dispensable".[11]

As late as November 1969 the Committee was advised that a fourth opera could not be accommodated within the budget. However, the London Chamber Opera was again available, on the same financial basis, but this time their production was properly in the Festival. The GLC also increased its grant.

It was a very ambitious programme, with two of the four productions being double bills, presented by the Park Lane Group. Delius's *Fennimore and Gerda* was combined with an unfinished children's opera by Richard Strauss called *The Donkey's Shadow*. Begun in the last months of his life for the local village school which his son and grandson had attended, it remained unfinished at his death. Many years later the Strauss family gave the school permission to re-examine Strauss's sketches and prepare them for a performance which took place in 1964; the Festival production was the first in this country. William Mann in

The Times dismissed it as a "pseudo-novelty", musically "quite feeble and seldom sounds like the late Strauss we know and love", but he thought the Delius "a moving and decidedly original opera".

Two Poulenc operas conducted by Roger Norrington, *La Voix Humaine* (written in 1959) and *Les Mamelles de Tiresias*, contrasted comedy and tragedy. The Tiresias/Thérèse joke, a setting of the 1903 play by Apollinaire, was first produced in 1947 and was receiving its first professional production in London. Colin Graham's witty English translation was used in which the audience is topically exhorted not merely to go forth and multiply but to 'make love instead of war'.

The London Chamber Opera's contribution was announced in a press release with the flourish that "this year we've discovered a manuscript of Scarlatti's baroque opera, *La Statira*, in the British Museum and it is getting its first performance in this country, probably its first performance anywhere since the early eighteenth century", to which Arthur Jacobs responded in *Opera*:

"This production took Alessandro Scarlatti out of operatic limbo, after which many of the audience must have wished him back there. I doubt, however, whether Handel's elder operatic contemporary ought to be judged on the strength of this plodding performance in Italian." [22]

A noted translator himself, Jacobs rode a particular hobbyhorse that opera should be sung in English; he grudgingly conceded that "its music – virtually all solo arias, plus expressive recitative – is well worth hearing".
Certainly the audience thought so: it was sold out.

Leoncavallo's version of *La Bohème*, the first *verismo* revival for many years, was judged by *Opera*'s Alan Blyth to "be a straggling, ill-constructed affair by comparison with Puccini's opera, but it has its merits." [23]

The RPO concerts at Swiss Cottage were not included in the Festival, evidently because the programmes offered were "not of sufficient interest to warrant their presentation". Two concerts nevertheless went ahead during the Festival period, and "with popular programmes there were good attendances…although the press were less than pleased about the lack of enterprise in the programme planning – in which we were not consulted." [24]

38 Ballet Rambert, in *Opus 65* created for the 1970 Festival (photo Alan Cunliffe, Rambert Dance Company Archive)

Newcomers were the recently formed Camden Chamber Orchestra, a group of young professional musicians conducted by John Lubbock. There was plenty of jazz, with concerts at the Cochrane Theatre and the Dankworth Big Band with Cleo Laine at the Swiss Cottage Odeon. They gave the first performance of Richard Rodney Bennett's 'Jazz Calendar' and sold more tickets than did the RPO concerts there. You could "spot the stars of the future", as the press release put it, in the Lunchtime Prizewinners' Recitals at Holborn Library Hall, one of whom was Imogen Cooper.

An experimental series of lunchtime guitar recitals of every possible style, including one by John Williams, at Holy Trinity Church, Kingsway, was very successful and proved popular with the working population of Holborn.

The modern dance programmes repeated their success: The Ballet Rambert [38] gave a 2-week season at the Jeannetta Cochrane Theatre, made possible by a grant from the Council; in token of their gratitude they created a new ballet especially for the Festival. Their performances, playing to 2,500 people, were sold out, while The London Contemporary Dance Company, 'at home' at their rapidly growing headquarters at The Place, had to extend their season by another week due to popular demand.

The Hampstead Theatre Club mounted a special Festival production of Rostand's *The Fantasticks* by Tom Jones and Harvey Schmidt, and also a late-night revue called *Take Me To Your Lieder* with Richard Stilgoe. There were films at Holborn Library on Friday evenings and late-night films at the Classic in Hampstead. Also at Holborn Library were talks, including one to mark Charles Dickens' centenary.

The Borough Librarian gave a glowing report to his committee: "This year's festival again demonstrated that the Festival continues to grow in range and in artistic standards whilst increasing the box-office takings." *La Voix Humaine* was recorded by the BBC. Over 26,000 tickets were sold, with an income of £13,365. New audiences had been brought in by the Ballet Rambert and the rock concerts. There was an overspend of some £3000 which was attributed to the rise in the cost of the operas; top ticket prices were still only £1 and had not increased for 3 years, so this would obviously have to be reconsidered. It was particularly noted that while the operas had attracted the largest audiences, many of the concerts were not so well attended.[24]

Yet again the national press was full of praise for the Festival and for Camden's role in London's artistic life, many commenting on how much could be achieved if other local authorities were to follow its example. As *Opera* put it:

"The enterprise of the London Borough of Camden in again staging its festival this month (opera, concerts, drama, and art exhibitions are included) is illuminated in a financial statement recently issued by the Borough. The proceeds of a 1d rate in Camden would be £140,500; Camden spends annually on the arts only an estimated £100,480, the equivalent of a rate of five-sevenths of a penny! (Local authorities may legally spend up to a 6d rate.) The average weekly cost per head of population is about 2d. The amount spent on the Camden Festival itself is £34,000. It becomes obvious that the Festival is not the product of 'extravagant' spending and that other authorities could maintain a comparable enterprise if they wished." [25]

The *Ham & High* agreed, and also pointed out that with income from the box office and various grants, the actual net cost to Camden was "barely £16,500…a minute sum compared with the Festival's fame and worth. Nobody, not even the meanest low-brow ratepayer, can complain that this is not real value for money". That still did not stop it aiming another broadside at the operas which "cost so much and are allowed year after year to scoop the cream off the budget. There is a need for fresh impetus and new ideas." [26]

One aspect was a genuine cause for criticism and in 1970 it drew a chorus of dissatisfaction, namely the limitations of the venues, in particular the Assembly Hall Audience dissatisfaction had been highlighted by the previous year's survey, and now the critics' patience – "we are so used now to the wonders of contrivance on the cramped stage of St Pancras Town Hall", as *Opera* put it in 1966 – was running out.

There was a "make do in spite of everything brigade", as Denby Richards described them, who were fond of the Assembly Hall.[27] However, Arthur Jacobs in *Opera* was fairly representative:

"The Town Hall acoustics now make it so difficult to put over the words… With the orchestra on floor-level, not in a sunken pit, this auditorium notoriously places the voices at a disadvantage, even with a conductor…skilful…in attempting to balance his forces. Our general gratitude to the London Borough of Camden for its festival should not prevent a protest against the continuing use of this hall. It simply cripples operatic pleasure. Why not hire the Collegiate Theatre, in the same area ?"

as was Alan Blyth:

"…notoriously unsympathetic acoustic. Why cannot Camden's opera transfer itself to the Collegiate Theatre which has a sunk pit and a raked auditorium?" [28]

The Festival team had even contemplated using the Shaftesbury Theatre for future opera performances. It would have given scope for longer runs and larger houses, but negotiations with the Arts Council during 1968 to make the theatre available came to nothing.

The Borough Librarian had ended his 1970 Festival report signalling that "a stage has now been reached at which widespread changes are both possible and desirable." The Working Party on the Camden Festival reported shortly afterwards, in June. It had considered every aspect of the Festival and interviewed several festival specialists, both national and local, as well as taking into account the suggestions made at the public meeting in 1968 and by representatives of local organisations. Noel Woolf had urged all his colleagues in Music & Arts to make their views known to the Council on how the arts should be organised, developed and run in Camden, "whether they want them run centrally under the hand of a council employee or whether they want to play a vigorous part themselves." [29]

M & A wanted the fringe events to be part of the main programme and included in the main festival brochure, but they were also anxious about being able to maintain their ability to have their say.

The Working Party's main finding was that the promotion of rare or neglected opera, on which the Festival's international reputation was based "should be maintained and that in addition the Festival should also concentrate on the visual arts and poetry". It pointed out that it was not possible to maintain an equally high standard in all art forms and it was usual for a Festival to specialise in particular areas. Concern was expressed at the neglect of drama, but it was hoped that the imminent opening of the Shaw Theatre in Euston Road and the participation of the National Youth Theatre which was to be based there would help strengthen drama in the Festival.

The Committee valued the Fringe events, which had an important part to play in the Festival "and should not be treated as a poor relation." The holding of "two separate programmes has caused many difficulties and has been a source of confusion to the public." The Fringe events would be combined with the main festival under the supervision of the Council's Arts staff; "close liaison should be achieved between the Council's Festival organisation and Music & Arts." A new member of staff should be appointed to the Arts Section who would work as an administrator for Music and Arts in Camden and also work with other local societies and the local community on arts matters. There should be one Festival programme in future, listing all events.

The working party considered that 4 weeks is unusually long for a Festival and that it should be shortened to 3 weeks. This would mean some reduction in the number of some events, but they are "not expected to be drastically curtailed". Planning should start earlier, at least a year ahead, in particular for the 1972 Festival when the Council would be participating in the All-London Festival. As the Festival audience was a working one, attending concerts in the evenings, rather than a 'holiday' audience as at Aldeburgh or Edinburgh, it was not advisable to try to cram in too much.

The idea of more outside sponsorship was also considered, particularly from large firms in Camden who "could have a greater identification with the Borough", as had happened with the Watney Mann sponsorship for *Under Western Eyes*.[30]

It was also suggested that Festival publicity needed to be improved "to generate more interest" and proposed that a freelance journalist be employed for this purpose during the Festival. The Borough Librarian and Treasurer rejected this, pointing out that it was unnecessary to spend more money on publicity when there was already wide coverage in the national press. M & A also countered the working party's suggestion that a Festival magazine should be produced, reminding them that sales resistance had been encountered to the increasingly large programme books, last produced in 1968 and sold for 2s 6d each. In 1970 a throw-away folder was produced instead. Generally, however, the working party's findings were welcomed.

At the same time William Maidment was examining the wider issue of the Borough's overall arts policy and in November produced a report called "Towards a Policy for the Arts".[31] He reminded Councillors that while there is a statutory duty to maintain libraries there was still no such duty to develop the arts, only the guidance that the Council *may* spend up to a sixpenny rate.

Coherent policies needed to be developed for the future. The Council was in the process of developing two major arts centres – the Swiss Cottage site, which was still at that stage planned to include a 2000-seat concert hall, and the new library and theatre at St Pancras – neither chosen by Camden Council but originating from commitments already made by the former boroughs before amalgamation. Clearly, Noel Woolf's criticisms had made some impression on Maidment because he acknowledged that while the borough was doing well in the provision of professional performances, it was doing less well in encouraging the amateur, or providing facilities for active participation in the arts, although the recent decision to appoint an Arts assistant to liaise with societies in the borough, as part of the recommendations about the Festival, would help.

He identified two major concerns: finding the right balance between the Council's provision of the different art forms, and whether it was justified to concentrate so much of the budget on the short Festival period, at the expense of activities throughout the year. Actually, in the Borough's overall expenditure on the arts, less was spent on music, including the operas, than on visual arts and drama, and most of it was concentrated on the Festival. For the two years 1969 and 1970 the budget for music was £28,887 and £30,324, for the visual arts £41,000 in each year while expenditure on drama overtook music, increasing from £21,000 to £33,000. With the Council already committed to Centre 42 at the Round House, Regent's Park Open Air Theatre, Hampstead Theatre and Unity Theatre, plus a number of smaller theatre groups, and with the Shaw Theatre nearing completion, Maidment considered that "careful discrimination should be exercised in accepting any further continuing commitments to traditional or experimental theatre in Camden. Theatre and various peripheral activities have been the most persuasive and effective 'lobby', but not necessarily the most deserving".

Other authorities were now developing programmes of support for the arts and beginning to organise festivals, which could in the future affect the position of the Camden Festival. It might be difficult to find dates that did not clash and for Camden "to remain outstanding amidst wider competition". It might be necessary to spend more to maintain the Festival's position. He suggested also that "it should be accepted that the festival in its present form may have to change after perhaps another four or five years. Plans should be made to increase the regular support for music."

Following these reports various changes to Committees were made. At Alderman Denza's suggestion a Music Advisory Panel was set up in February 1971 to advise the Arts Sub-Committee and "act as a forum for discussing new ways of developing the musical life of the Borough". It was to consist of the advisors who were already co-opted onto the Arts Sub-Committee: Felix Aprahamian, the music critic, John Cruft of the Arts Council, the composer Wilfred Josephs and the conductor Stanford Robinson, with Jack Henderson and Denza himself as chairman. In response to concerns that the interests of music were too dominant amongst the advisory members of the Arts Sub-Committee, an Advisory Panel on the Visual Arts was also established and Susanna Capon was co-opted to strengthen drama representation.

Another important innovation was to require more detailed reports showing a breakdown of all money spent by the Council on the arts.[32]

For Noel Woolf, however, it was time to go. At a Music & Arts committee meeting in September 1970 he announced he would not stand for re-election as "he felt many of the changes implicit in the future development of M & A could be better handled by a new Chairman." His last contribution as chairman was the suggestion that Camden Council should be invited to nominate two councillors to be co-opted on to the M & A executive so that "they would have a better understanding of M & A's difficulties". At the same meeting Patrick Gilbert, who was to take over as chairman, expressed the view that "there should be more professionalism" in the M & A contributions.[33]

1971

1971 was the year that the Camden Festival moved into the streets, signalling (as one press report put it) "the transformation of the North London Borough into the liveliest place in town. Plans for the £37,000 fiesta show a huge new section of outdoor events ranging from a ballet performed by mobile mechanical cranes to a touring storyteller to street theatre groups. All this will be staged alongside the usual festival fare of high quality theatre, opera dance, jazz, poetry, exhibitions and happenings. For the first time pop music and music hall feature in the official programme". The brochure and publicity material were redesigned, and the Festival Diary grouped events under the headings Music, Theatre, Exhibitions, For Your Children, In the Open Air, In Historic Settings and By Local Organisations.

The official opening in April was a major event, timed to coincide with the opening of the new St Pancras Library and Shaw Theatre by Princess Anne, complete with specially commissioned sculpture by Keith Grant. This project, like the civic centre at Swiss Cottage, had begun many years ago when St Pancras had planned a new Central Library and assembly hall in the Euston Road. When Camden Council came into being, it was decided instead to build a civic theatre which, it was thought, could be done without extra cost. Only after the building was under way did the Council start to think about its appropriate use. After much discussion it was decided to lease the theatre at a peppercorn rent to the National Youth Theatre to run a programme of inexpensive theatre for young people.

Although the Working Party had recommended a shortening of the Festival to 3 weeks and the programme had been scaled down accordingly, it somehow ended up lasting 4 weeks anyway. Considerable cuts had been made to keep to the budget allocation of £40,000, and the programme looks rather thin compared with previous seasons. Orchestral, chamber and ensemble music and film were all eliminated and there were only three operas, which was a cause of heated argument within the Committee in the preparatory stages. There were three choral concerts; three organ recitals at Hampstead parish church; lunchtime concerts at Holy Trinity, Kingsway; prizewinners' recitals; and concerts at Fenton House featuring early keyboard instruments.

The celebrity recitalist was Segovia.

M & A also presented several attractive Poetry and Music events including three commemorating the 150th anniversary of Keats's death and also a recital by the Glenilla Arts Group and the Helicon Ensemble. London Contemporary Dance gave their season at The Place and PLG presented Avant Garde Jazz at the Collegiate theatre with the London Jazz Composer's Orchestra, one of the most unusual ensembles in contemporary music. Founded in 1970 by Barry Guy, it was "designed to couple the anarchic instrumental methods of the atonalist with the formal restraints of composition. The participating musicians form something of a *Who's Who* of British improvisers."[34] With the incorporation of the fringe events into the Festival there was a noticeable change of balance, a large proportion of the programme consisting of pop concerts, music hall, and street events. It also included a programme for children during the Easter school holidays which was considered very successful.

39 Valerie Masterson in Rossini's *Tancredi* at the 1971 Festival (photo Donald Cooper)

Michael Alfandary sent an interesting application to stage the pop concerts,[35] proposing "to arrange concerts with recognisable musical objectives and with a predetermined stylistic structure rather than presenting a hotch-potch of artists based on promotional values alone. Our aim will be to commission a group to compose and perform a specific work for the Festival." He suggested that a guarantee of £1,500 would be necessary. In the end it would appear that the "promotional values" won the day as Peter Bowyer presented a Camden 'Pop' festival at the Round House to audiences totalling 16,000, at no cost to the Festival.[36]

There was an effort to achieve a wider geographical spread of art exhibitions – in 1970 they had been concentrated too much in Hampstead – with suggestions that open spaces such as Russell Square and the concourse of Euston Station be investigated. In addition to the usual Camden Artists there were Hoffnung drawings at the Swiss Cottage Library and an exhibition to mark the centenary of the acquisition of Hampstead Heath, jointly mounted by the Camden History Society and the Heath and Old Hampstead Society. Hampstead Photographic Society showed in both 1971 and 1972. At the other end of the borough there were shows with a Japanese theme at the Ansdell Gallery in Covent Garden, and at the Crafts Centre of Great Britain in Earlham Street there was craftwork from the newly established studios in what had been warehouses for Covent Garden market.

The Hampstead Theatre mounted a production of *Vincent*, a play about Van Gogh. They also played host to a company from Los Angeles, who staged a late-night revue called *Raisins and Almonds*, to Soho Theatre for lunchtime performances of John Grillo's *Blubber*, and to Hampstead Drama Guild for *An Italian Straw Hat*. The Gatehouse Theatre in Highgate also participated, with *The Sand Kitchen* by Richard Wall.

The three operas were moved to the Collegiate Theatre, which from now on became the main venue for fully staged productions, although the old Assembly Hall was still occasionally used for concert performances of opera. Another Haydn opera, *La Fedeltà Premiata*, was given its first performance in this country in a production brought from the 1970 Holland Festival by Park Lane Group, conducted by David Lloyd-Jones. Rossini's *Tancredi* [39] was revived by Basilica Opera, and Opera Concerts further explored the *verismo* repertoire with Cilea's *Adriana Lecouvreur*, not seen in London for some 50 years. The Arts Sub-Committee was not entirely happy with these choices, considering them to be too "similar in style and/or period and language, and the presentation of one modern opera was urged". The cost of these productions was approximately £6000 each while income from a full house at the Collegiate was only £930. An interesting postscript to Leonard Marcus's career is the appearance of his name as General Manager of Opera Concerts.

The 1971 Festival closed with an event which harked back to the Festival's earliest days at St Pancras: a Jumbo May Day Carnival organised by the Positive Movement especially for children at Parliament Hill Fields, attended by 3000 people. Attendance figures for all the events excluding the eight exhibitions was 48,805, 16,000 of them for the week of pop concerts and films.

A new concern surfaces in the Council report on the Festival: the aim to "reach a wider Camden audience", perhaps sparked by the findings of the *Ham & High* survey of four years before about where the audience lived. A scheme was introduced to give Camden residents priority booking at special rates, and 48% of the tickets were sold through it. The box-office receipts for operas showed an improvement on the previous year in spite of the move to a smaller theatre: *Tancredi* was completely sold out in advance. So also were the Segovia concert, the prizewinners' recitals, the Glenilla Arts Group concert and the concerts at Fenton House.

The Festival had featured on the front page of the *Sunday Times* and on BBC TV Nationwide, and the 1971 report ended on an upbeat note:

> "The best response to the Festival is undoubtedly a response to quality. The Festival can apparently obtain an audience for any sort of artistic activity provided it is of the highest possible standard. It is with this in mind that the 1972 Festival is being prepared." [36]

There was a greater drive for publicity, with advertising hoardings, badges for children, door-to-door mailing and car stickers, although the latter two were not so successful.

In an end-of-year report on the eve of the festival, in March, Christine Stewart-Munro reviewed the changes that had taken place in the last nine months. In particular, she mentioned the new method of early approval of content by allocating budgets to each category of events, so that the Festival team could proceed with their job of working out the details.

Immediately the festival finished in May 1971, local elections resulted in another switch of political control, back to Labour domination. Enid Wistrich was the new chairman of the Libraries Arts and Recreation Committee; the vice-chairman was Councillor Needham. Members of the Arts Sub-Committee included Alderman Luigi Denza and Councillor du Mont, while Christine Stewart-Munro and John Richardson stayed on as advisory members. It was clear that the Festival formula was still not right and the new team set in train a further report, issued in November 1971, which was to change the format yet again. Music & Arts was becoming increasingly concerned about its future role, feeling that the Hampstead Festival had lost its impact. They had started planning for 1972, but they began to feel less and less welcome. Maidment sent them a patronising letter in September quoting at them the statement in the June report of the Camden Arts Sub-Committee that artistic activity must be of the highest possible standard. He also rubbed in the impression that they were not wanted by saying that he understood that neither Hampstead Theatre nor the Shaw was available to them. Patrick Gilbert of M & A appealed to Councillor du Mont for help:

> "It is no secret that Henderson would much prefer Music & Arts not to take part in the festival, just as it has been obvious for some time that the [Hampstead] Theatre Club would prefer the Societies not to have their Music & Arts Weeks there. I realise that Henderson wishes to establish a reputation in the Festival World…and this I find quite acceptable because he is competent and he does run a good Festival. I can also see his anxiety about the participation of amateur societies, good as they may be – and some of them are very good. An alternative was for M & A to have a separate Festival Fortnight in the autumn, but, on the whole, I would prefer to join in the main Event.…The position at the

40 Logo of Music & Arts in Camden

41 Festival brochure 1972

moment is unsatisfactory... could you advise us of the best way of setting about producing a happier relationship with the Arts Department." [37]

After much discussion as to what their future role should be, whether they should alter the way Music & Arts weeks were run or even whether they should continue at all, they decided to press Camden for a grant for a full-time administrator, but this was refused. The questions were left unresolved, and the 1972 Festival was the last to feature any M & A events. After struggling on for several more years they faded away. However, the coming together of M & A and the St Pancras Festival radically influenced the future direction of the Festival. M&A left a lasting legacy, having introduced to it a completely different style of popular event.

1972

The 1972 Festival opened the Greater London Arts Association's London Festival, a combination of the Festivals of London co-ordinated by the GLAA. It had in fact been the brainchild of Patrick Gilbert of Music & Arts, who had made the suggestion as early as 1968. With a hugely increased budget of £50,000, Camden pulled out the stops to ensure a good showing, with a specially hired press and public relations consultant. A scheme was introduced to give the borough's library-card holders reductions on their tickets.

Big orchestral concerts returned. At the Swiss Cottage Odeon the London Symphony Orchestra celebrated the Diaghilev centenary, and the New Philharmonia presented a Viennese evening, while the Royal Philharmonic gave a children's concert at the Round House. The Celebrity Recital was given by Elisabeth Schwarzkopf accompanied by Geoffrey Parsons, both of whom lived in Hampstead. There was a Danish theme, with a special Danish exhibition at the Camden Arts Centre organised by the Danish Embassy and also a concert by the Danish Chamber Orchestra. Still in its May slot a large open-air programme was arranged with free events such as a Hot Air Balloon and two special Festival commissions: an event called *May Rising* by a group called The Welfare State and Bruce Lacey's *Incredible Sound Machine*. Other elements of the Festival such as poetry and film were strengthened. Peter Bowyer again presented pop concerts at the Round House.

The operatic programme, back to four productions, one of which was a double bill, was the most ambitious and varied yet, with a departure from tradition by moving outside the Borough to the Sadler's Wells Theatre in collaboration with the Delius Trust. In return for a £3000 guarantee against loss from Camden the Trust bore most of the cost of a production of Delius's *Koanga* [42]. There were three performances, with Charles Groves conducting a cast of top-rank singers, and the possibility of a recording by EMI. At the Collegiate, Opera Concerts presented a double bill of Massenet's *La Navarraise* and Rachmaninov's *Aleko*, and Park Lane Group returned with Smetana's *The Secret*. The Delius and the Smetana were broadcast live by the BBC.

Another novelty was "late night opera", bringing the first appearance at the Festival of Opera Rara. This company was started by Patric Schmid and Don White in 1970 and has since earned world-wide fame and respect for its work in promoting the forgotten operas of the 19th century, in particular of the *bel canto* repertoire. Camden festival provided their first opportunity to mount a fully staged production, Donizetti's comic opera *Le Convenienze Teatrali*. Requiring only piano accompaniment and therefore reducing financial risk, it was presented in a shortened version as a late-

42 Sketch for Delius's *Koanga* (Festival 1971) by Peter Rice

night show on five consecutive nights at the Collegiate, starting at 10 pm. Translated as *The Prima Donna's Mother is a Drag*, the piece contains a remarkable burlesque role for a baritone singing falsetto as the mother [43] and was a huge success. *Opera's* critic, Arthur Jacobs, entered into the spirit of the thing:

> "There was a hilarious finale when the Mother led them in a piece...presented as part of a supposed *Boadicea Regina d'Inghilterra*. "I do it in English" announced the Mother, "so that I'll get a good review from *Opera* magazine". You have, Mr Aspinall, you have!" [38]

The post-Festival report to the Committee again drew attention to the fact that it was due to the "continual emphasis on quality that the general standard of performance during the Festival compares with that of any festival in this country." The number of tickets sold was the highest ever, with many events sold out: the Schwarzkopf concert, a Latin American evening by John Williams, a series of events at Fenton House, Hampstead Music Club's two concerts of Victorian music in costume at Burgh House, a concert by Maria Farandouri, and the children's concert at the Round House. All the performances of *Koanga* were virtually sold out and, as the report to the Committee pointed out, Sadler's Wells holds three times as many as the Collegiate.[39]

It was hoped that this London-wide festival would become a regular event. In the event it was the only such attempt. The reality was the "very grave financial problems which beset all London local authorities at this time".[40] Arts activities throughout Britain were increasingly starved of funds as the country went from one financial crisis to another, and by the end of the 1970s any such thoughts had entirely evaporated.

The Committee's Report[41] of November 1971, in a thorough and careful assessment of the Festival in the context of all the Borough's arts commitments, concluded that another radical overhaul was needed. The Council's commitment to drama at the Shaw Theatre and the Hampstead Theatre Club amounted to £68,000; the visual arts programme at Arkwright Road and at the Swiss Cottage and other libraries cost around £40,000. But there was no continuing provision for music, even though most of the Council's prestige for arts activities was based on its reputation for presenting music. The role of the Festival "had become obscured in recent years because it included so many varied events". Its new May slot caused problems for the operas because there were too many other Festivals going on at the same time, yet it was still too early in the year for the fine weather needed for the outdoor events.

It was proposed to divide the Festival into three separate sections. The music Festival, with the operas, would return to its old slot in February/March. The more populist elements of the programme would be planned as a series of neighbourhood festivals, with local community participation in the summer when the big outdoor events could take place. A new third element was to be a special Autumn Theme Festival, concentrating on one particular subject such as visual arts, drama, dance or film which should not require a high level of subsidy from the Council, either because the relevant organisations already had grants from the Council or because the activity itself was not expensive to promote. Together with the long-standing Junior Festival – begun in 1962 by St Pancras – every November, this would distribute activities throughout the year. It would also mean that a larger number of Camden residents would become involved in, and be entertained by, the Festival than had hitherto been possible. It was recommended that in view of the expansion of activities thus envisaged, expenditure should be maintained at the 1972 level of £50,000, of which £30,000 would be allocated to the music Festival.

43 Michael Aspinall, with Mary Hill at the piano, in Donizetti's *Le Convenienze Teatrali* (Festival 1972) (photo Donald Cooper). *Opera* commented "Look out, Danny La Rue! Michael Aspinall is on your heels, and he can sing too."

Holding the Festival in April/May had been far from ideal for the planning of the operas and had diminished box-office receipts by 14%. Camden found itself in competition with other festivals, in particular Glyndebourne, both for audiences and for the services of singers, and stage and production crew. Even in February there had been problems, with companies working in the Festival vying with each other for the services of a limited pool of available performers. As to the chorus, Patric Schmid remembered, it was sometimes not so much a case of auditioning but going on bended knee to beg singers to take part! Now the Festival could go back to "its work of 'discovery', recover its identity and capture the musical imagination of everyone in and around London with an adventurous programme".

Jack Henderson had given careful thought to the future of the opera programme. In his contribution to the report he "stressed the importance of paying attention to the history and development of opera in planning for future Festivals"; the commitment to modern music must be maintained and the organisers must endeavour to find audiences for new work. He would have liked to repeat the Sadler's Wells experiment, with a second production in 1973 using an internationally known cast, while concentrating the smaller-scale works at the Collegiate. He advised the Committee: "There are a number of operas which are well worth revival but which demand singers of the highest quality and with great experience. They are not suitable for the format of the Collegiate Theatre, admirably though that suits less mature singers". There were proposals from Opera da Camera for the revival of 18th-century English operas which "require stylised staging, a small orchestra and a cast of manageable proportions...at a rather lower cost" than that of the works recently presented. Purcell's *Indian Queen* was proposed and as a contrast, a piece by a 20th-century composer such as Wolf-Ferrari or a non-Italian composer such as Chabrier. Henderson also suggested exploring work by contemporary composers such as Henze who were producing work which avoided "conventional operatic trappings but which offer a musical and dramatic experience".[41]

The *Ham & High*, still in critical mode, put a rather misleading gloss on this report in its Heathman's Diary. It was "wrong to concentrate all the events we promote in a short Festival period" and "growing criticism...of the Festival has been reflected in a gradual decline in box-office takings".[42]

Christine Stewart-Munro immediately wrote in to refute this, pointing out that Festival audiences had in fact increased overall year on year.[43]

But more than just the Festival was being reorganised. After the 1971 local elections and the change of administration, the Arts and Libraries Department itself came under scrutiny from its new Committee. It had grown tremendously since 1965, acquiring responsibility for a whole range of outdoor activities such as sports grounds and open spaces in addition to libraries, museums, and art galleries, and there was a need for rationalisation. In 1970 it had been renamed the Libraries, Arts and Recreation Committee. During 1972 it was completely restructured. Under the new title of Leisure Services it was split into two divisions, each with its own Sub-Committees: Libraries and Arts, and Recreation and Open Spaces. Many new people appeared on the new Leisure Services Committee including its chairman, Frank Dobson, bringing with them new priorities and preoccupations. As the decade unfolded these moved ever further from the ideals and purpose of the original Festival founders and from now on the Festival's importance within the Council was diminished. Even finding the reports on it in the Council minutes is difficult, buried as they are amongst fishing, cricket, building works and all manner of other activities which were now the responsibility of the single department.

Notes for chapter 4

1 *The Musical Times* Dec 1967 (vol 108, no.1498), Editorial.
2 *Opera* May 1962 (vol 13 no.5) p 334.
3 *Opera* May 1967 (vol 18, no.5) p 417.
4 *Camden Journal* Apr/May 1969 (vol 4, no.6) p 1.
5 *Ham & High* 16.5.69
6 *Opera* Jul 1981 (vol 32 no.7) p 679.
7 Libraries, Arts and Amenities Committee minutes 3.7.69 LAA/69/48 Agenda item 4b.
8 *North London Press* 9.5.69.
9 *Ham & High* 6.6.69.
10 Letter from Keith Martin to Jack Henderson, 28.6.68 (Keith Martin Archive, see ref. 12).
11 Report of Camden Arts Sub-Committee 3.9.69 LAA/69/60 Agenda Item 1/15.
12 Report prepared jointly by M&A and HAC, July 1969 (Keith Martin Archive)
13 *Ham & High* 13.6.69 "Beyond the Fringe".
14 *North London Press* 9.5.69.
15 *Ham & High* 7.11.69.
16 *Ham & High* 22.3.68, p 9.
17 *Ham & High* 17.10.69.
18 *North London Press* 27.3.64.
19 *Ham & High* 16.5.70.
20 *Evening Standard* 5.5.70.
21 *Ham & High* 8.5.70.
22 *Opera* Jul 1970 (vol 21 no.7) p 679.
23 Ref. 22, p 680.
24 Libraries, Arts and Amenities Committee minutes 29.6.70 LAA/70/54) Agenda item 5a.
25 *Opera* May 1970 (vol 21 no.5) p 382.
26 *Ham & High* 20.3.70 "The cost of culture".
27 *Ham & High* 26.5.72.
28 Ref. 22, pp 683, 681.
29 Memorandum 21.1.70 to M&A members (Keith Martin archive).
30 Working Party report to Libraries and Arts Committee LAA/70/35a 8.6.70 Agenda item 20b.
31 Libraries, Arts and Recreation (LAR) Committee minutes LAR/70/106 23.11.70 Agenda Item 10.
32 LAR minutes LAR.71/47 22.3.71) Agenda item 16b.
33 M&A minutes 4.9.70 (Keith Martin Archive).
34 1980 Festival programme notes.
35 Letter from Alfandary to Keith Martin 4.9.70 (Keith Martin Archive).
36 LAR minutes 9.9.71 LAR/71/72 Agenda item 15.
37 Letter of Patrick Gilbert 1.10.71 (Keith Martin Archive).
38 *Opera* Jul 1972 (vol 23 no.7) p 660.
39 Leisure Services Committee minutes, 12.6.72 LS/72/5, Agenda item 5b.
40 Chairman GLAA and Westminster Councillor, letter to London LAs about the 1972 London Festival. ASC minutes 4.2.71 (Keith Martin Archive).
41 LAR minutes 10.11.71 LAR/71/105 Agenda Item 5.
42 *Ham & High* 3.12.71.
43 *Ham & High* 10.12.71.

5 Triumph over adversity (1973–1980)

[Notes for chapter 5 are on p 92]

Clouds were gathering as the country's growing economic problems began to affect local authority expenditure. In 1973 the OPEC quadrupling of oil prices triggered an economic crisis and the 3-day week. For the arts, the optimism of the mid-1960s was draining away as arts subsidies remained at a standstill and inflation began to erode budgets. Funding for the arts failed even to keep pace with the official inflation rate, and any idea of the arts as a growth area was set aside. Chairman of the Arts Council Patrick Gibson wrote an anguished letter to *The Times* pointing out that

"We still have far to go before the arts reach all those whose lives can be enriched by them, but there has been a real growth in the range of people reached and their spread across the country, and it will be a tragedy if this process is halted."[1]

In the years that followed there was much argument about inflation statistics and minimum needs.

It was also a time of growing controversy on the whole subject of the character and nature of the arts: what were they? who were they for? The GLC produced a discussion paper called *Leisure for Londoners*[2] which declared: "London can and must provide rich and comprehensive leisure opportunities within the reach and means of all its residents and visitors"; it also acknowledged that there was an audience of millions for theatre and opera.

Camden's new Leisure Services Committee initiated several reports of its own on arts policy. A Leisure Services Position Statement issued in March 1973 examined all the various areas of cultural activity which the Council funded.[3]

It stated that there was "a lack of detailed information on the demand for services", including music and opera provision, a curious observation since it was, in fact, the one area of Council provision where demand was well documented because of the Festival.

By May 1973 Frank Dobson had become leader of the Council and John Lipetz had taken over as Chair of Leisure Services. A Community Arts Working Party that included Councillors Leila Campbell, John Lipetz and Ivor Walker was initiated. Its report, issued in April 1975, seems innocuous enough but it contains ominous indications for the future. It speaks of "a feeling voiced by a growing number of artists and organisations interested in the arts that traditional art forms have little relevance for a large proportion of the population". The Committee's Discussion noted: "In these days of financial stringency, it is most welcome to find organisations which do not see direct financial support as the prerequisite to their successful participation in the life of the Borough."

1973

In 1973 the Festival hit a low point. It emerged from the latest reorganisation reduced both in scope and budget and scaled down to 2 weeks. It was no longer a Festival of the Arts, just a Music Festival, with a greatly diminished range on offer and only two operas. Fully staged drama productions had gone, never to return, as had the regular presentation of visual arts and the shows devoted to Camden Artists. In his report to the Committee the Director had made it clear that there would be "grave difficulties" in keeping up past standards with such a reduced budget.[4] There were even difficulties in securing dates at the Shaw and Collegiate theatres now that the Festival had returned to its original February/March slot. Chamber music at the Everyman had gone, as had the prizewinners' concerts, poetry and jazz. The Swiss Cottage Odeon was no longer available for orchestral concerts and the RPO had in any case lost its grant from the London Orchestral Concert Board for this purpose. The *Library Journal*, which had for so many years reported on the Festival and all the Library department's activities, was stopped.

The new administration's very different perceptions of the arts in general and the Festival in particular soon became apparent.

The rearrangement dividing the Festival into three sections had been specially devised to give greater scope for programmes of popular entertainment; the introduction of the summer neighbourhood festivals with their own budget was supposed to cater for this. Nevertheless it was now announced that "an innovation in this Festival will be a series of seven variety shows and entertainments held at Community Halls throughout the Borough and a large-scale Variety Show at the Town Hall, Euston Road".[5] These events were free, and tickets were distributed amongst tenants' associations and other similar local organisations. There was also an evening of Progressive Pop and a cabaret dance at Holborn Assembly Rooms.

The main programme was built around the specific theme of the human voice, with an exploration of three contrasting styles of vocal music – the Purcell era, late-19th-century French operetta, and contemporary post-serial, post-Beatles music. "All three are linked by a concern with declamation…and a satirical sense of humour."[6] Choral concerts were given by the Hampstead Choral Society and the Saltarello Choir. There was an evening entitled *Melodramas* with Joan Greenwood and Rhondda Gillespie. The exhibition at Swiss Cottage Library and lectures at the Collegiate Theatre and the Holborn Library all concentrated on subjects of operatic interest. The "humorous" side was provided by an evening of musical theatre of the 1920s called *Romance to Rhythm*; a concert of Victorian music and verse called *Voices and Verses* with Anne Howells, Ryland Davies and Cyril Luckham; the King's Singers, and Michael Aspinall, who returned with a tribute to Dame Clara Butt. The "post-serial" element was an Open Rehearsal of works by new young composers presented by the Society for the Promotion of New Music, and a concert of electronic music with works by Luigi Nono and Thea Musgrave, with Jane Manning, presented by the Park Lane Group.

London Contemporary Dance Theatre presented a 2-week season, and Shura Cherkassky gave a piano recital at the Assembly Rooms. Other music consisted of smaller-scale events such as had featured in the cost-cutting 1971 Festival, with a series of lunchtime concerts at Holy Trinity Church, Kingsway featuring lute and guitar, and organ recitals at St Dominic's Priory.

Under Jack Henderson's expert guidance the operas maintained and increased their interest. Desmond Shawe-Taylor commented in *The Observer* that "Although this year economically reduced from three to two productions, the Camden Festival has scored a pair of bull's-eyes".[7] Purcell's *The Indian Queen*, presented by Opera da Camera, was thought to be the first stage revival since the 18th century. *Opera* wrote: "On the whole it was a musically delightful evening" although the plot "is to modern taste mere posturing of patriotic and amorous expression and the dialogue is never far from banality (the audience could scarce suppress an ironic cheer at 'Thus die all rebels!')".[8] The cast of actors and singers included Maxine Audley and John Tomlinson.

Opera Rara were back with "Offenbach's *Robinson Crusoe* [44], brilliantly produced by William Chappell in an amusing translation by Don White, with a great personal triumph for Sandra Browne as Man Friday, with her full, richly tinted voice, her zest and enchanting stage personality."[7]

The opera performances were completely sold out, but the increasing trend towards sparse attendance at concerts of modern music was noted by *Opera*'s Arthur Jacobs:

"The Camden Festival's three performances of Purcell's *The Indian Queen* were all sold out – a remarkable and heartening testimony to the London public's appetite for rare opera, even outside the readily accepted Italian conventions. When this is set beside the poor bookings for some of the Camden Festival concerts, one may wonder if this enterprising municipality will not decide to turn its annual event simply into an opera festival".[8]

More surprisingly, even with free tickets, attendance at the variety shows was also disappointing. The Director of Libraries and Arts was "requested to analyse the attendance figures and to report on publicity and distribution of tickets for each event to reveal why there was such vacillation in attendance figures for the variety shows… to assist in planning the next series."[9]

The *Ham & High* critic felt that "…despite a number of very successful events and some good experiments, the right formula still eludes the planners. The festival did not by any stretch of the imagination have a corporate spirit, an identity. A balanced festival surely should present the unusual, rare music of the past and music of the present and future, performed by local artists of which Camden has many,…possibly using one of

44 Offenbach's *Robinson Crusoe* (photo Donald Cooper) "What can be said of Sandra Browne as Man Friday except that she is entirely charming?" (*Country Life*, March 1973) L to R Ian Caley, Sandra Browne, Sandra Dugdale

our excellent local orchestras such as the Camden Chamber Orchestra, whose absence from the whole Festival was strange." [10]

The second component of the new arrangements, the Neighbourhood Festivals, was very successful. A pilot scheme had been undertaken with the community in Somers Town in 1972, and in 1973 several summer Festivals took place involving local communities in their own streets, and although they were not without problems they were generally a great success story.

Film was chosen for the first Autumn Theme Festival. It started with the high hope that it would "involve and reach everyone who has any interest in films and lives or works in the Borough – a large majority". [11] It was run by the writer and critic John Baxter and devoted to British films, the aim being "to show an industry which despite economic adversity continues to reflect Britain on the screen with skill, insight and enthusiasm." It focused on three areas of interest: British Cinema Now, Fantasy/Reality and Radical and Alternative.

It immediately ran into trouble when at the last minute one of the films to be shown (*England, Whose England?*) was discovered to be a piece of racist propaganda. A special screening was held for councillors and representatives from Camden Committee for Community Relations, and the National Council for Civil Liberties was also invited. There was unanimous agreement across the political divide that the film was incompatible with efforts to foster good community relations. It was withdrawn from the Festival and the Attorney-General was informed of the content and the possibility that an offence had been committed under the 1965 Race Relations Act. But the problems did not end there. The whole festival was a complete flop. It was plagued by technical problems and public apathy; screenings were rarely more than half full and often virtually empty – even an appearance by Eric Sykes drew only 60 people. It lost £7000 and was bitterly criticised by councillors at the next meeting of the Arts Sub-Committee: Councillor John Lipetz called it a fiasco.[12] John Baxter had been brought in specially, and the idea of having an 'outside' artistic director was now called into question. A report was commissioned "on arrangements to be made

45 Helen Lawrence and Francis Egerton in Storace's *The Comedy of Errors*, 1974 (photo Jerry Young). Courtesy of the author

in the event of an outside director being appointed in future with particular reference to establishing the respective responsibilities of the outside director and the Council".[13]

Yet another report, entitled *The Development of Community Arts*, was submitted by a Leisure Services Programme Planning Group at the end of the year.[14] It attempted to analyse what is meant by 'community arts' and concluded that it would "imply the presentation of artistic products which speak in a more vernacular language at low cost or free of charge and in an environment which militates against social inhibitions". It questioned "not the principle of promoting the arts, but frequently the methods".

> "It is a costly operation for a poor man to go to the theatre; and once there he is likely not to understand the 'artistic' statement because it is not couched in a 'language' into which he has been educated. In addition he is likely to be surrounded by an audience consisting of people from a background alien to his own."

As far as the Festival was concerned it raised the question "as to whether the content is in fact still valid in the current form of presentation". But it did suggest that perhaps it could be presented purely as an opera season "perhaps achieving greater impact in an area where Camden has already attained some pre-eminence and won an established market", echoing the view which had been put forward[8] in *Opera*.

1974

In 1974 momentum began to recover. Despite a standstill budget of £30,000 and continuing political upheaval and governmental anti-inflation regulations making large cuts in the Leisure Services Department, the Festival regained its form, and another period of steady achievement began.

Opera productions increased to three; two of them, *The Comedy of Errors* by Stephen Storace [45] and *Torquato Tasso* by Donizetti [46], received fully staged productions at the Collegiate Theatre. The Donizetti provided one of those legendary moments of back-stage drama when the leading lady cancels at the last moment. Margareta Elkins was taken ill on the afternoon of the opening night and the likelihood of finding a singer who knew the part was remote – the whole point of the Camden Festival being that no-one knew these operas. However, someone reminded Patric Schmid that Janet Price was a superb sight-reader and might be persuaded to stand in. She consented and travelled up from Bristol with 4 hours to spare, but what to do on stage? A second heroine saved the day. Joyce Castle, wife of the leading tenor Bruce Brewer, and herself a singer, had attended many of the rehearsals and felt she could remember enough of the moves to walk the part on stage while Janet Price sight-sang it from the wings. As one of the critics declared, her performance at 4 hours' notice was "a feat past belief". One of the performances did eventually have to be cancelled due to illness.

An attempt to control the number of complimentary tickets, which at an average of 80 for each opera was getting out of hand, somewhat misfired. Critics are traditionally offered a pair of free tickets, so the Festival organisers tried asking them to pay for the second ticket. William Mann of *The Times*, not so enamoured of the performance of *Torquato Tasso* and unmoved by Janet Price's heroism, used his review to make a dig:

"Having paid for a seat, as critics seldom are asked to do, I felt like a lonely, amorous man who saves two pounds for a sensational night out, only to be faced with an inanimate rubber doll in bed while the voice of the favourite sex-symbol murmurs endearments from a gramophone record."

Chelsea Opera Group contributed to the Festival for the first time, starting a collaboration which lasted until 1985. Because they concentrated on concert performances, they were able to bring large-scale operas to the Festival at minimal cost. With the smaller theatre and raised performance standards, staged performances of large works were no longer financially feasible. As money got tighter over the coming years this group's contributions enabled the Festival to have an extra opera within the budget. Their first presentation was Hindemith's *Mathis der Maler* at the Assembly Rooms.

The rest of the programme was similar to that of the previous year under the headings Lectures, Recitals, Dance, and Concerts, and there was an interesting programme of Opera Films, much as there used to be in the old St Pancras days. There was another series of 'Club Nights' which were advertised on separate sheets, including an appearance by Anne Shelton at the Assembly Rooms.

Concerts included a programme of music and words to commemorate the 150th anniversary of the death of Lord Byron, and orchestral music was back with the return of the Camden Chamber Orchestra, now called the Orchestra of St John's Smith Square, with their conductor John Lubbock. A concert by the Amadeus string quartet had to be moved out of the Assembly Hall to the smaller Collegiate Theatre because a general election was called; Camden Library members were given the opportunity to buy tickets for it at half price. Among the talks was a personal appearance by the legendary British opera singer Joan Cross in conversation with Lord Harewood, also at the Collegiate. Plans to put on a Viennese evening with Elisabeth Schwarzkopf and the Philomusica Orchestra did not materialise.

The Committee report[15] records "the most satisfactory financial result in the Festival's history", with 3000 more paid admissions, even though there were many free tickets and reductions for old age pensioners, children and students. 50,000 Festival brochures were printed at a cost of £1,231.

All the operas were fully booked, as were the choral concerts, the Amadeus and the London Contemporary Dance Theatre at the Shaw, which had to lay on an extra matinée in response to demand. Production costs of the operas had now increased to about £7,000 each with box-office receipts of about £1,800.

46 Christian du Plessis and Margareta Elkins in *Torquato Tasso* (Donizetti), 1974

Top ticket prices were still only £2.

There was one jazz concert, but the main jazz event of the year was in the Autumn Festival, when jazz was chosen for the 'theme'. There had been quite a lengthy correspondence in the *Ham & High* the previous year complaining of the Festival's neglect of jazz – although again this was not strictly true, as jazz had been included regularly since the beginning. However, at John Dankworth's suggestion representatives from the Jazz Centre Society met the Festival team to discuss plans. Their brief was that "any events organised should involve or primarily be arranged for Camden residents" [15] and as a result the Camden Jazz Festival began. A brilliantly successful programme emerged, with a spectacular feast of all the best in jazz, staged mainly at the Round House and featuring leading jazz musicians such as Mike Westbrook, Stan Tracey and many others. There were also films, Poetry and Jazz, and a series of free events. Nearly 6000 people attended the various events and the net cost to the Council was £8,869. Jazz Week was henceforward a fixture in the calendar, becoming part of the main Festival from 1976 onwards.

As to neighbourhood festivals, 23 were held in the summer, giving local communities the opportunity to get involved; they were considered very successful with a high standard of entertainment. A sum of £10,000 was allocated in 1975 for the neighbourhood festivals, part of which came from departments such as social services because of the community element and part from engineering, as road closures were involved. By 1986, the Council was spending over £40,000 on neighbourhood festivals, funded from the Community Arts vote.

1975

The programme guide of the 21st Camden Music Festival in 1975 trumpets the achievements of the Festival in no uncertain terms – perhaps in response to the rising undercurrent of critical murmurs in other quarters of the Council. The policy of presenting adventurous repertory and the encouragement of young artists is restated, as is the list of achievements: the rediscovered operas and the famous 'discoveries' amongst the singers who sang them. Despite problems at the Collegiate with noise penetrating from

47 Meyerbeer's *L'Etoile du Nord* (1975) L to R: Deborah Cook, Alexander Oliver, Bonaventura Bottone and Janet Price (photo Donald Cooper)

other parts of the building, which almost ruined one performance, they were rewarded with endorsement by the music press.

"Once again the Camden Festival has proved that great artistic profit can result from modest financial outlay; *Il Re Pastore* [Mozart] and *L'Etoile du Nord* [Meyerbeer] [47], each presented in its original language, provided remarkably enjoyable evenings." (*Opera News*)[16] Philip Hope-Wallace in *The Guardian* strongly recommended the Meyerbeer as "a good collector's piece and exactly what a Camden opera occasion should be" and the Mozart opera "worthily celebrated the 200th anniversary of the work".[17] Chelsea Opera Group's concert performance at the Assembly Rooms of Bizet's *The Pearl Fishers* for the centenary of the composer's birth was not so well received.

Ways of economising on the operas were sought. For years the department had tried to interest other local authorities to take productions after they had been mounted at the Festival, but hardly any other boroughs had the courage to run such events. Different ideas were tried out in the next few seasons: running operas in repertory or reviving previous years' shows. In 1975 *Torquato Tasso* was revived, but for the critics its novelty had already palled:

> "Saturday's opening night was fraught with disaster – even the bed fell off its beer crates, as the crazed, imprisoned poet flung himself on to it – the piece is at the very best middling Donizetti".[17]

Eventually, such ideas were abandoned because the point of the Festival was to see something new.

There was the usual selection of concerts, dance, lectures, films, and recitals, and a concert by the Parlour Quartet with a programme of Victorian drawing room music. It had been planned to present a series of contemporary British orchestral music with performances by the New Philharmonia, the London Symphony nd the Royal Philharmonic Orchestras. Negotiations were held with the Arts Council and the London Orchestral Concerts Board, but evidently financial constraints did not allow it.

Neither was there any jazz. Following the huge success of the 1974 Jazz Week, The Jazz Centre Society had asked Camden to consider repeating it in 1975 but were told money was not available. It was decided instead to present a monthly series of jazz evenings at the Shaw Theatre and arrange for a jazz section in the 1976 Festival. In the event the performances at the Shaw were cancelled.

Not only was the budget being tightly held down but it was now having to be split between the Autumn Theme Festival and the Neighbourhood Festivals, leaving only £31,000 for the main Festival. Ticket prices were still relatively low, with the top price at £2.50 (in 1971 it was £1.50). The operas were all sold out and the audience increased by 3,500 over all.

William Maidment retired as head of the Library Service in 1975 and was succeeded by Frank Cole. Both he and Christine Wares, who succeeded him in 1982, were keenly interested in the arts and very supportive of the Festival. Thus it was able not just to survive the various upheavals of this period but to maintain its momentum, explore new directions and improve.

1976

The 1976 Festival had an American theme to mark the bicentenary of the Declaration of Independence, and two American operas were presented. The US Embassy in London contributed £100.

Jack Henderson had secured the British première of Menotti's opera *Maria Golovin* with the composer himself as producer. But while there was praise for performance and the production, *Opera* asked "what can have possessed the programme planners to stage this really terrible opera?" However, two sold-out concert performances of George Gershwin's *Porgy and Bess* at the Assembly Rooms restored the balance, with two more "I heard him there first" performances for the festival:

> "The vigour and total lack of inhibition that characterized both the orchestral playing and choral singing must be put down to Simon Rattle's inspired conducting…Willard White was an outstanding Porgy".[18]

There was also the first production for over a century of Thomas Linley's opera *The Duenna* based on Sheridan's play.

Continuing the American theme, there was a performance of Coleridge-Taylor's *Hiawatha*, a concert of American symphonic music by the Young Musicians' Symphony Orchestra, and six concerts of American and British contemporary music presented by the Park Lane Group with a distinguished roster of musicians. Jazz was back in the Festival with six concerts at the Shaw Theatre featuring American jazz, all sold out, and there was a Sunday evening programme of music from American musicals not yet heard in Britain. Finally there was a Jazz Band Ball with Humphrey Lyttelton and his Band and The Crouch End All Stars.

Negotiations with the Arts Council for a series of contemporary British orchestral music had continued and now came to fruition with full sponsorship of two concerts, one by the New Philharmonia and one by the Royal Philharmonic Orchestra at the Round House. Henderson had again persuaded Elisabeth Schwarzkopf to perform for the Festival, and she was to have given two recitals of Hugo Wolf Lieder there. In the end she cancelled, but Henderson was able to get equally starry replacements in Victoria de Los Angeles and Rita Streich.

There was a large choral contribution, with six concerts at various churches throughout the borough which attracted large audiences, as did London Contemporary Dance Theatre Week at The Place. Yet again it was noted that none of the contemporary music concerts was well attended.

Over the next few years the programme

settled into a well-structured pattern, grouping events under headings. Artistically it went from strength to strength, and under Jack Henderson's guidance this period was another golden era. New ideas were easy to slot in and there was a wide variety of imaginatively programmed music from every era. There was a return to the large glossy programme books, edited by Festival Director James Miles, which themselves provide a comprehensive record of the artistic achievement of this period. Opera remained the focus of the Festival, but three other elements now began to grow in importance: Jazz Week, International Music and Dance, and Music in Historic Buildings.

Festival Operas between 1977 and 1983

A new generation of opera companies had by now grown up, five of which provided the main fare in the following years: Chelsea Opera, Opera Rara, Park Lane Group, Phoenix Opera, and Abbey Opera. Other companies such as Kent Opera and the New Opera Company made single appearances. Despite the ever-present anxiety about finance the next few years saw an extraordinary variety of interesting works from every period, performed to the highest standard and, on occasion, making imaginative use of unusual locations in the borough. Representatives from the Royal Opera House and English National Opera regularly attended performances and took up works they liked.

For the Jubilee Year in 1977 Opera Rara came up with the first of Donizetti's so-called Tudor operas, *Il Castello di Kenilworth* [48]; and continued mining the seam of forgotten *bel canto* operas for the Festival with varying success until 1983. Max Loppert in the *Financial Times* found Donizetti "at his dullest and theatrically least remarkable" in *Il Castello di Kenilworth*, but the composer's double bill of *La Romanziera* and *Francesca di Foix* in 1982 [49] were found by Rodney Milnes in *Opera* to be "delightful comedies, with fine music". One of their more eccentric productions was Cimarosa's *Gli Orazi ed I Curiazi* [50] which involved laying down two tons of sand on the stage, which promptly started sifting through the cracks in the stage floorboards into the orchestra pit, causing havoc for the instrumentalists below. It also took up too much rehearsal time and thus

48 Yvonne Kenny and Bridget Bartlam (kneeling) in Donizetti's *Il Castello di Kenilworth* (1977)

49 Costume design for the King in *Francesca di Foix* 1982

detracted from the success of the show, as was noticed by the critics. The singers' "efforts were insistently undermined by a wayward and haphazard production" (*Daily*

50 Nan Christie and Diana Montague (kneeling) in Cimarosa's *Gli Orazi ed I Curiazi*, 1977 (photo Donald Cooper)

Renaud by Sacchini was the choice and in 1982 *Adriano in Siria* by Johann Christian Bach, who lived most of his life in London and was buried in the graveyard of St Pancras Old Church. This performance, the first in modern times, marked the bicentenary of his death. It was conducted by Charles Mackerras with a distinguished cast including Ann Murray, Eiddwen Harrhy and Ryland Davies.

The Park Lane Group had a huge success with its 1978 production of Offenbach's *La Grande Duchesse de Gerolstein*, described by Rodney Milnes in *What's On in London* as a

> "masterpiece from Offenbach's best period, a combination of delirious, toe-tapping musical invention and social satire…When Patricia Routledge was announced for the title role, legitimate mezzo sopranos were casting themselves from top-floor windows all over London. While sympathising with their disappointment, I welcome Miss Routledge with open arms. She can sing more than well enough, but her acting is something else…devastatingly demure and unutterably lady-like in everything she does, gets her laughs with a twitch of a lip muscle, or the flickering of an eyelash. This was a great comedy performance…I haven't laughed so much for years." [20]

In 1979 PLG gave Delius's *Fennimore and Gerda* its second production at the Festival (the first was in 1970). But it failed again, not because it was not well sung (with Rosalind Plowright as Fennimore)

> "nor because its orchestral beauties were not fully realised by the Park Lane Music Players, they were; but because, as Sir Thomas Beecham rightly believed, it is an unviable piece for the theatre….For once I wished that the diction of the principals had not been so good".[21]

The Delius Trust gave a guarantee of £4,500 towards the cost. It was paired this time with Stravinsky's *Mavra* [51]. Park Lane Group continued producing operas for the Festival until 1986.

Phoenix Opera provided productions for the Festival between 1978 and 1983. *La Spinalba* by Almeida in 1978, with Della Jones, received rave reviews from everyone while the British première of Paisiello's *Don Quixote*, adapted by Hans Werner Henze, was the first presentation of opera "in the round" on the new stage at the Round House in 1979. Thelma Holt became

Telegraph) which was "ridiculously inept" (*Sunday Times*). Apparently, the sand eventually ended up under a re-laid patio in someone's garden!

In 1979 the Festival celebrated its 25th anniversary with an increased budget and the beginning of a collaboration with BBC Radio 3 which resulted in the broadcast of operas from three Festivals. The first was Mozart's early *Mitridate, Rè di Ponto*: the Camden performance was its British première, with Philip Langridge, Felicity Lott, Ann Murray and Felicity Palmer in the cast.[19] In 1981 director of the building in the mid-1970s and persuaded a grant out of the Arts Council to improve the performance space, exploiting its shape for theatre in the round. Although this entailed a reduction in seating capacity from 950 to 600 it meant that everyone could see the performance properly. Henze was

51 Stravinsky's *Mavra* (1979)

52 Costume design by Terence Emery for Wolf-Ferrari's *School for Fathers*

particularly keen for the opera to be staged there and was generous with his help in solving the artistic problems. The staging by director Tom Hawkes included "a *coup de théâtre* with the flying horse Hippogryff".[21] In 1981 *Crispino e la Comare* by the Ricci brothers was so successful that Peter Stadlen in the *Daily Telegraph* was moved to declare "The first operatic offering of this year's Camden Festival positively made me look forward to paying my rates." In 1982 Phoenix produced *Eritrea* by Cavalli in a realisation specially made by Jane Glover from the sole manuscript score in the Biblioteca Marciana in Venice. The cast included Sally Burgess, James Bowman, Johanna Peters and Sandra Browne. Their last contribution to the Festival was Wolf-Ferrari's *School for Fathers* in 1983.

The New Opera Company appeared just once at the Festival in 1980. Rodney Milnes wrote in *Opera* of Nino Rota's *The Italian Straw Hat*

"Some eyebrows were raised at the New Opera Company's mounting so light a work…but after tilling the fields of high art all these years they have surely earned themselves a bit of fun – as indeed have their audiences. And it is no use complaining that Nino Rota's *farsa musicale* is insubstantial: it is meant to be. All great fun and just the job for the Camden Festival, though I doubt whether the piece has the substance to survive in the general repertory."[22]

A new 1000-seat concert hall, the Logan Hall, designed by Sir Denys Lasdun for the University of London's Institute of Education in Bedford Way, also became available in the mid-1970s. Unfortunately its acoustic was not much better than that at the old Assembly Hall and it drew just as much criticism:

"London's new concert hall, a jumped-up lecture theatre hewn deep from the bowels of Bloomsbury with an insistently humming air-conditioning system that can't make up its mind whether to blow ice-cold, lukewarm or no air at all at you; the humming is constant, and so is the dryness of the conditioned air, which made the singers a bit jumpy."[23]

"If London has a killer hall, guaranteed to ruin any performance of music there, it is Logan Hall. Monstrously ugly in an aseptic way, it has the acoustics of a match box with its forehead-low ceiling and sound-damped walls." [24]

Nevertheless from 1978, when the first Festival event there was a celebrity recital by Rita Hunter, it was used extensively by the Festival for operas, recitals, jazz and Music and Dance.

After Verdi's *Vêpres Siciliennes* with John Tomlinson at the Assembly Hall in 1977, Chelsea Opera gave most of their performances at the Logan. They championed Tchaikovsky's *Mazeppa*, with Mark Elder conducting, Dvorak's *The Jacobin* and an important performance of *Lady Macbeth of Mtsensk* by Shostakovich:

"The tumultuous applause from what must have been Camden festival's largest audience reflected not only the power and skill of the Chelsea Opera Group's performance, but also the warm welcome for their enterprise that followed the long years of waiting for any performance at all." [24]

Both *Mazeppa* and *Lady Macbeth* appeared at the English National Opera within a few years. Two rare Richard Strauss operas, neither part of the mainstream repertoire, were given a hearing: *Feuersnot* in 1978 and *Friendenstag* in 1985. British composers were not neglected: in 1982, to celebrate Walton's 80th birthday, Chelsea opera performed *Troilus and Cressida*, and in 1983 Britten's *Gloriana*.

Abbey Opera's first presentations at the Festival were also concert performances: the British première of *Antony and Cleopatra* by Samuel Barber in 1982, Cilea's *Adriana Lecouvreur* in 1984 (last performed at Camden in a staged production in 1971) and Boito's *Nerone* in 1985. In 1983 one of the most unusual presentations, both for Abbey Opera and for the Festival, was at the Nereid Gallery at the British Museum, combining both the Music in Historic Buildings and opera strands of the Festival. This was a concert performance of a double bill of 20th-century one-act operas, *Notturni ed Alba* by John McCabe, and Stravinsky's *Oedipus Rex*, which looked wonderful with the Nereid Monument as the backdrop [53]. The great Wagnerian tenor Alberto Remedios sang the title role of Oedipus, but he was also engaged at Covent Garden to sing the First Armed Man in Mozart's *Magic Flute* on the same night. As the Museum is only a short distance from the Garden he felt he could manage both: in an echo of events at the *Ernani* performances of 1963 he sang Oedipus and then raced in a taxi down to the

53 The Nereid Monument at the British Museum, used as backdrop for Stravinsky's *Oedipus Rex* in 1983

Royal Opera House, arriving in time to go on stage as Armed Man.

Hampstead artist Milein Cosman's drawing of Stravinsky conducting appeared in the programme of *Oedipus Rex* as it had in an an exhibition of her work in the 1982 Festival ([63], p 91).

Jazz, 1976 and after

After the success of the 1976 Jazz Week, jazz was firmly back in the Festival, presented in collaboration with The Jazz Centre Society. Founded in 1968, the Jazz Centre received Arts Council funding and became the largest single promoter of modern jazz in Britain. Over the years Camden's Jazz Weeks came to be as noted and popular a feature of the Festival as the opera, with performances by some of the most exciting musicians on both sides of the Atlantic. "The borough of Camden could justly claim to be the local authority most friendly to jazz in the London area, if not the whole of Britain" wrote Kevin Henriques in the *Financial Times*.[25] Among the many greats who appeared were Bobby Hackett, Wild Bill Davidson,

Art Blakey, Johnny Griffin, Dexter Gordon, the World Saxophone Quartet, and Gil Evans [54].

The Festival's 25th Anniversary year, 1979, presented a particularly rich programme, and a new jazz work, "Conversations with the Blues" was commissioned from Ian Carr, a Camden resident [55]. The Festival scored a triumph by presenting the first performance in Britain of the almost legendary Art Ensemble of Chicago [56], a major force in the jazz world. In addition Chet Baker, the creator of West Coast 'cool' school trumpet style,

54 Dexter Gordon, Gil Evans (R), Johnny Griffin. Three jazz musicians who appeared in Camden Festivals

appearing in Britain for the first time for many years, "played two hours of utterly mesmerising music." [25] Many new groups and artists such as Trevor Watts [55] with his Moiré Music and Courtney Pine were also given their opportunity, as was new work by Ian Carr, Mike Westbrook and Barbara Thompson. As the Festival programme of 1985 put it: "it has attempted to reflect as much as possible the richness of the British scene. Most of the leading 'local' musicians have appeared at some time – often giving a

55 Trevor Watts. and Ian Carr, stars who appeared at the 1979 Jazz Week

56 Art Ensemble of Chicago, a coup for the 1979 Festival

timely fright to the visitors." Perhaps the writer had in mind the opening of the 1977 Festival Jazz Week at the Shaw, as described in *New Musical Express*:

> "The Camden Music Festival got off to a vaudeville start amid flat irons and howls of contumely and derision. With a vociferous section of the audience there to see the Clark Terry Big Band, four to the bar and no messin', there was precious little toleration for the opening set from Keith Tippett's Ark [57]. "Rubbish!" "Gerroff!" "Play some Jazz!": thus spake the *arbiter elegantiarum*".[26]

The issue was over Free Jazz, a movement led by artists such as the American saxophonist Ornette Coleman and pioneered in Britain by Gavin Briars. Arising out of developments in the 1950s, it abandoned harmony in a move to look back beyond jazz, beyond the blues and other related music, to the folk-like work song.[27] The *Express* continued:

> "Maybe it was the absence of a stated beat, maybe it was the emphasis on trance and texture....The dust-up raises a lot of questions. Were the leavers threatened or merely bored? Is Free Music, unsupported by the record companies and communications networks, doomed to remain a minority cult? How far, if at all, should the musician regard himself as an entertainer? One thing is sure – music that was played with sincerity and an open spirit was received with a closing of ranks."[26]

As Ronald Atkins said in *The Guardian*: "The truth is that your average big-band enthusiast has always been a bit conservative".[28] However, Miles Kington in *The Times* the same day, while condemning the bad-mannered behaviour, thought Keith Tippett's offering "a pretentious load of twittering solemnity". The season was filmed for BBC2's Lively Arts programme.

From 1978, Jazz Week was staged at the Round House until it closed in 1984, when performances transferred to the Shaw and then to Logan Hall, which brought both benefits and problems. Logan Hall had 180 more seats than the Round House, but was not geared to cope with this kind of event. "The Festival administration spent a great deal of time smoothing relations between the Institute, the musicians and National Jazz Centre officials' conflicting ideas and intentions".[29] For Camden, the cost of jazz weeks was minimal as the arrangement was based on an undertaking to guarantee against loss, and in most years the bands played to capacity audiences. The programme books contained copious and informative programme notes about all the performers and their musical styles.

The Festival Ball, not held since the old St Pancras days, was revived in 1976 as

57 Keith Tippett, founder of Ark, which was given a rough ride at the 1977 Festival

the Jazz Band Ball. Humphrey Lyttelton, who first played at the Festival in 1957 in its St Pancras days, George Melly with John Chilton's Feetwarmers and The Crouch End All Stars joined by Wally Fawkes and Sheila Collier were great favourites over the years. It was held either at the Round House or the Camden Centre (the old St Pancras Assembly Hall). The last took place in 1985 with the Victor Sylvester Orchestra, when it was simply called the Festival Ball.

Other genres

Contrary to the complaints by some people about the lack of lighter, popular entertainment in the Festival, such programmes had been and continued to be featured regularly. Furthermore, the Festival team devised them with the same care and innovative approach as for the rest of the programme. In 1977 Robert Tear and Benjamin Luxon gave evenings of Victorian songs and ballads at the Shaw Theatre to a capacity audience. An evening of music hall was staged "In Celebration of Hampstead Town Hall" for its centenary in 1978, and there was Old Time Music Hall in 1980. There was cabaret at the Shaw and many novel programmes such as French operetta, entitled "from Adam to Madame". In 1984 there was a "popular classics tour" with the Chamber Music Players of London, who gave a series of concerts in the Hampstead, Primrose Hill and Abbey Community Centres and at Lauderdale House. The "lollipop" programme ranged from Lennon/McCartney, Bach and Vivaldi to Johann Strauss. The legendary cabaret singer and actress Elizabeth Welch was interviewed in 1985 at Holborn Library.

An innovation from 1979 was International Music and Dance, originally conceived as a showcase for the arts of Britain's ethnic minorities, but eventually promoting performers from all over the world

"Someone ought to strike a medal of honour for Camden Council! How many other London boroughs would bother to promote a week of International Folk Music and Dance in these government-inspired austere times?" [30]

The Programmes contained extensive

58 Los Awatinas from Bolivia, appearing in International Music and Dance, 1979 Festival

59 Samulnori from Korea (1979)

with fascinating programmes – "world music" before anyone had thought of that label. Such evenings had of course been pioneered by the Festival in its St Pancras days, with performances by the great Ram Gopal and the Asian Music Circle in 1960 and evenings of International Dance. Now it was re-launched and continued every year until 1987, either in the Shaw, the Camden Centre, or the Round House. The first one in 1979 was partly financed from the proceeds of the Camden Lottery. This truly was music which could rarely be heard elsewhere, and the range of visitors to the Festival was extraordinary. It was greeted with acclaim in the press, the following extract from *Music World* in 1983 being typical:

and instructive notes about all the performers and their music. Some were groups based in London, such as the Barnet Cypriot Dance Group, London Turkish Theatre Folk Dancing Group, Bible Way Tabernacle Youth Orchestra and Mayapi (refugees from Chile). Others travelled in especially. Los Awatinas from Bolivia [58] became great favourites, appearing on three occasions. They sang in native Quechua and Aymara languages as well as in Spanish, playing percussion and wind instruments dating back to Inca times and string instruments that were brought to Bolivia from Spain. Samulnori from Korea [59] was one of the last generation of Namsadang folk troupes in a tradition that had virtually died out; their repertoire included music from various provinces of Korea, each area having its own distinctive rhythmic and musical patterns. The Jing Ying Soloists came from Hong Kong, and amongst the many Indian musicians (e.g. [60]) who played was the distinguished sitar player Imrat Khan. "Sweet Honey in the Rock" was an American group described in the Programme as

> "an orchestra of voices performing Gospel, jazz blues, African roots songs. Despite some of their themes – lynchings, false imprisonment, coups and discrimination – Sweet Honey's music is anything but oppressive." [31]

English contributions included Bob Copper, a member of the famous family of traditional folk singers from Sussex with Sam Sherry, the noted Lancashire clog dancer, the Northumbrian piper and fiddle player Kathryn Tickell, and John Kirkpatrick, melodeon player.

The Greek contributions in 1982 and 1983 were unusual in that they featured contemporary composers rather than folk music. In 1982 Theodorakis's music was performed with Haroutune Bedelian, the New Chamber Choir and Soloists conducted by Christos Pittas, who was also a composer. In 1983 the composer Yannis Makropoulos conducted his own setting of a work by the Greek poet Solomos called *The Free Besieged* with the St Sophia Cathedral Choir and a group of Greek instrumentalists and singers. The subject was the Siege of Missolonghi in 1826 during the Greek War of Independence. Both these performances were subsidised by large grants from the Greek Ministry of Culture. On another occasion the great singer Maria Farandouri performed.

In 1983 and 1984 a variation on the presentation of these events was tried, with performers touring to different venues in the borough. There was a Folk Music Tour taking English and Irish folk music out to community venues: The Irish Centre, Highgate New Town Community Centre and West Hampstead Community Hall. In 1984 the English Folk Music and Morris Dancers [61] repeated the exercise, visiting Lauderdale House, The 48 Club, Boundary Road and the Swiss Cottage and West Hampstead Community Centres. The Jazz Band Ball also took off, in 1984 leaving the Camden Centre and going on tour round the borough playing at three different venues.

60 Tabla player (1979 Festival)

61 Morris dancers (1984 Festival)

Choral concerts & chamber music

Music in Historic Buildings was another innovative idea based on a programme first introduced in 1971 and developed from 1978. It gave many people the chance to see the interiors of buildings not always open to the general public at the same time as listening to some beautiful concerts. In addition to the Nereid Gallery at the British Museum already mentioned, Staples Hall and the Great Halls at Gray's and Lincoln's Inns, Old St Pancras Church, Keats House, Burgh House, Fenton House, Lauderdale House, the Midland Hotel (the glorious neo-gothic pile at St Pancras Station), and the Thomas Coram Foundation were all used. The music was often matched to the period of the venue, and produced some very interesting programmes ranging from seldom-heard Gothic French and English 12th- and 13th-century works, to the 20th century. A wide range of performers could be heard, from chamber choirs and ensembles to solo recitalists. There were evenings of music and poetry in full costume such as *Samuel Pepys Esquire* at Gray's Inn in 1979. Evelyn Barbirolli (oboe) played at Burgh House both in 1979 and 1981; Barbara Jefford and Gwen Watford devised a programme called *Four Nineteenth-Century Women Poets* for Keats House in 1982; The Songmakers' Almanac gave an evening of songs and readings about every aspect of London Life called *The Dream City* at the Great Hall of Lincoln's Inn.

In addition to the Poetry and Music events in historic buildings, other themed programmes were also devised. John Carroll presented two: *The Sun King*, with Gwen Watford, Marius Goring and John Westbrook, at Hampstead Theatre in 1979, and in 1980 *What's the Use of Poetry?* with Judi Dench and Michael Williams at the Shaw Theatre.

Choral concerts continued every year with a nucleus of local groups. The conductor Julian Williamson had founded the Camden Choir in 1972 to provide amateur choral singers with as varied a repertoire as possible, and in 1978 he founded the Camden Chamber Choir to perform *a capella*. These and the Highgate Choral Society at St Michael's, Highgate, were regulars, as was the Hampstead Choral Society at St John's, Church Row until it folded in 1981. In addition to the standard oratorio repertoire these choirs, in the spirit of the Festival, unearthed some interesting unknown works such as Krenek's *Deutsche Messe*, Vaughan Williams's *Epithalamion* written in 1957, a *Stabat Mater* by the 17th-century composer Bononcini, *Shields of Faith* by Bliss, the first performance of Alun Hoddinott's *Lady and the Unicorn*, John Gardner's *Cantata for Easter* and many more. Their main conductors [62] were Brian

62 Local conductors Brian Wright, Julian Williamson, Martindale Sidwell

Wright at Highgate, Julian Williamson at Camden and Martindale Sidwell at Hampstead. The Council did not bear the full cost of these concerts, but gave a small grant, and, like the Jazz week, undertook to guarantee against loss on box-office income. Since they were nearly always well attended this arrangement enabled the Festival to include these concerts at minimal cost, although programme content was closely scrutinised by Jack Henderson.

20th-century music

Performance of 20th-century music and encouragement of living composers had of course been one of the earliest objectives of the Festival and was an integral part of the programming. Most of the organisations devoted to promotion of new work were given opportunities by the Festival. Park Lane Group, Music In Our Time and the Society for the Promotion of New Music appeared regularly. Every format was tried to promote the success of these concerts, sometimes listing them under obvious titles: '20th-Century Music' or 'Contemporary Music'. Many composers, some of whom lived locally, were given opportunities for first performances and young musicians from the London music colleges were also encouraged.

The Divertimenti string orchestra appeared in the Festival every year from 1977 until 1985. It was founded in 1974 by Emmanuel Hurwitz, and the artistic director from 1978 was Nicholas Kraemer. Their programmes featured 20th-century repertoire alongside well-known works. Based at the Rosslyn Hill Chapel in Hampstead, they played in 1983 and 1984 at the Shaw and The Place and in 1985, sponsored by the Wellcome Foundation, they played a series of three Family Concerts at different venues round the borough. Their 1981 and 1982 concerts were financed by their own efforts and were at no cost to the Festival.

In 1984 five 'Contemporary and Orchestral' concerts were presented which included the Endymion Ensemble with a special tribute for Harrison Birtwhistle's 50th birthday and introduced the North Camden Schools Orchestra for the first time. The Orchestra grew out of the strong tradition of music-making at the William Ellis and Camden Girls' Schools. They were brought together in 1981 under the auspices of the ILEA Music Centre for an orchestral workshop which was so successful that it was decided to create a full orchestra from the best school players in the North Camden area. Michael Ashcroft and Colin Durrant, the Music Directors at the two schools, were the conductors, and the orchestra performed again in the 1985 Festival.

Their choice of soloist for their first concert at the Festival in 1984 was the cause of an unusual political imbroglio. Malcolm Binns was due to play the Rawsthorne First Piano Concerto but there was embarrassment at the Festival office when in March his name appeared on a United Nations list of people who had recently performed in South Africa, then at the height of the apartheid era, and subject to boycotts from many quarters including various artists' associations. Camden asked him to sign a declaration stating that he did not intend to perform there again. Although he assured the Council that he was opposed to apartheid he was not prepared to do this. It was considered that "in the light of these circumstances, and given that the children performing in the concert might be particularly affected by any demonstration, it is not appropriate that Mr Binns should appear in the Festival." [32] The controversy reached the Letters page of *The Times* with protests from Bryan Magee, president of the Critics' Circle, composer Alexander Goehr and Francis Routh the organiser of the concert, and was a rare occasion when anything connected with the Festival drew criticism of the Council. It was difficult to find a pianist to replace Binns because the Rawsthorne piece was seldom played, but fortunately Eric Parkin was able to

63
A drawing of Stravinsky by the Hampstead artist Milein Cosman shown in the 1982 Festival exhibition

take over the performance. Malcolm Binns had to be paid as well.

Exhibitions

Exhibitions remained a feature of the Festival nearly every year, but they were now focused exclusively on subjects connected with music, opera and musicians. In 1977, 1980 and 1983 stage sets and costume designs were the subjects. Four exhibitions were devoted to composers: Michael Tippett 1981, Benjamin Britten 1983, Delius on the fiftieth anniversary of his death in 1984, and drawings and sketches by Hampstead artist Milein Cosman of Stravinsky [63] at the Camden Arts Centre in 1982.

In 1984, also at the Camden Arts Centre, the Hampstead Artists' Council

64 Wally Fawkes, aka "Trogview", jazz clarinetist and cartoonist, self-portrait

organised an exhibition of the original gouache drawings by Wally Fawkes **[64]**, who was the cartoonist "Trogview" and a jazz musician (one of the Crouch End All Stars). In 1985 a retrospective of the Camden Festival itself was mounted at the St Pancras Library/Shaw Theatre foyer.

From time to time other, more unusual programmes were presented that did not fit any of these categories. In 1979 it was puppet shows by the Hungarian State Puppet Theatre and Drak Puppets from Czechoslovakia, with special performances for schools. In 1980, Apollo Children's Concerts – a trust established in 1977 to bring a new, lively and informal approach to concerts for children – presented two concerts at the Shaw Theatre with Richard McNichol, flautist with the London Philharmonic Orchestra, and the Alberni Quartet.

Notes to chapter 5

1 Ref. 5 (see p 13), p 26.
2 GLC Publication No.71680454, Feb 1973.
3 Leisure Services Committee LS 73/91.
4 Camden Arts Sub-Committee minutes 15.3.72 LAR/72/36 Agenda item 5.
5 *Ham & High* 12.1.73.
6 Libraries and Arts Sub-Committee 12.6.72 LS 72/8 Agenda item 6b.
7 *The Observer* 11.3.73.
8 *Opera* Apr 1973 (vol 24 no.4) p 371.
9 Leisure Services Committee minutes 25.4.73 LS/73/137 Agenda Item 16a.
10 *Ham & High* Mar 1973.
11 Ref.4, Agenda item 5a.
12 *Ham & High* 30.11.73.
13 Council Minutes 10.10.73 Vol 10 Report of Leisure Services Committee p 650.
14 *The Development of Community Arts* LS/73/243 12.12.73 Agenda item 4.
15 Leisure Services Committee minutes 3.4.74 LS/74/74 Agenda item 12.
16 *Opera* May 1975 (vol 26 no.5) p 485.
17 *The Guardian* 24.2.75.
18 *Opera* May 1976 (vol 27 no.5) p 488.
19 *Opera* May 1979 (vol 30 no.5) p 493.
20 *What's On in London* 31.3.78.
21 Ref. 19, p 497.
22 *Opera* May 1980 (vol 31 no.5) p 497.
23 Edward Greenfield in *The Guardian* 24.3.81.
24 *Opera* Jun 1984 (vol 35 no.6) p 696.
25 *Financial Times* 27.3.79.
26 *New Musical Express* 16.4.77.
27 New Grove's Dictionary. Entry "Jazz 14 The 1960s" in Vol 9 p.576
28 *The Guardian* 29.3.77.
29 Leisure Services Committee minutes 7.6.84. Report on the Camden Festival 1984.
30 *Music World* 7-19 April 1983.
31 Festival programme 1986, International Music and Dance section.
32 Council Minutes, Vol 21. Answer to Question No.4, 29.2.84.

6 Decline and fall (1983–1987)

[Notes for chapter 6 are on p 109]

The 1980s saw no diminution of the financial problems. The Local Government Act of 1980 brought in a new system of strict central government control and regulation over local authority capital expenditure, imposing ceilings on all outlay – the notorious 'rate capping'. A tight framework required detailed monitoring from 1981. Camden, famously to the left politically, and in its heyday a model of what enlightened social policy could achieve, was beginning to lose its way. The response of its then political leaders to the constraints was to become ever more entrenched in dogmatic attitudes which allowed no way out, while continuing to make financially disastrous expansionist plans.

The problems mount

Council meetings were dominated by the constant need to look for cuts in all services. Libraries were under continual threat of closure, with drastic cuts in opening hours, and the Shaw Theatre and Library [65] became a drain on the Council's resources. The theatre had opened with high hopes in 1972, but it was soon realised that its design was defective, with too little wing or backstage space, no green room or rehearsal space, dreadful acoustics and continual problems with the air-conditioning equipment. In 1981 its Arts Council funding of £52,000 was withdrawn and in 1982 the £25,000 GLC grant was lost. The resident company, the National Youth Theatre, also lost its £15,000 grant. Camden was contributing £180,000. Anxious that this valued local resource should not be lost to the Borough, the Council tried several options to keep the theatre alive, including leasing it to a commercial company and running it directly, before it was finally closed down and the whole building sold off in 1988.

65 St Pancras Library, and The Shaw Theatre, 100 Euston Road (triennial report of the Director of Libraries and Arts,1971)

Soaring inflation made accurate forecasting of Festival costs difficult; they constantly escalated above the original estimates while the imposition of VAT on theatre tickets in 1979 reduced income. The cost of staging an opera rose from £7,000 in 1974 to £25,000 in 1980 and nearer to £40,000 by 1985. Between 1978 and 1979 the gross Festival budget nearly doubled, from £54,000 to £100,000, although the net costs were still only £22,778 and £33,900 respectively. Of this the Arts Council contributed £12,000 and the GLC £6,000. Other sponsorship was negligible at a little over £5,000.

There was also a Camden Lottery which ran for a few years from 1978, the proceeds being earmarked for social, recreational and environmental objectives. It raised at least £200,000 in the first 15 months and some small sums were used to fund projects in the Festival. In 1979 Camden joined the London Lottery Club, comprising twenty London boroughs and run by Littlewood's. But by May 1980 legislative restrictions had destroyed its viability as a commercial proposition.

When budgets first began to overrun in the late 1970s it was still possible to squeeze money from other areas of the Council's budget to make up the shortfall, seldom more than £2,000 or £3,000. But by 1980 this had risen to £13,000.

There was no great extravagance or excessive artists' fees, and the operas still played to packed houses every year. But ticket prices were kept relatively low – £6.50 was the top price in 1980 – and with no suitable larger theatre in the borough the seat capacity could not be expanded. All the companies that presented operas in the Festival were in fact working at the financial margin. They often tried to find operas which did not need a chorus; if they had to use one they used music students or young professionals at the lowest possible cost. Chelsea Opera Group was and is based on an amateur chorus. However, opera is labour-intensive. Twenty players might be required even in a pared down orchestra, and they have to be paid Musicians' Union rates, which had increased by 16% in 1980. Equity was also negotiating higher fees for its members. Many of the artists were still prepared to work for a fraction of their normal fees or even for expenses only, just as they had in the early St Pancras days of the Festival, but there were sets to be built, costumes and lighting to be arranged, and all the personnel undertaking these tasks had to be paid. One way of cutting costs on these elements was to give students an opportunity to try their hands at, for instance, designing and making costumes.

The Festival team, conscious of the urgent need to raise more money or make cuts if the Festival was to continue, examined every available possibility. The *Ham & High* spelt it out in a 1980 editorial:

"While Bernard Levin may castigate Camden with just cause for its profligacy whenever the occasion arises, as a committed man of music he never hands out a bouquet for the borough's consistent support for the arts.…We are pleased to set the balance right. For the Festival was again a resounding success, an event of which Camden can be proud, some 20,000 people attending it. But in these days of restraint there is little doubt that councillors will be looking for further festival savings next year.…Since the operas are responsible for £50,000 of the festival's £68,000 production costs they obviously make a tempting target. But cut them out and you undoubtedly cut the heart out of the festival. It may be hard for politicians, particularly Labour politicians, to see any benefits in these prestigious events but they have earned Camden a reputation for artistic enlightenment.…The one major area where Camden must do more – and do it far more effectively – is in seeking sponsorship for the festival. If Camden truly believes in the future of its splendid festival then it has to become more entrepreneurial and less dogmatic in both its political and cultural thinking." [1]

Elements of the festival such as the celebrity concerts began to disappear. In 1977 Elisabeth Schwarzkopf [66] made the Festival the occasion of her last recital appearances with two concerts at the Assembly Rooms. She announced and explained the programmes herself, which according to the Festival brochure were to be "songs which Sir Thomas Beecham would have called 'lollipops'". In 1978 Rita Hunter gave her first London recital at the Festival at the newly built Logan Hall. In 1979 there were two celebrity recitals, both at the Logan Hall, featuring old friends of the Festival: Janet Baker with Geoffrey Parsons, and Cleo Laine with John Dankworth. Nicholas Kenyon described the latter in the *Financial Times* as a "riotously successful evening…the Camden Festival presented Cleo Laine's first solo recital in 1966 and here she was 13 years later – successful without having stopped being nice; brilliantly accomplished without having lost a mite of popularity". The last two were in 1980, both at the Shaw Theatre: Elaine Strich and Alan Jay Lerner presented the great lyricists of the musical in a programme entitled *The Lyricist as Poet*, introduced by Benny Green, and Marian Montgomery gave a programme called *From Bach to Blues and Back Again*. Neither attracted good audiences.

Lunchtime recitals, which had been a feature of the Festival from its earliest years, were also dropped after 1980, not without much heart-searching. Such concerts are often problematic, but in more affluent times the Festival organisers felt they could carry the cost. Churches – St Pancras, St George the Martyr and Holy Trinity were the main venues – were not ideal for such events, with their poor sightlines and lack of heating. In 1980 the recitals were moved to the Shaw Theatre, where there were much better facilities including a snack bar, but despite the wide publicity, well-known artists playing for a reduced fee, and cheap admission rates audiences still failed to materialise – seldom more than 50 people except for the concerts by John Williams, Julian Bream and Imogen Cooper. One of the last concerts in 1980 was Tommy Reilly playing the harmonica at the Shaw.

The Music Panel suggested that cost might be reduced by asking students from the London music colleges to give the concerts, but the officers pointed out that artists' fees were only a small proportion of the costs: there were also printing, advertising, hall hire, and officers' time. It required two officers 3–4 hours to set up and clear the event and this amount of time and work could no longer be justified. And if established artists could not attract an audience, students certainly would not. It was more sensible to concentrate on events that attracted a good audience and gave the Festival a distinctive flavour. The only lunchtime event to continue was Christopher Bowers-Broadbent's organ recitals at St Pancras Church.

The Everyman series of morning recitals was also failing to attract audiences despite a distinguished array of artists including the Coull String Quartet with the clarinettist Jack Brymer. Whereas in 1977 John Williams's guitar recital had sold out on postal bookings and the Medici String Quartet had played to 80% capacity, by 1980

audience take-up was too small to justify continuing.

Dance, which had been a regular feature of the Festival, was missing in 1981, 1982 and 1984. Talks and films too, dwindled from the programmes. In 1983 there were three talks complementing the

66 Elisabeth Schwarzkopf, from a photograph in the 1972 Festival brochure

exhibition about Britten: a biographical study by Dr Wilfred Mellors, a discussion of the opera *Gloriana* with Joan Cross and Norman del Mar, and a talk on the composer's music for film. The next year was the last: Wilfred Mellors returned to discuss the blurring of the sexes in contemporary pop, Joseph Horovitz talked about writing music for television, and Henry Pleasants spoke on recordings of great singers of the past, all at Holborn Library. In 1978 there was a selection of films of dance and opera and in 1979 a season of operettas on film, all at Holborn Library, but after that film disappears.

However, simply cutting things could not provide a long-term solution. The drastic reduction of the programme and increase of ticket prices for the 1981 Festival did not go unnoticed. Philip Sommerich asked in the *Ham & High*

"Is it still a Festival? Gone are the lunchtime concerts, the ventures into cabaret or new music, the celebrity recitals and the cosy Sunday morning quartet performances at Hampstead's Everyman cinema. Can this still be the same event, which, begun by St Pancras

Council in 1954, catapulted artists...
and forgotten operas to fame?" [2]

The fraught world of commercial sponsorship needed to be tackled, as the *Ham & High* had suggested:

"Camden had long taken a view that it should be the sole financing body (together with other state subsidy organisations) of its artistic programme, but the hardening economic climate and notice of the strides being made by other arts organisations into the commercially rewarding area of sponsorship caused the borough to reverse this view." [3]

James Miles, who had been appointed as a new Senior Arts Officer in 1978, had experience in obtaining sponsorship at Greenwich. He knew that such strategies were not an easy or assured route and required much time and forward planning. Neither were they straightforward: there had already been controversy in 1979 over advertisements in the programme from cigarette manufacturers. Soaring inflation rates made any forecasting difficult because if costed plans were drawn up sufficiently early for fund-raising strategies to work, prices had risen by the time any money was received. However, Miles set to work and was soon having some success. Firms such as Butterworths, Standard Telephones & Cables, Marks & Spencer and many individual law firms were willing to give small amounts to sponsor the Music in Historic Buildings concerts. Opera sponsors were also increasingly found: Marks & Spencer again and also Greycoat London Estates, Town and City Properties, Legal and General Assurance and the Sterling Trust all helped at various times.

By 1983 the amount had risen to £15,000, but the highest ever achieved was £28,000 in 1986, not enough to justify the huge effort required to find it or to make much impact on the costs, which were rising much faster. The fact was, as James Miles explained in the *Ham & High*:

"Sponsors want charismatic names and celebrity recitals to hang their names on – but we do not feel these are the sort of events we should be doing, as they happen in London anyway." [4]

Another strategy was to establish the Festival as a Charitable Trust, to make it easier to attract finance from foundations and business organisations. The arrangements were finalised by November 1981 and the Board of Trustees included Councillors from all the political parties:

Anne Robertson, Chair of the Leisure Services Committee, and her opposite number Michael Brahams, Derek Jarman, Chair of the Music Advisory Panel and his opposite number Tony Kemp. The Mayor, the Leader of the Council (Roy Shaw, a keen opera enthusiast), and the Leader of the Opposition (Tony Kerpel) were nominated Council representatives. The independent members included Charles Alexander, Director of the Jazz Centre Society, the music critic Felix Aprahamian, John Woolf of the Park Lane Group, Gerald Isaaman, Thelma Holt, Liz Forgan, Anne Wood of Phoenix Opera the indomitable Luigi Denza who was now over 90, and a representative from the Arts Council. Ivor Walker, who had resigned as a Councillor in 1981, became Chairman of the Board. The Festival remained part of the Council's direct promotions and the Leisure Committee still exercised control over the budget and programme content.

Cultural democracy: élitism versus populism

Financial turmoil was not the only problem to affect the Festival. There were wider controversies surrounding the role of the arts, and various theories developed around 'cultural democracy' as opposed to the 'democratisation of culture'. The music world itself had been going through a long period of crisis stemming from what Hans Keller called the Schönberg Trauma,[5] taking contemporary music down ever more obscure and incomprehensible byways into which later-20th-century audiences were unable or unwilling to go. A writer in *Time Out* in 1977 said "Camden has always paid too much attention to the stagnant centre of modern music"; for him, Varese and Stockhausen would have been preferable. However, for the concert-going public what the critics thought was no longer relevant. The failure of concerts of new music to attract audiences is a recurring theme through Festival reports and, as the destructive arguments about 'élitism' in the arts in general grew ever more strident, audiences for other performances of music were increasingly affected.

At the same time, a new and influential generation of 'community artists' such as Sue Braden in the 1970s held that it was patronising even to make opera or

Shakespeare available to the people because it had no relevance for them:

> "The so-called cultural heritage which made Europe great – the Bachs and Beethovens, the Shakespeares and Dantes, the Constables and Titians – is no longer communicating anything to the vast majority of Europe's population. It is not that these cultural forms are above people's heads but that it is a bourgeois culture and therefore only meaningful to that group." [6]

But as Terry Eagleton, former Thomas Wharton Professor of English Literature at Oxford University, has pointed out, in deciding for others what they may or may not appreciate, the populist trend setters were equally patronising and élitist:

> "Like élitists, such populists assume that cultural meanings are fixed. Like élitists too, they confuse 'bourgeois culture', in the sense of doctrines like possessive individualism, with values like the appreciation of Verdi."

and

> "It is not on the whole the content of such culture that radicals should complain of, but its function. What is objectionable is that it has been used as the spiritual badge of a privileged group." [7]

Such voices were making themselves heard at Camden from the late 1960s, and dominated the new Leisure Services Committee after 1972. Their constant undercurrent of criticism became ever more insistent, gradually eroding confidence in the whole basis of the Festival. They demanded "assistance for a wider spectrum of the arts – 'popular' arts such as film, as opposed to esoteric ones such as opera." [8]

Again, "Activities in culturally deprived areas such as Camden Town, Kentish Town and Kilburn should be stimulated" [yet Camden Town and Kentish Town had, after all, been part of the borough of St Pancras and a short distance from the Assembly Hall, the Working Men's College and other venues where the Festival and many other activities had always been available][9] and "Some members expressed doubts as to whether the range and scope of the Festival for 1975 was a fair representative of musical activity and public interest." [10]

By 1975, there was already talk of closing down the Festival. Although admitting that the Festival "has been proved to meet a real demand" the Committee, now chaired by John Lipetz, decided that

> "The programmes of the music festivals are too narrow in their scope....We have given particular consideration to the advantages of holding a Festival or, alternatively, of allocating the financial resources to a programme of events throughout the year....We have agreed that the Festival should continue in 1976. We feel, however, that its programme should be broadened and have accordingly asked the officers to put forward proposals for discussion." [11]

In 1978 yet another policy statement on the future of arts and entertainments in Camden was issued which provoked the following directive from the Committee:

> "Officers were instructed to bear in mind the recommendations of the Community Arts Working Party to broaden the range of activities, in particular in the area of 'popular entertainment' with greater emphasis on regular presentations of music hall;[12] the meeting wished to give emphasis to the need to develop music hall in the borough and to finding a permanent venue for it."

There was even a proposal for a one-week 'popular stars Festival' with artists of the calibre of Val Doonican and Morecambe & Wise. However, this was not supported "as it was felt that this form of entertainment was already provided by commercial enterprise." [13]

While councillors seemed intent on pushing "pop" music, officers apparently were not. In June 1979 the Director of Libraries tells the Committee that "It has been our policy to present a traditional pantomime [eschewing] blue jokes, endless references to TV shows and other features which have in recent years turned what passes for pantomime into a glorified variety show or pop concert." [14]

In 1982, whilst acknowledging that the festival was "the most successful yet in terms of high box-office returns (many events being sold out) excellent press coverage and artistic merit", the committee, under the chairmanship of Councillor Sandy Wynn, nevertheless advised "the Camden Festival Trust, which has been set up to advise the Council on the Festival programme...that the Committee wishes to see the nature of the Festival extended to give it a more community-based approach." [13]

Again in 1985 the Festival team were "asked to look into involving the elderly, disabled and the 16-30 year olds" in their programming.[15]

Yet nearly £40,000 was already being

allocated to Neighbourhood Festivals established specifically to provide "community-based" popular programmes.

In 1984 £16,000 was siphoned off from the Festival budget to fund the Christmas Pantomime, without any consultation with the Festival team or the Chairman of the Trust, Ivor Walker. He wrote to the Chief Executive asking for an explanation, and the reply reveals all too clearly the change of attitude towards the Festival:

> "I understand the Committee suggested that when considering the programme again the Trust avoids providing costly functions which attract small audiences and therefore require large subsidies. I take this to be a reference to the operas provided last year and those programmed for 1984, which incidentally represents some 70 % of the estimated expenditure but only 44% of the estimated income." [16]

But according to the figures in the Council records, this was simply not true. The total estimated budget for the 1983 Festival was £130,200, of which £65,000 (i.e. just under half) was allocated to opera. The total estimated box office income was £30,900, of which over half, £16,000, was from the operas; box office receipts for International Music and Dance were estimated at £10,000. The estimated expenditure on operas in 1984 was less, at £55,000. With regard to content, the 46 Festival performances were evenly balanced between operas and concerts on the one hand and Jazz, International Music and Dance and other "popular" evenings devoted to tap dancing and folk music on the other. Audience size was dictated by venue capacity, and all performances were well attended.

Furthermore, that £65,000 had paid for three opera productions, while in 1983 the single pantomime had cost £53,000, of which less than half – £25,000 – was recouped at the box office.

The truth is that while the total budget for Arts and Entertainment during the early 1980s increased by 123% to £606,000, the Festival budget during the same period was held down or reduced (between £59,000 and £65,000 net). That this was deliberate is spelt out in the Council minutes: "the allocation of funds.....reflects Council policy".[17] Struggling to produce the 1984 Festival on the slashed budget the team understandably overspent by £9000. There was no sympathy from the Director of Finance who, whilst acknowledging that £16,000 of their budget had been withdrawn, damned them with the comment that "control over this expenditure was clearly inadequate".[17]

This unrelenting criticism was accompanied by an increasing obsession with the make-up of the audience and a reversal of the urbane view developed by St Pancras councillors early on. While originally they had thought of the Festival as being primarily for the local area, when they saw the impact it was having they were very happy to embrace the results of their success. In 1960 the borough minutes record with pride a comment in *The New Statesman* that "these functions serve a wider audience than the ratepayers of St Pancras. But London's cultural life would be much richer if all the Metropolitan Boroughs were as generous".[18] In 1965 John Richardson had declared that the Festival was "for London as a whole – not just for our borough".[19] In 1968 Jack Cooper, announcing that year's Festival, said: "We expect people to come to Camden",[20] and the Council published a guidebook for tourists to encourage people to come to the borough to sample, amongst other things, its theatres.[21] The 1971 report recommending the provision of Neighbourhood Festivals had specifically noted that they would attract people to Camden.

An officers' report of 1975 on Leisure provision in the borough provided a balanced and careful consideration of the questions: who is to benefit, where are the gaps, and who is best suited to make provision? In discussion of the first point it posed the question "should the Council provide mainly for Camden residents or should it also cater for the needs of non-residents working in the borough?" and reminds Councillors that the Library Service was obliged by statute to be available to all who wished to make use of it and that the borough boundaries are "mainly an administrative convenience" and cannot be enforced in any way as to who uses services, whether arts or book provision.[22]

Nevertheless, a parochial view that had first emerged in 1971 now began to take hold, to the effect that if Festival events attracted audiences from outside the borough the Council should not be spending money on them. Schemes for priority booking for Camden residents were devised and in 1977 the first week of postal bookings was reserved for Camden residents, which brought in receipts of £2,700, approximately 10% of the box office.

The criticisms could not be justified as a response to any great outcry by local ratepayers against Council extravagance on the Festival. It is usual when there is an issue of great concern for people to write not only to their Councillor but to the local newspaper as well. There is no evidence that the people of Camden ever complained about the Festival, either through the Letters columns in the local press or anywhere else; there were seldom any letters about the Festival other than from a small number of people, already mentioned, with a vested interest.

Yet other topics connected with the arts drew large numbers of letters of objection – and, on occasion, praise. In 1970 the open-air art exhibition was thought to be sub-standard and provoked a correspondence in the *Ham & High* lasting several weeks. When local Parliamentary candidate Geoffrey Finsberg reopened Keats House in March 1971, many angry letters accused the authorities of allowing him to use it as a political platform. The proposals to build a concert hall as part of the planned civic centre at Swiss Cottage provoked many letters against the idea, as did Camden's grant to the Hampstead Theatre Club in 1966 – all on the grounds of waste of taxpayers' money. There were also many letters to the *North London Press* in 1968 in support of a project to open a theatre in St George's Church, Tufnell Park, some comparing Camden's attitude towards funding the arts favourably with that of Islington.

In reality, the Festival continued to bring enormous prestige to Camden, particularly when the Council was under fire from all quarters for its failing management. In 1968 Councillor Cooper acknowledged in his introduction to the Festival Guide that: "Wherever in this country the Borough of Camden is mentioned people tend to think first of the Festival".[23] By the late 1970s and '80s it was about the only thing left which countered the negative image of Camden to outsiders, as the many examples of comment in the press bear out. The following are typical:

> "Despite its poor public relations and organisation, the Camden Festival gives an annual service in presenting operas we would not otherwise see in enterprising productions." (*The Tatler*, 1974)
> "Say what you will of Camden Council, its Festival remains above reproach." (*Evening Standard*, 1981)
> "As a South Londoner I don't know what else the Camden Council gets up to, but their record on the arts is beyond reproach. To their annual spring festival is now added a Winter Season also under the expert guidance of Jack Henderson....Were every borough to follow Camden's example, London would indeed be the musical capital of the world" (*The Spectator*, January 1983).

Dick Witts, the last Festival Director, summed it up in 1987: "in what other area does our embattled borough win so much glory unclouded by acrimonious criticism?" Yet from the 1970s onwards, much time had to be spent behind the scenes simply justifying the Festival's existence. There was no cause for the criticisms; the audiences were not small. Despite the Committee's refusal to acknowledge it, the 'esoteric' operas played to capacity audiences of thousands year in, year out – the best any promoter of entertainments of whatever kind would hope for. It was the supposedly "popular" events, such as the film festival and many of the "popular" entertainments inserted into the programmes which often failed to attract audiences.

It is clear from the selectiveness of these concerns, directed as they were specifically at the operas and concerts, that there was more to them than simply care for ratepayers' money. When audiences for the Jazz Week or the International Music and Dance or other popular programmes failed, not only were no such reservations expressed about the programming, but officers were instructed to make sure the audiences came next time. Nor was any concern shown when large sums of money were spent in later years to bring in popular entertainers from overseas. In the restructuring of 1973, Neighbourhood Festivals had been established with their own budget specifically to provide for popular programming, supposedly leaving the Camden Festival to concentrate on the operas and concerts for which it was famous. Yet new targets were now being set which the Festival had never been intended to reach, based on unproven assumptions that flew in the face of all available facts. The real aim of these persistent critical calls appeared not to be, as claimed, to broaden the range of the Festival but to narrow it.

A strange new anti-arts coalition had developed amongst the political classes: those on the Right who had never seen any point in the arts and certainly were opposed to their public funding were now joined by an element on the Left who derided the arts as "bourgeois culture". It is notable that

I D Tomisson, whose view as expressed in a letter to the *Ham & High* in 1969 (Chap 4, p 62) was that "pop music will replace classical music", was a member of the Leisure Services Committee in the early 1980s.

Such arguments understandably caused a crisis of confidence among politicians, both national and local, who had a responsibility to fund the arts, and it cannot have been easy for the Camden councillors to steer a path between them. The achievement of the Festival and the prestige it had brought to the borough was evident; yet now they were being told that it was all wrong, out of date and 'élitist'. As one ex-Camden Arts Officer said "If you say the arts are élitist it saves you having to fund them." It is to the credit of the Council as a whole that the Festival was kept alive for so long through the ideological and financial turmoil.

By 1983 Jack Henderson was increasingly being sidelined. Although he had nominally been Head of Arts Activities his main interest had always been the Festival, other officers taking responsibility for the year-round programme. In 1982 he was downgraded to Music Advisor and in March 1985, after several months' absence due to illness, he retired from the Department. He then became a Trustee of the Festival. Save for a three-line passing reference in a report to Committee of September 1985 his achievements appeared to be unacknowledged by the Council.

1984: the beginning of the end

In 1984 The Arts Council wrote to all its clients asking what their reaction would be to a 25% cut in funding. Nothing demonstrates better the change of attitude towards the Festival than the response minuted in the Committee report:

> "If the cut was due to the ACGB withdrawing funding, then it is possible that Camden, seeing ACGB funding as a form of recognition of the Festival's national standing, could withdraw funding from certain areas of the Festival." [24]

The pride and self-confidence of the old St Pancras days had all but gone.

The last three Festivals had a very different feel to them. The "popular" content of the programmes had increased so much that by 1985 it far exceeded the operas or concerts.

1985

The 1985 Festival was launched with warnings both in press releases and in the programme about the effects of rate-capping: the headline of the press release was "**Cash, cuts and culture in the community**", and it went on

> "The Government's proposals for rate-capping Camden and the abolition of the GLC pose a very real threat to the 1986 and subsequent Camden Festivals. They are a serious attack on the continuity and quality of the Festival, but Camden is determined that the Festival will continue to flourish into the 1990s."

In the programme book the Chairman of Camden's Leisure Services Committee, Richard Sumray, explained: "The Festival costs Camden's rate-payers about 30p a head to put on. Not a lot, is it? Yet this is exactly the sort of thing that the Government's Rate Capping Proposals [67] are aimed at." The total budget for the Festival now stood at £162,900. With increased ticket revenue, Arts Council and GLC grants, sponsorship and other income the actual net cost to Camden was estimated at £61,000. To set that in context, the Leisure Services Department's over-all budget in 1985 was £1,314,000.

Only one fully staged opera was mounted in 1985, Mozart's *La Finta Semplice* – a resounding success both artistically and at the box office. The production cost £36,000. Three other operas were given in cost-cutting concert performances, with a return to the Nereid Gallery of the British Museum for Caccini's opera *L'Euridice*, presented by the New London Consort, where once again the monument provided a stunning backdrop. Although this and the previous event there in 1983 were huge successes artistically, they were logistical nightmares for the Festival staff, who had to get everything set up between the museum's closure for the day at 5:30 pm and the start of the concert, and remove everything again immediately the concert finished. The cost was £4,000, and £2,300 was recouped at the box office.

Contemporary music was represented by a weekend of workshop rehearsals and lectures at the Shaw Theatre called *Towards a Theatre of Sound* with the West Square Electronic Music Ensemble exploring composing techniques using electro-acoustic materials and computers. This was presented by the Society for the Promotion of New Music and the Electro-Acoustic Music Association. Audiences were barely 25% of capacity.

Notwithstanding the remarks to Ivor Walker that operas were "costly functions which attract small audiences" the operas played to capacity houses, as did most of the four concerts in historic buildings and the three choral concerts. The box-office take for the one staged opera production of £7,838 exceeded its estimate by £2000. It was the audiences for the pop events that yet again were disappointing – acts such as the two-woman band *Ova* blending "music and political awareness", Lord Eric's Agor MMBA playing "African high life music with an exciting blend of traditional dancing and drumming", Shirley and Tony Menary with songs from musicals to operetta, The Screaming Abdabs with Jeremy Hardy in cabaret. While the reggae of Far 1 Upsetter Militant Rockers attracted a good audience, others were as low as 13% of capacity. Allowing politically motivated dogma to decide artistic programming is a dangerous and futile game. Even the Jazz and the International Music and Dance programmes failed to attract the usual crowds. The National Jazz Centre, which took financial responsibility for the Jazz Festival, found itself with a deficit of £9,600.

1986

At the end of 1985 a new Festival Director was appointed, and the Festival was expanded to three weeks, "flying in the face" as *Classical Music* put it, "of dark rate-capped times",[25] although the real reason was to enable the Jazz Week to take place at the Council-owned Shaw Theatre, thereby saving money on the rental charge. Dick Witts, still in his 20s, with a fresh view, was full of ideas – some of them imaginative, thoughtful and fun – on the radical wing of the arts, and determined to stir things up. As a musician he spanned the worlds of classical, pop and jazz, having begun his career as a percussionist in the Hallé Orchestra. He had also worked as a presenter on the TV rock programme the Oxford Road Show. He aroused dislike and admiration in equal measure.

He wanted the Festival to "represent and reanimate" the Borough:

"This is how a Festival should be: a confluence of events, each extraordinary,

67 Calman cartoon in the 1986 Festival brochure

that offers more than the sum of its parts, that help build relations between us, and that offer a good time yet disclose a better one (should our minds be so receptive)."[26]

and again

"I think we should be looking at the relationship between current trends, the relationship between our concerns with historical attitudes, the way those change over the years."[27]

He tended to view things as either "progressive" or "reactionary". The 1986 Festival – some of which had already been put in place before he took over – was "the most varied and progressive so far."[28] Park Lane Opera's production of Mozart's *La Finta Giardiniera*

"was attractively staged in a conventional manner....In contrast to the recent development in authentic, 'Urtext', revitalised productions of Mozart, this was a reactionary production."[29]

He was aware that the Almeida Festival was collapsing, and saw an opportunity for Camden to move into that artistic territory. In his view the Festival's operatic content needed a thorough shake-up; the local theatres were not suitable for opera and in any case he considered that the producers had run out of operas to put on. "With the expansion of both the large and the small opera companies in Britain, Camden has simply lost its place" he told *Classical Music*.[30] He considered it necessary to go for music theatre – in particular the American product, in order to bring the best of the work in these fields in the last 50 years or so to the Festival.

> "This year's operas are all of this century and none of them are operas, strictly speaking. Camden has chosen operas where society explains itself through music. This is surely why the London Borough of Camden and its sponsors, in enlightened manner, support such opera, as a total creative act that offers a full image of how things are and might be for the better. There is one more reason for this choice. While some festivals plod around the operatic scrapyards so trainspotters can tick off yet more rare items from their Kobbé Guides, this Festival wishes to be useful and to serve the future of music in Britain." [31]

There was some truth in this. After 30 years the Festival's operatic offerings were probably scraping the barrel and were now costing huge sums of money to produce. As long ago as 1972 Denby Richards thought there had been enough of 19th-century revivals, and the choice of works needed to change:

> "What St Pancras and Camden have done for neglected operas of the past they could now do for neglected composers of our own time." [32]

Although the availability of the Collegiate Theatre and Jack Henderson's unerring instinct for attractive programming had reinvigorated the Festival throughout the 1970s, some of the works were judged not worth reviving. It is clear that a rethink was necessary, particularly in view of the financial situation. Witts identified six "areas of neglect" in the operatic repertoire which could be exploited: Public Opera, Venice 1637–1670; Revolutionary Opera, Paris 1790–1820; Magic Opera, Germany 1830–50; Decadent Opera; Social Opera in Germany, France and USA 1925–40; and Modern Classics, including Berio, Nono and Philip Glass.[33]

While all this looked very interesting on paper the promise was not fulfilled. Witts's attempt to "serve the future of music in Britain" with two contemporary pieces of music theatre, *Phantastes* by Paul Barker and *Other Voices* by Steven Medcalf and Chris Willis, misfired Critical opinion was unanimous:

> "It is some while since the contemporary music theatre has produced an evening quite so dismal as the one endured at The Place."(*Daily Telegraph*)

> "True to Camden form, they will probably never be seen or heard again."(*The Guardian*)

The *Financial Times*, whilst acknowledging that the Festival was "bravely mounting a double bill of new works" found that "the two together made a pretty grim evening." [34] The other Festival offerings - a Kurt Weill double bill presented by Abbey Opera, the Mozart opera and Rimsky-Korsakov's *The Snow Maiden* given by Chelsea Opera were highly praised by all the press and played to the usual packed houses.

Another of Witts's ideas was to match programmes to venues more closely. This resulted in one particularly innovative and memorable presentation in the Music in Historic Buildings series. A performance of John Cage's *Apartment House 1776* was planned to take place in the famous Glass House, home of the architect Michael Hopkins, built in 1976 in Downshire Hill, Hampstead. Commissioned for the 200th anniversary of the American Revolution, Cage's work "is structured as though we are in a building of that style and of that year. Each room seems to be peopled with representatives of the various communities of that time…who can be heard singing or playing the ritual music with which they are identified." However, at the last minute the GLC refused to give a public performance licence and the event had to be transferred to the Diorama in Regent's Park. Concert-goers were given a quick tour around the Hopkins home and then taken by coach to the Diorama. Paul Griffiths in *The Times* gives the flavour of the event:

> "We had Gregory Rose offer strange dismantled versions of hymns and marches from 1776….One knows how Cage is. Dick Witts, responsible for music at the Camden Festival, cheerfully excused a late change in the venue as "somehow appropriate" for Cage…. Just by making a hash of things one enters into the spirit of Cage."

It attracted capacity audiences.

The American theme was maintained in other programmes: the Amati Ensemble with 'England New England' music of the 18th century on authentic instruments at the

Thomas Coram Foundation; The Landini Consort with 'Columbus and the Court of Spain' at the Hall of Lincoln's Inn; and 'Amerigo, his America' given by the London Pro Musica, at Gray's Inn Hall. Christopher Bowers-Broadbent came up with 'The All American Organ' for his recital at St Pancras Church, and there were the usual Dance, Other Concerts (two orchestral concerts) and Other Voices (choral concerts) sections.

The Jazz Week [68], which was programmed by John Cumming and Jean Davenport, attracted the highest praise in all sections of the press for being "even by its own high standards unusually substantial." (*The Times*) It included an evening devoted to women musicians, and BBC Radio 3 recorded several of the shows.

Witts was equally forthright about the community arts element, which he renamed Street Levels: "We're rather aggressive about the term 'community'. It's seen as a middle-class term for working-class culture" (interview in the *New Statesman*). More than 40% of the budget was given over to the popular elements of the Festival, but box-office income for many of these events, particularly the Street Level programmes and three of the Music and Dance programmes, was disappointing – or as the officer's report puts it "these were examples of audience resistance to what appeared to be sound programming". This was despite the fact that these events had been moved "from community centres to more professional, better equipped venues".[29]

Witts told the *New Statesman* that "Compartmentalism has been one of the blocks of British creativity, which is why music theatre is in such a bad state in Britain. Cross-fertilisation is what we're after." (cf. [69]) But the author of the article commented that the Festival "gives little sign this year of achieving this goal. Without a central focus, it was hard to find a sense of cohesiveness".[35] Certainly, the way the publicity was handled did not help; separate publicity leaflets were issued for each section of the programme, none of them giving any inkling of the other components. It was difficult to know from the opera and concert programme that there were also the Jazz Festival, Street Level events, the International Music and Dance programme, a Young Festival which had been launched very successfully in 1985, and a programme of events called Music and Film. This drew strong criticism from Sandy Broughton, who had been brought in as press consultant and

68
Art Blakey, who took part in the 1986 Jazz Week

found she was having to hand out six separate leaflets, rising later to twenty! "On top of this, the Festival programme was produced in two parts, neither of them comprehensive of the whole Festival."

She also gives an insight into other problems behind the scenes:

"A major problem for the Festival is one common to arts event of all kinds – who is it for? The answer to that question should never be seen in over-simplistic terms. If an internationally celebrated musician is performing within the Festival, for example, this adds to the prestige of the Festival for all concerned and adds to, not detracts from, the local level. In any event pressure for the Festival to be 'used', whether by local politicians or by vested interests within the community, should be resisted and the aims, once agreed by the Festival Trust and the Administrator, supported by all concerned....The importance of the festival...is not stressed sufficiently. Overall awareness throughout the whole of the Council might be achieved via induction courses".[29]

Support within the Council for the festival, which had been Borough's flagship annual

quart-sized Festival from a pint-sized pot." [29]

There was, understandably, friction between Dick Witts and the Board of Trustees, who by now felt they had made a terrible mistake. He was concerned at the membership of the Camden Festival Trust, many of whom he felt had been there too long, were behind the times and standing in the way of the sort of revitalised programming he wanted to pursue which would, in his view, attract much greater Arts Council funding. The feeling was mutual, as the Board mostly regarded his ideas as far too radical and a betrayal of what the Festival was supposed to be about. As *Classical Music* put it, Witts had a reputation for "[creating friction] between himself and the Establishment." [36]

Meanwhile, the Council was descending into ever greater chaos, with regular reports in the local press of officers demoralised by political interference, huge staff increases and turnover, creative accounting, and a lack of corporate direction and supervision, while a divided political leadership argued over how to deal with the problems. Early in the year the district auditor wrote to the Council warning it "to bring future revenue expenditure and available resources into balance." [37]

69 Calman cartoon on the front of the 1986 Festival brochure

event for 30 years, had so declined that "induction courses" were now needed!

Allocation of press and complimentary tickets had apparently again got out of hand. This drew comment in *Punch* whose "request for a very modest number of press tickets" was refused: "Is this plain stingy or just plain amateur, or perhaps a consequence of some past feud with a denouncer of Camden Council?" Abbey Opera suffered particularly, as nearly £3,000 worth of tickets were handed out.

The disaster of 1986 was that the budget was overspent by £32,000. Voluminous reports were produced trying to explain how it had happened, but Camden's Director of Finance was clear that "this overspending results, at least in part, from lack of financial control". He pointed out that "it is necessary to be realistic about what can be achieved within the given budget". However, since 1981 there had been virtually no increase in Camden's net contribution to the Festival budget and as the Senior Arts Officer, James Miles, pointed out in his report, "The officers have for several years been attempting to produce a

1987

It was not a good basis on which to start the Festival in 1987. Perhaps the fire which engulfed Witts's office just before it started, destroying files, photographs and other materials relating to the Festival, was an omen. In a desperate attempt to ease the budgeting problem the Festival was moved to the end of March so that it would span two financial years and take money from the following year's budget to cover the deficit. However, this device was accompanied by a further expansion of the estimated budget by £67,000, bringing it to £289,000. It has been said that the thinking behind these manoeuvres was the expectation that a Labour government was about to be elected and would bail everybody out. Whatever the theory, warning bells were already being sounded by the Director of Finance: "It follows that without further equivalent resources being available in future years, the level of Festival budget could not be sustained." [38]

At a time when audiences were increasingly hard to attract, Dick Witts's programme, the first and last for which he was solely responsible, did not help. It impressed the Arts Council sufficiently for them to raise their grant, on the basis of its "integrated series of five operas, all progressive works of the 20th century" and a "more wide-ranging, thematic, and progressive [programme], with a dynamic profile, as well as being risk-taking, thoughtful and highly successful".[39]

But it was a risk too far. Although there were many interesting programmes some of which were highly praised, its financial weight sank the Festival. Out of 83 events in the Festival there were only eight concerts, and even the concerts in historic buildings had gone; the emphasis was now on Jazz, International and Urban Trax – yet another name for the "popular" programmes – on which large sums of money were spent to bring in artists from all over the world. The availability of the Town and Country Club in Highgate, which seats about 2000, made it possible to recoup the expenses at the box office. Attendance figures for International Music and Dance were again disappointing, but special sponsorship of £18,000 to cover the airfares at least made the budget balance.

The Young Festival was repeated with several attractive and novel programmes such as cartoon films, Latin-American music and Chinese puppets, but no attempt at the sort of programme which Youth and Music used to offer.

The operas were a similar mix to the previous year: rediscovered Kurt Weill, a controversial new opera by the American composer Robert Ashley, and a Benjamin Britten double bill. The two Kurt Weill operas were acclaimed by the critics, especially the first fully staged performances of *Silverlake* [70], banned by the Nazis in 1933. This was an outstanding artistic success, hailed by the press as a major discovery with plaudits for the company, Abbey Opera, and its cast and musical director, Antony Shelley. Unfortunately for them it was a financial disaster. Despite a good first-night house and the brilliant reviews, which compared their performances favourably with the 1980 New York staging, audience attendance was only around 70% for the rest of the run, and with too many complimentary tickets still being handed out they did not achieve their necessary box-office income.

70 Costume and set designs by Lez Brotherston for *Silverlake* (1987) (courtesy Abbey Opera)

Happy End, in a production by the Welsh company, St Donat's Music Theatre, played to capacity houses but at The Place, which has only 250 seats. The Britten one-acters, at All Hallows Church in Gospel Oak, also suffered from the exaggerated claims in the publicity material:

> "Provocative staging, stunning costumes and décor were promised by the French company Volte Face for *Curlew River* and the *Prodigal Son*, but nothing of the sort materialised…'Provocative' is hardly the word to describe either production, but in the case of the *Prodigal Son* we were offered a refreshingly untraditional view of the work." [40]

The critic of *The Independent* commented

> "If operas are to live as art rather than petrify as chunks of history, they cannot be constrained within the terms of their original production. The question, though, is whether reinterpretation serves the work or merely cakes it in cosmetics". [41]

Unfortunately, the general consensus appeared to share his verdict that the "style is the undoing of both presentations which, alas, subside into designer's camp".

Witts's claim in his report to the Committee that *Atalanta* by Robert Ashley "has revitalised opera as an art form by using its ability to play with time and language" [33] was also not borne out, to judge by its reception. The production, which was brought over from America with its composer, who performed the leading role, played to a half-empty theatre. David Cairns in *The Sunday Times* described the evening under the heading "What happened to the flying saucer?":

> "The electronic sound and the relentless rhythmic and melodic patterns are of numbing monotony. As for the words, most of them were droningly inaudible. Of Atalanta, Max Ernst, architecture, the flying saucer, or any of the work's supposed preoccupations I could detect no sign. The lighting changed constantly but nothing else happened".

But he added: "All the same, I liked the way Camden is willing to try new things". [42]

Opera's critic liked Blue Gene Tyranny's solo electric keyboards: "always good value – some of his wilder virtuoso flights scurrying from cloud to cloud, were really quite impressive", but shared the general view of the performance as a whole:

> "If *Atalanta* had not been so long, and so pretentious, it might have carried the day with certain zany 'alternative' charm."

Challenged by the *Ham & High* about the negative reception of this much vaunted piece Witts is reported to have said

> "In five years' time people will recall *Silverlake*, but in 25 years' time they will recall *Atalanta*"; it is "years beyond the thought that now exists in British composition." [43]

One of the most successful concerts was a collaboration with the Royal Academy of Music, which staged a Messiaen Festival the week before the Camden Festival started. It was arranged that their last concert would also be the first concert of the Festival. Heralded in the guide as "Messiaen in Camden" the composer himself attended the concert at St Pancras Church, which was given by the Manson Ensemble and received a standing ovation from a full house. The 5-hour event included a performance of his *Des Canyons des Etoiles* and a conversation between Messaien and Felix Aprahamian.

Another novel programme given by Divertimenti at the Everyman included music by Sallinen, Michael Nyman and Bernhard Herrmann's Suite from Hitchcock's *Psycho*, with short films and stills, preceded by a 'meet the composer' talk and followed by an evening of related films.

The dance programme was perhaps one of the most unusual things ever to appear in any Festival and another example of Dick Witts's imaginative programming at its best: a work called *Waterproof* performed by the *avant-garde* French group Astrakan at Swiss Cottage Baths. As Witts reported:

> "Safety regulations and other factors led to extremely complicated budgetary and technical problems in the unique staging, lighting, video and sound rigging around the pool. The work [by Daniel Larrieu] was a sensational success and the Festival has been nominated for a SWET Award for this production. A film version was shown on Channel 4". [39]

The line-up of jazz stars was a major coup for the Festival with a residency by the American Ornette Coleman, the creator of free jazz, joined by Gavin Briars, Charlie Haden, Carla Bley and a host of others [71]. Some of the musicians also participated in workshops and Coleman gave a lecture at the Holborn Library.

There were two exhibitions: photos of jazz musicians at St Pancras Library, with headphones to play the music at the same time; and at Swiss Cottage Library, the life and work of Paul Robeson.

For the first time in the Festival's history audience numbers overall were down. Some attributed this to the confusingly designed advance publicity, printed in such small typefaces that it was difficult to read. Sandy Broughton's advice was not taken; the programme books were still in separate parts,

none making any reference to the other parts of the Festival. Choral Societies were dismayed "that their concert programmes consisted of single hastily prepared sheets of paper which gave scant details of the works to be sung." [43]

Witts blamed the office fire which had destroyed all the programme notes and the slowness of the societies to provide him with replacements. However, there was clearly more to it than that; everything, including the Kurt Weill operas, was misleadingly dressed up as "alternative" or "cutting edge". If it was supposed to attract new audiences it only served to put off the old one. Abbey Opera certainly attributed their problems to this approach, and the *Ham & High* in a post-Festival article noted that "the artistic policy has veered from catering for affluent opera buffs to enticing sensation-seeking yuppies" and some of the events were of "dubious artistic worth".[43]

Questioned on this point by the *Ham & High*[43] Witts maintained that people had not understood his intention to "provide a concept Festival exploring the various ways that text is conveyed in music. Such themes will replace the traditional way the Festival was departmentalised into opera, classical concert, ethnic or jazz events". He went on to say that "the Festival's publicity machinery had collapsed after a glitzy press launch" and to go with the new image he was trying to create there would need to be an injection of more professional expertise with more use of consultants for publicity, promotion of sponsorship and technical production. But for over 30 years, until he arrived on the scene, these things had been managed without any problem.

This article also told of mismanagement at some Festival events, in particular the Jazz nights, with "audiences left standing in the rain for doors to open on chaotically organised concerts". Witts was quoted as saying that the Festival needed a concert venue of its own in order to fulfil its new [sic] role as an innovative and high-profile series of events. The paper's editor had some sarcastic words to say on this:

"Mr Witts is a man who is totally and rightly uninhibited about the fact that Camden is rate-capped and more than £100 million in debt. Among his top priorities is the acquisition by the Council of its own venue….It is good to come across a man whose bold vision fairly takes the breath away – but we are a bit dubious about

71 Jazz stars Ornette Coleman, Charlie Haden and Carla Bley (1987)

whether a building of suitable prestige can be found within the borough boundaries. Mr Witts may have to look further afield – to the Albert Hall perhaps. Or wouldn't that be large enough?" [43]

The budget limits were observed, but the next year's money had already been spent. By this time Camden Council was in dire straits financially, badly managed, committed to interest payments on disastrous foreign bank loans, and wrong-footed at every turn by government restrictions. Every single area of council activity suffered drastic cuts over the next year, with many job losses, and it was impossible for the Festival to remain unscathed. Since no-one at the Festival office had seriously considered how to save the Festival by reducing its cost, the only discussion was whether to slash the year-round arts programme or the Festival; both could not be justified. In the prevailing anti-intellectual climate it was inevitable that the Festival would go.

The only consideration recorded in the decision to give the Neighbourhood Festivals priority over the Camden Festival seemed to focus on the same obsession that

"the year-round programme of Arts and Entertainments reaches a larger number of Camden residents than the Camden Festival, which is enjoyed by many non-Camden residents. We have agreed therefore that the year-round programme of Arts and Entertainments be given priority over the Camden Festival within the budget for the next year."

There was no consideration of what the quality or content of any of these programmes might be.[44]

Ironically, no sooner had this decision been taken than the following report was made to Council, headed *The Cultural Industries*:

"The importance of this sub-sector of tourism has only recently been realised. Figures show that, nationally, employment in this sector is the fastest growing and contributes £1 billion per annum to the balance of payments. It embraces music, specialist museums, the theatre, design etc. – all of which are active in Camden but which have not been seen as important and expanding economic sectors requiring specific strategies." [45]

Perhaps it is time after 17 years to ask some questions about the ending of the Festival. Did it have to die? Could it have been saved? Times were bad, it is true, in a period of economic decline but the financial problems were only one element – albeit an important one – in the final reckoning. The ground had been prepared by a changing perception of 'culture' in general and of 'classical music' in particular that had more to do with new values and attitudes then taking hold.

The drive towards more so-called 'popular' and 'accessible' culture has been achieved at a cost which perhaps its advocates had not anticipated. It coincided with the rise of a dominating belief in the virtue of 'market forces' with their constant demand for new, simple and easily disposable products to yield a rapid economic turnover. Far from broadening cultural choices, it has narrowed them. As Hugh Jenkins warned[46] in 1979, in the search for maximum profit "merchand-isers identify their markets and serve them with products *which must be easily assimilable*, widely acceptable and highly profitable" (my italics). Bill Holland, director of Universal Classics and Jazz UK, the parent company of Decca, succinctly spelt out what this has

meant for music in a recent interview[47] in *The Times*: "We're in the business of turning a profit for the shareholders. Working in the business teaches you that your favourite music shouldn't be based on genre, it should be based on sales." The kinds of arts and culture that demand time for contemplation and intellectual engagement simply do not fit into this brutal system, which has commodified every area of our lives. Indeed, in his recent study *Who Needs Classical Music?* Julian Johnson suggests[48] that 'classical' music is a form of cultural resistance to the value-free relativism of the marketplace and therefore by its very nature poses a threat to that system. He asks, despairingly perhaps:

"What does it mean that a society cares so little for things of the mind, that concert halls and libraries become increasingly empty?"

Back in 1979, Hugh Jenkins accused the politicians of complicity in this process and concluded that it had "re-opened, deepened and widened the culture gap",[49] the very one the founding fathers of the Festival sought to bridge. With their vision of a Library Service at the centre of the cultural life of the Borough catering for all tastes and all ages, Krishna Menon and his colleagues at

St Pancras, followed by John Richardson at Camden, had set out to make our rich cultural heritage available to all, in all its diversity. Their extraordinary achievement, and its astonishing success, is a matter of record.

It is a tragedy that the process was halted, and London's cultural life is greatly the poorer. However, nothing can diminish the scale of that achievement, which remains a glowing page in the history of Camden.

Notes to chapter 6

1. *Ham & High* 18.4.80.
2. *Ham & High* 13.2.81.
3. Report to Music Advisory Panel October 1980, part of LS 80/188.
4. *Ham & High* 14.3.86.
5. Hans Keller *Music, closed societies and football* Toccata Press 1986.
6. Sue Braden *Artists and people* Routledge & Keegan Paul 1978.
7. Terry Eagleton *The idea of culture* Blackwell Manifestos 2000 pp 121 and 52.
8. Report of Arts Sub-Committee 15.2.71 LAR/71/28 Agenda item 8.
9. End-of-year report of Camden Arts Sub-Committee 22.3.71 LAR/71/47 Agenda item 16b.
10. Leisure Services Committee minutes 3.10.74 LS/74/216 Agenda item 12c.
11. Council minutes 15.1.75 (vol 12) Policy for future Festivals p 16.
12. Council minutes 19.4.78 (vol 15) Leisure Services Report p 259.
13. Leisure Services minutes 9.3.78 LS/78/83 Agenda item 4b.
14. Leisure Services Committee Report 27.6.79 Agenda Item 6.
15. Leisure Services Committee minutes 13.6.85.
16. Letter 12.7.83 from the Chief Executive.
17. Leisure Services Committee Report 7.6.84 Agenda Item 9
18. Borough minutes 8.2.61 p 4; *New Statesman* 31.12.60.
19. *North London Press* 22.1.65.
20. *North London Press* 12.1.68.
21. Announcement, *North London Press* 9.2.68.
22. Leisure Services Committee 21.5.75 LS/75/179 Agenda item 4. Report of the Leisure Provision Programme Area Working Group.
23. Programme guide 1968.
24. Council minutes 29.2.84 (vol 21) Report of Leisure Services Committee p 15.
25. *Barlines* 8.2.86.
26. 1987 Festival programme.
27. Transcript of interview on BBC Radio 4 Kaleidoscope 13.3.86, Camden Festival Archive.
28. Committee minutes 16.7.86 (vol 23) Report of Leisure Service Committee p 162.
29. Leisure Services Committee minutes 12.6.86 LS/86/90 Agenda Item 4a.
30. *Classical Music* 8.3.86 "Camden's Lease of Life".
31. 1987 Festival programme.
32. *Ham & High* 26.5.72.
33. Leisure Services Committee minutes. Preliminary programme report June 1986, LS/86/91 Agenda item 4b.
34. *Financial Times* 20.3.86.
35. *New Statesman* 28.3.86 "Little Boxes".
36. *Classical Music* 8.3.86.
37. *Ham & High* 20.2.87.
38. Leisure Services Committee minutes 6.11.86 LS/86/212 Agenda item 11. Camden Festival 1987.
39. Leisure Services Committee minutes 30.6.87 LS/87/78 Agenda item 6a. Camden Festival.
40. *Opera* Jun 1987 (vol 38 no.6) p 691.
41. *The Independent* 6.4.87.
42. *Sunday Times* 12.4.87.
43. *Ham & High* 17.4 87.
44. Leisure Services Committee minutes 10.11.87 Agenda Item 8.
45. Leisure Services Committee minutes 20.5.88 Agenda item 17 "Employment and Training Strategy in Tourism".
46. Hugh Jenkins *The Culture Gap: An experience of government and the arts* Marion Boyars 1979.
47. Quoted in *The Times Saturday Magazine* 28.6.03 "Roll over, Beethoven".
48. Julian Johnson *Who Needs Classical Music? Cultural choice and musical value* OUP 2002, p 57.
49. Ref. 46, pp 19–20.

Appendix 1 Operas and operettas produced at the Festivals

1955
Haydn Orfeo ed Euridice

1957
Handel Alcina
Mozart La Clemenza di Tito

1958
Handel Theodora
Mozart Idomeneo
Sharp-Foster Lord Bateman

1959
Cimarosa Il Matrimonio Segreto
Handel Alcina

1960
Blacher The Tide
Milhaud The Sorrows of Orpheus
Haydn Il Mondo della Luna
Mozart Idomeneo

1961
Carissimi Jephtha
Carissimi The Story of Hezekiah
Carissimi The Story of Job
Chabrier Une Education Manquée
Verdi Un Giorno di Regno
Menotti The Medium
Rossini L'Italiana in Algeri

1962
Arne Artaxerxes
Back Crane Feathers
Bizet Dr Miracle
Verdi I Masnadieri

1963
Britten Noye's Fludde
Rossini La Pietra del Paragone
Smith Ulysses
Verdi Ernani

1964
Cherubini Pigmalione
Gluck Iphigénie en Aulide
Haydn L'Infedeltà Delusa
Verdi Aroldo

1965
Britten Noye's Fludde
Debussy Pelléas et Mélisande
Monteverdi Il Ritorno d'Ulisse
Rossini Il Turco in Italia
Tate The Lodger

1966
Donizetti Maria Stuarda
Haydn L'Incontro Improvviso
Henze The End of a World
Henze Miracle Theatre
Henze A Country Doctor
Verdi Il Corsaro

1967
Donizetti Marino Faliero
Hindemith There and Back
Massenet Sapho
Holst The Wandering Scholar
Maconchy The Sofa
Mozart Lucio Silla

1968
Mozart The First Commandment
Mozart Il Sogno di Scipione
Rimsky-Korsakov Mozart & Salieri
Tchaikovsky Iolanta
Rossini Elisabetta Regina d'Inghilterra
Three medieval music dramas (see p 113)

1969
Berlioz Beatrice and Benedict
Joubert Under Western Eyes
Rossini La Donna del Lago
Scarlatti/da Capua double bill

1970
Delius Fennimore and Gerda
Strauss The Donkey's Shadow
Leoncavallo La Bohème
Poulenc La Voix Humaine
Poulenc Les Mamelles de Tirésias
Scarlatti La Statira

1971
Cilea Adriana Lecouvreur
Haydn La Fedeltà Premiata
Rossini Tancredi

1972
Massenet La Navarraise
Rachmaninov Aleko
Smetana The Secret
Donizetti Le Convenienze Teatrali
Delius Koanga

1973
Offenbach Robinson Crusoe
Purcell The Indian Queen

1974
Donizetti Torquato Tasso
Storace The Comedy of Errors
Hindemith Mathis der Maler

1975
Mozart Il Rè Pastore
Donizetti Torquato Tasso
Meyerbeer L'Etoile du Nord
Bizet Les Pêcheurs de Perles

1976
Menotti Maria Golovin
Thomas Linley The Duenna
Gershwin Porgy and Bess

1977
Monteverdi Orfeo
Donizetti Il Castello di Kenilworth
Verdi Les Vêpres Siciliennes

1978
Offenbach Grand Duchess of Gerolstein
Almeida La Spinalba
R Strauss Feuersnot

1979
Delius Fennimore & Gerda
Stravinsky Mavra
Paisiello/Henze Don Quixote
Mozart Mitridate, Rè di Ponto
Dvorak The Jacobin

1980
Rota The Italian Straw Hat
Grétry Zémire et Azor
Tchaikovsky Mazeppa

1981
L & F Ricci Crispino e la Comare
Cimarosa Gli Orazi ed i Curiazi
Sacchini Renaud
Puccini Manon Lescaut

1982
Donizetti Francesca di Foix
Donizetti La Romanziera
Cavalli Eritrea
J C Bach Adriano in Siria
Walton Troilus and Cressida
Barber Antony and Cleopatra

1983
Wolf-Ferrari School for Fathers
Pacini Maria Tudor
Britten Gloriana
Stravinsky Oedipus Rex

1984
Vivaldi Juditha Triumphans
Delius Margot la Rouge
Lecocq Dr Miracle
Cilea Adriana Lecouvreur
Shostakovich Lady Macbeth of Mtsensk

1985
Mozart La Finta Semplice
Caccini L'Euridice
Boito Nerone
R Strauss Friedenstag

1986
Paul Barker Phantastes
Richard Hawkins Other Voices
Mozart La Finta Giardiniera
Rimsky-Korsakov The Snow Maid
Weill The Protagonist
Weill The Czar has his photograph taken

1987
Robert Ashley Atalanta
Britten Curlew River
Britten The Prodigal Son
Weill Silverlake
Weill Happy End

Appendix 2 Opera casts, companies, and costs

c, conductor; p, producer (term used until c.1986); d = director; des = designer
All Chelsea Opera Group performances were concert performances.
Many of the singers listed also appeared in Festival concerts.

1955
Haydn *Orfeo ed Euridice*
(*L'anima del filosofo*)
Impresario Society
David Galliver
Niven Miller
Derek Hammond-Stroud
Heather Harper
Ellen Dales
c: Dr Hans Ucko

1957
Handel *Alcina*
Handel Opera Society
Monica Sinclair
Joan Sutherland
Emerentia Scheepers
John Noble
Miles Amherst
John Carvalho
John Kentish
c: Charles Farncombe
p: Anthony Besch

Mozart *La Clemenza di Tito*
Impresario Society
Heather Harper
Monica Sinclair
Geraldine Frank
David Galliver
Derek Hammond-Stroud
Belva Broditsky
c: Dr Hans Ucko
p: Anthony Besch

1958
Mozart *Idomeneo*
Impresario Society
Adele Leigh
Nancy Evans
Arda Mandikian
John Stoddart
Derek Hammond-Stroud
Alexander Young
c: Dr Hans Ucko
p: Douglas Craig

Handel *Theodora*
Handel Opera Society
Cost approx £1000
Geraint Evans
Helen Watts
John Kentish
April Cantelo
Monica Sinclair
c: Charles Farncombe
p: Anthony Besch

Sharp/Foster *Lord Bateman*
New Opera Workshop
Alan Lyne
Peter Hemmings
Kenneth Bowen
Ray Spelmann
Noelle Barker
Jill Nott-Bower
Heather Godden
c. Alan Boustead
p: Colin Graham

1959
Cimarosa *The Secret Marriage*
Impresario Society
Frederick Williams
Edgar Fleet
Doreen Hume
Norman Platt
Doreen Murray
Johanna Peters
Ian Paterson
c: Dr Hans Ucko
p: Richard Stuart Flusser
des: Michael Young

Handel *Alcina*
Handel Opera Society
(concert perf.)
Heather Harper
(replacing Joan Sutherland)
Margreta Elkins
Josephine Veasey
John Noble
Marion Studholme
John Kentish
c: Charles Farncombe

1960
Haydn *Il Mondo della Luna*
Group Eight Productions
Cost £3814
Marcello Cortis
John Kentish
Julian Moyle
April Cantelo
Mary Illing
Laura Sarti
c: Adrian Sunshine
p: Douglas Craig
des: Ralph Koltai

Double Bill
Group Eight Productions
Cost £577
Blacher *The Tide*
Donald Campbell
Mary Illing
Edward Byles
Julian Moyle
c. Myer Fredman
p: Rowland Holt-Wilson
des: Christopher Gotch

Milhaud *The Sorrows of Orpheus*
John Cameron
Jeanette Sinclair
Terence Conoley
Shirley Minty
Denis Wicks
c: Myer Fredman
p: Peter Harwood
des: Jane Kingshill

Mozart *Idomeneo*
Impresario Society
(concert perf.)
cost £533
Ilse Wolf
Jeanette Sinclair
Arda Mandikian
David Galliver
Derek Hammond-Stroud
John Dobson
c: Dr Hans Uckof

1961
Carissimi
Three musical morality plays:
Jephtha,
The Story of Hezekiah,
The Story of Job
Handel Opera Society
Cost £266
Marjorie Biggar
(replaced Jean Evans)
Kenneth Bowen
(replaced Duncan Robertson)
Eileen Poulter
Margaret Smith
Norman Lumsden
c: Charles Farncombe
p: Charles Craig

Chabrier/Menotti double bill
Group Eight Productions
Cost £808
Une Education Manquée
Maria Zeri
Bernard Dickerson
Bernard Turgeon
The Medium
Monica Sinclair
Peggy Castle
Audrey Deakin
Rita McKerrow
George Macpherson
Tony Calvin
c: Myer Fredman/Bernard Jacob
p: David Gauld/Anthony Besch
des: Christopher Gotch/Peter Rice

Verdi
Un Giorno di Regno
Impresario Society
Cost £2523
Bettina Jonic
Cynthia Jolly
Eric Garrett
Alfred Hallett
Derek Hammond-Stroud
James Atkins
John Hauxvell
Patrick Costeloe
c: Dr Hans Ucko
p: Michael Geliot
des: Jennifer Agnew

Rossini
L'Italiana in Algeri
Group Eight
Cost £836
Jean Allister
Angela Rubini
Laura Sarti
Heinz Danziger
Derek Hammond-Stroud
Dennis Wicks
Edgar Fleet
c: Peter Gellhorn
p: Rowland Holt-Wilson
des: Jane Kingshill

1962
Verdi
I Masnadieri
Philopera Circle
Cost £1371
Pauline Tinsley
Niven Miller
Jack Irons
Edward Byles
Gerwyn Morgan
David Winnard
c: Franz Manton
p: David Gauld
des: Lily Manton

Appendix 2 continued

c, conductor; p, producer (term used until c.1986); d = director; des = designer

Bizet/Back
Double Bill
Group Eight
Cost £1399
Bizet *Dr Miracle*
Michael Maurel
Anna Pollack
Kenneth Bowen
c: Myer Fredman
p: Anthony Besch
des: Peter Rice
Sven-Erik Back
Crane Feathers
Connell Byrne
Carol Rosen
Andre Dorval
Dennis Wicks
c: Sven-Erik Back
p: Peter Harwood

Thomas Arne
Artaxerses
Handel Opera
  Society
Cost £1338
Barbara Holt
Heather Harper
John Stoddart
Johanna Peters
Mary Thomas
John Littlewood
c: Charles
  Farncombe
p: Norman Ayrton
des: Dawn Pavitt

1963
Verdi *Ernani*
Philopera Circle
cost £1475
Pauline Tinsley
Edward Byles
John Rhys Evans
Susan Gray
George
  Macpherson
Alex Hood
John Jackson
c: Franz Manton
p: David Gauld
des: Lily Manton

Britten
Noye's Fludde
Finchley Children's
  Music Group
Owen Brannigan
Edith Coates
Kenneth Loveless
Elaine Pearce
Rosalind Tennyson
c: John Andrewes

Rossini
La Pietra del
Paragone
Group Eight
cost £1316
Derek Hammond-
  Stroud
Heinz Danziger
Laura Sarti
Patricia Clark
Noel Mangin
Duncan Robertson
Dennis Wicks
Elizabeth
  Bainbridge
c: Myer Fredman
p: Rowland Holt-
  Wilson
des: Christopher
  Gotch

John Smith
Ulysses
Handel Opera
  Society
Cost £1346
Johanna Peters
Maureen Keetch
  (replaced Wendy
  Baldwin)
Margaret Neville
David Palmer
c: Charles
  Farncombe
p: Douglas Craig

1964
Verdi *Aroldo*
Opera-Concerts
Cost £1445
Anne Edwards
Nasco Petroff
Michael Maurel
Joseph Beachus
Noel Mangin
Jennifer Cox
David Fisher
c: Gerald Gover
p: John Cox
des: Margaret
  Bedford

Gluck
Iphigenia in Aulis
Philopera Circle
cost £1497
Geoffrey Chard
Glennis Halliday
Martin Lawrence
Elaine Blighton
Gerald Stern
Wyndham Parfit
c: Franz Manton
p: Geoffrey
  Connor

Cherubini
Pygmalion
(concert perf.)
Philomusica
  of London
Cost £845
Maureen Lehane
Janice Chapman
Doreen Price
John Noble
c: Joseph Horovitz

Haydn
L'Infedeltà Delusa
Handel Opera
  Society
Estd cost £1409
Patricia Clark
Mary Thomas
Adrian de Peyer
Kenneth Bowen
Eric Shilling
c: Charles
  Farncombe
p: Colin Graham
des: Terence Emery

1965
Rossini
Il Turco in Italia
Handel Opera
  Society
Philip Langridge
Sheila Amit
Raymond Hayter
Eric Shilling
Jennifer Eddy
Benjamin Luxon
Stuart Burrows
c: Charles
  Farncombe
p: Michael Geliot
des: Jennifer
  Agnew

Britten
Noye's Fludde
Finchley Children's
  Music Group
Norman Lumsden
Sheila Rex
Trevor Antony
c: John Andrewes

Debussy *Pelléas*
et Mélisande
Opera Concerts
Clare Walmesly
David Hughes
Michael Maurel
Joseph Rouleau
Maureen Morelle
Maria Zeri
Heinz Danziger
c: Gerald Gover
p: Dennis Maunder
des: Judith Ebert

Monteverdi
Il Ritorno d'Ulisse
Basilica Productions
Walter Dinoff
Elizabeth
  Bainbridge
Clare Walmesly
Laura Sarti
John Kentish
Margot Barry
Bernard Dickerson
John Walton
Yvonne Minton
William McKinney
c: Frederick
  Marshall
p: Rowland
  Holt-Wilson
des: Helen Spankie

Phyllis Tate
The Lodger
Group Eight
Emyr Green
Yvonne Minton
Audrey Attwood
Peter Leeming
David Hillman
c: Myer Fredman
p: Peter Harwood
des: Jane Kingshill

1966
Donizetti
Maria Stuarda
Opera Concerts
Cost £3487
Cynthia Jolly
Marie Landis
David Hillman
Bryan Drake
Lawrence Richard
Beryl Cook
c: Gerald Gover
p: Dennis Maunder
des: Gerald
  Kitching

Haydn
L'Incontro
Improvviso
Handel Opera
  Society
Cost £2604
Peter Bamber
Margot Barry
Josephine Barstow
Patricia McCarry
Edward Byles
Frank Olegario
Frederick
  Ketteridge
Michael Warren
Michael James
Wyndham Parfitt
c: Charles
  Farncombe
p: David Gauld
des: Terence Emery

Appendix 2 continued

c, conductor; p, producer (term used until c.1986); d = director; des = designer

Hans Werner Henze
Three one-act operas
The End of a World, Miracle Theatre, A Country Doctor
Basilica Opera
Cost £4044
John Cameron
Edmund Bohan
Monica Sinclair
Dorothy Dorrow
John Kentish
Noel Noble
Geoffrey Chard
Angela Moran
William McKinney
John Rhys Evans
Norman Knight
Peter Leeming
David Barney
Robin Bell
John Broome
c: Frederick Marshall
p: Rowland Holt-Wilson
des: Helen Spankie

Verdi
Il Corsaro
Opera Viva
Cost £2822
Donald Smith
Noel Noble
Jeannette Sinclair
Pauline Tinsley
Bryan Drake
Joseph Beaches
Dennis Conway
Peter Lea
c: Leslie Head
p: Tom Hawkes
des: Andrew & Margaret Brownfoot

1967
Donizetti
Marino Faliero
Opera Viva
Cost £4126
Paolo Silveri
Malcolm Shaw
David Parker
Rae Woodland
George Macpherson
Gwynne Sullivan
Jack Irons/Anthony Bremner
Gwenyth Annear
c: Leslie Head
p: Tom Hawkes
des: Jane Kingshill

Three comic operas
Holst
The Wandering Scholar
Hindemith
There and Back
Elisabeth Maconchy
The Sofa
Irwell Opera
Cost £3216
Neil Howlett
Gwenyth Annear
Ronald Evans
Emlyn Ellis
Elizabeth Denning
Dorothy Wilson
Joseph Ward
Sasha Abrams
Phillip Hooper
John Coles
David Lennox
Joy Evans
Monica Sinclair
Sydney Reid
Marion Mead
Robin Bell
Elizabeth Thomas
Jean Southern
Gene West
Neil Jenkins
Duncan Reece
c: Joseph Horovitz
p: Dennis Arundell

Mozart
Lucio Silla
Handel Opera Society
Cost £3741
Margaret Curphey
Julien Pike
Richard Conrad
Angela Jenkins
Rhonda Bruce
c: Charles Farncombe
p: H Powell Lloyd
des: Jennifer Pocknell

Massenet
Sapho
Opera Concerts
cost £3391
Milla Andrew
Adrian de Peyer
Joy Domzalski
Paschal Allen
James Christiansen
Maria Zeri
David Lennox
Frank Olegario
c: Gerald Gover
p: Dennis Maunder
des: Gerald Kitching

1968
Rossini
Elisabetta, Regina d'Inghilterra
Opera Concerts
Cost £3676
Alexandra Browning
Maurice Arthur
Malvina Major
Beryl Cook
Leo Kernan
Terence O'Rourke
c: Gerald Gover
p: David Giles
des: Kenneth Mellor

Mozart double bill
Il sogno do Scipione;
The First Commandment
Handel Opera Society
Cost £3724
Bernard Dickerson
David Palmer
Margaret Smith
Patricia Clark
Teresa Cahill
c: Charles Farncombe
p/des William Chappell

Russian double bill
Park Lane Group
Cost £5039
Rimsky-Korsakov
Mozart & Salieri
Norman Lumsden
Kenneth Bowen
Robert Mundy (violin)
Tchaikovsky
Iolanta
Noreen Berry
Josephine Barstow
Jenny Hill
Kay Olive
Oliver Broome
Frederick Bateman
Noel Noble
Anthony Raffell
Norman Welsby
Adrian de Peyer
c: David Lloyd Jones
p: Geoffrey Connor
des: Juanita Waterman

Three medieval music dramas
Planctus Mariae, Visitatio Sepulchri, Peregrinus
Pilgrim Players
Jean Allister
Patricia Clark
Thelma Godfrey
Edgar Fleet
Geoffrey Shaw
Frederick Westcott
David Read
Quem Quaritis Singers
c: Roy Jesson
p: E Martin Browne
des: Monica Peckham

1969
Rossini
La Donna del Lago
Opera Concerts
Kiri Te Kanawa
Gillian Knight
Maurice Arthur
Robert Lloyd
John Serge
Linda Hutchison
Terence O'Rourke
Keith Wright
c: Gerald Gover
p: Tom Hawkes
des: Peter Whiteman

Appendix 2 continued

c, conductor; p, producer (term used until c.1986); d = director; des = designer

Berlioz
Beatrice and Benedict
Park Lane Group
Erica Busch
Maureen Keetch
Jean Temperley
David Kane
Robert Bateman
Geoffrey Chiswick
Roderick Leyland
John King
John Gibbs
Michael Strobel
 (spoken part)
c: Ivor Keys
p: Geoffrey Connor
des: Dacre Punt

John Joubert
Under Western Eyes
New Opera Company
Noelle Barker
Noreen Berry
Meriel Dickinson
Margaret Gale
Clare Walmesley
Alan Charles
Nigel Douglas
John Hauxvell
David Lennox
Robert Lloyd
Norman Lumsden
William McAlpine
c: Leon Lovett
p: Michael Geliot
des: Christian Edzard

Scarlatti/da Capua double bill
Agar ed Ismaele; Esiliate, La Zingara
London Chamber Opera (with London Opera Centre)
Donna Faye Carr
Alison Hargan
Laureen Livingstone
Jane Plant
Delia Wallis
David Harrison
Edward Sadler
Jacob Witkin
c: Lionel Friend
p: Philippe Perrottet

1970
Scarlatti
La Statira
London Chamber Opera
Janet Gail
Alison Hargan
Lilian Watson
Marjorie McMichael
Robin Donald
Malcolm Rivers
Geoffrey Talbot
c: Lionel Friend
p: Philippe Perrottet
des: Susan Blaine/ David Fielding

Leoncavallo
La Bohème
Opera Concerts
Cost £4757
Doreen Cryer
Dorothy Iredale
Valerie Morgan
Graham Allum
Anthony Baldwin
David Clyde
Alex Hood
Peter Lyon
Graham Nicolls
David Norris Smith
John Truleaux
c: Gerald Gover
p: Brenda Stanley
des: Reginald Woolley

Poulenc double bill
La Voix Humaine
Les Mamelles De Tirésias
Park Lane Group
Cost £5864
Joan Davies
Angela Hickey
Anne Pashley
Thomas Hemsley
Neil Jenkins
John Kitchener
Kevin Miller
Dan Klein
c: Roger Norrington
p: Anthony Besch
des: John Stoddart

Delius/Strauss double bill
Fennimore and Gerda; The Donkey's Shadow
Park Lane Group
Cost £6899
Marjorie Biggar
Nan Christie
Margaret le Foe
Tom Allen
Graham Allum
Robert Bateman
Christopher Davies
Jack Irons
c: Myer Fredman
p: Basil Ashmore
des: Elroy Ashmore

1971
Haydn
La Fedeltà Premiata
Park Lane Group
Cost £5829
Lissa Gray
Janet Price
Victoria Sumner
Angela Hickey (replaced Sally Strane)
Bernard Dickerson
Raymond Hayter
David Hillman
Anthony Raffell
c: David Lloyd-Jones
p: Patrick Libby
des: John Fraser

Rossini
Tancredi
Basilica Opera
Cost £6080
Maureen Morelle
Maureen Lehane
Valerie Masterson
Edward Byles
Malcolm Rivers
Graham Allum
c: Frederick Marshall
p: Roland Holt Wilson
des: Berkeley Sutcliffe

Cilea ***Adriana Lecouvreur***
Opera Concerts
Cost £5500
Milla Andrew
Dorothy Iredale
Wendy Pollock
Patricia Westwood
Paschal Allen
Bernard Dickerson
Kenneth Collins
David Jennings
Julian Moyle
Graham Nicholls
c: Gerald Gover
p: Brenda Stanley
des: Elaine Anderson

1972
Rachmaninov
Aleko
Massenet
La Navarraise
Opera Concerts
Cost £6545
Joyce Blackham
Ruth Gurner
Alice Robiczek
Frederick Bateman
Myron Burnett
David Fieldsin
Powell Harrison
Malcolm King
Thomas Lawler
Peter Lyon
c: George Badacsony/ Gerald Gover
p: Dennis Maunder
des: Gerald Kitching

Smetana
The Secret
Park Lane Group
Cost £7445
Joan Clarkson
Victoria Sumner
Paschall Allen
Adrian de Peyer
Ronald Murdoch
Alan Opie
Anthony Raffell
Malcolm Rivers
Anthony Thompson
c: Vilem Tausky
p: Ian Watt-Smith
des: Sue Plummer

Delius ***Koanga***
Delius Trust
Jean Allister
Claudia Lindsey
Powell Harrison
Eugene Holmes
Anthony Raffell
Gordon Wilcock
c: Charles Groves
p: Douglas Craig
des: Peter Rice

Appendix 2 continued

c, conductor; p, producer (term used until c.1986); d = director; des = designer

Donizetti
Le Convenienze Teatrali
Opera Rara
Michael Aspinall
Lissa Gray
Peter Lyon
Rosemary Williams
Robert Carpenter Turner
Sylvia Eaves
David Fieldsend
Paschal Allen
Wyndham Parfitt
James Phillips
Mary Hill (piano)
p: Michael Winter
des: Anthony Holland

1973
Purcell
The Indian Queen
Opera da Camera
Cost £6121
Helen Attfield
Maxine Audley
Valerie Baulard
Anne Pashley
S James Adams
Richard Angas
Kevin Smith
John Tomlinson
c: Steuart Bedford
p: Peter Lehmann Bedford
des: Moshe Mussman

Offenbach
Robinson Crusoe
Opera Rara
Cost: £6544
Sandra Browne
Sandra Dugdale
Enid Hartle
Janet Price
Ian Caley
Noel Drennan
Peter Lyon
Wyndham Parfitt
c: Ian Macpherson
p: William Chappell
des: Anthony Holland

1974
Storace *Comedy of Errors*
Opera da Camera
Cost £6000
Marie Hayward
Helen Lawrence
Anne Wilkens
Kenneth Bowen
Christopher Davies
Francis Egerton
Stuart Harling
Malcolm King
Richard Stilgoe
John Tomlinson
c: Steuart Bedford
p: Peter Lehmann Bedford
des: Bruno Santini

Donizetti
Torquato Tasso
Opera Rara
Cost £7000
Alexandra Browning
Margareta Elkins/ Janet Price
Bruce Brewer
Noel Drennan
Christian du Plessis
William Mason
Andrew Snarski
c: Kenneth Montgomery
p: William Chappell
des: Anthony Holland

Hindemith
Mathis der Maler
Chelsea Opera Group (concert perf.)
Victor Godfrey
Geoffrey Shovelton
Nan Christie
Richard Gandy
Michael Rippon
Geoffrey Pogson
Adrian de Peyer
Milla Andrew
Richard Angus
Sarah Walker
William Armstrong
c: Roderick Brydon

1975
Mozart
Il Rè Pastore
Park Lane Group
Cost £7500
Anne Pashley
Elizabeth Gale
Kenneth Bowen
Anthony Rolfe Johnson
Della Jones
c: David Lloyd-Jones
p: David William
des: Alan Barlow

Donizetti
Torquato Tasso
Opera Rara
Cost £7520
Milla Andrew
Janet Hughes
Noel Drennan
Christian du Plessis
Jeffrey Talbot
Peter Lyon
Andrew Snarski
c: Steuart Bedford
p: William Chappell
des: Anthony Holland

Meyerbeer
L'Etoile du Nord
Opera Rara
Alexander Oliver
Malcolm King
Bonaventura Bottone
Janet Price
Deborah Cook
Alan Watt
Roger Bryson
Graham Clark
Lissa Gray
Susanna Ross
Bruce Ogston
c: Roderick Brydon
p: Adrian Slack
des: Anthony Holland

Bizet
Les Pêcheurs de Perles
Chelsea Opera Group
Cost: £300
Jennifer Smith
Geoffrey Pogson
Michael Halliwell
Paul Danagher
c: Philip Sims

1976
Thomas Linley
The Duenna
Opera da Camera
Cost £11,200
Elizabeth Gale
Kate Flowers
Sheila Rex
Kenneth Bowen
John Fryatt
John Gibbs
Keith Lewis
Graeme Matheson Bruce
c: Lionel Friend
p: William Royston
d: Bruno Santini

Gian-Carlo Menotti
Maria Golovin
Park Lane Opera
Cost: £12,416
Alison Hargan
Maureen Morelle
Rosalind Plowright
Ian Caddy
Bernard Dickerson
Richard Chadwell
c: Nicholas Braithwaite
p: Gian-Carlo Menotti/ Michael Rennison
des: Anthony Holland

George Gershwin
Porgy and Bess
Chelsea Opera Group
Cost £1031
Laverne Williams
Willard White
Dorothy Ross
Clementine Patrick
Dinah Harris
Malcolm King
c: Simon Rattle

1977
Monteverdi
Orfeo
Kent Opera
Cost: £9180
Rosemary Hardy
Gloria Jennings
Patricia O'Neill
Rosalind Plowright
Patricia Taylor
Jean Temperley
Nigel Beavan
David Clyde
Wynford Evans
Kenneth Francis
Philip Griffiths
Robert King
Peter Knapp
William Mason
Eric Roberts
Ian Thompson
c: Roger Norrington
p: Jonathan Miller
des: Bernard Culshaw

Donizetti
Il Castello di Kenilworth
Opera Rara
Cost: £10,850
Janet Price
Yvonne Kenny
Bridget Bartlam
Maurice Arthur
Christian du Plessis
Clive Harre
c: Alun Francis
p: Patrick Libby
des: Anthony Holland

Verdi
Vêpres Siciliennes
Chelsea Opera Group
Cost: £873
Margaret Haggart
Mary Hamilton
Adrian de Peyer
William Elvin
John Tomlinson
Andre Hoelet
Anthony James
Edgar Charlebois
c: John Matheson

1978
Offenbach *The Grand Duchess of Gerolstein*
Park Lane Group
Cost: £18,198
Patricia Routledge
Meryl Drower
Emile Belcourt
Bernard Dickerson
David Hillman
John Gibbs
c: Vilem Tausky
p: Christopher Renshaw
des: Tim Goodchild

Almeida
La Spinalba
Phoenix Opera
Cost: £7670
Helen Walker
Della Jones
Johanna Peters
Kate Flowers
Norman Welsby
Geoffrey Pogson
Richard Berkeley Steele
Alan Watt
c: Michael Lankester
p: Tom Hawkes
des: Malcolm Pride

Appendix 2 continued

c, conductor; p, producer (term used until c.1986); d = director; des = designer

Richard Strauss
Feuersnot
Chelsea Opera Group
Cost: £558
Eilene Hannan
Michael Lewis
Nigel Robson
Graeme Matheson-
 Bruce
c: Nicholas
 Braithwaite

1979
Mozart
Mitridate,
Rè di Ponto
Camden Festival/
BBC Radio 3
Cost: £3239
Philip Langridge
Marie Slorach
Susan Kessler
Felicity Lott
Ann Murray
Felicity Palmer
(replacing Caroline
 Friend)
Anthony Roden
c: Gyorgy Fischer

Double bill
Park Lane Opera
Cost: £24,864
Delius *Fennimore*
and Gerda
Rosalind Plowright
Christopher
 Booth-Jones
Justin Lavender
Gerard Delrez
Karen Stone
Catherine Benson
Adrian Thompson
Tim Yealland
Shirley Mason
Delith Brook
Joy Puritz
Janis Kelly
Peter Savidge

Stravinsky *Mavra*
Penelope Mackay
Ian Caley
Noreen Berry
Sarah Walker
c: Michael
 Lankester
p: David Williams
des: Annena
 Stubbs

Dvorak
The Jacobin
Chelsea Opera
 Group
Anthony Ransome
Ann-Marie Connors
Roger Bryson
Graeme Matheson-
 Bruce
Marie McLaughlin
Keith Lewis
Jacek Strauss
Roderick Earle
Prue Roper
c: Stephen Barlow

Paisiello/Henze
Don Quixote
Phoenix Opera
Cost: £19,000
Kenneth Bowen
Alan Opie
Alison Hargan
Johanna Peters
Geoffrey Pogson
Alan Watt
Kate Flowers
Rae Woodland
c: Jan Latham-
 Koenig
p: Tom Hawkes
des: Ralph Koltai/
 Annena Stubbs

1980
Nino Rota
The Italian
Straw Hat
The New Opera
 Company
Cost £26,256
Edward Byles
Terry Jenkins,
Stuart Kale
Malcolm Rivers
Anne Pashley,
Michael Follis
Sandra Dugdale
Julia Parker
Terry Jenkins
Anne Collins
Michael White
Paul Hudson
Ray Scally
Michael Fitchew
c: James Judd
p: Anthony Besch
des: Peter Rice

Grétry
Zemire and Azor
Phoenix Opera
Cost £25,000
Kate Flowers
Phyllis Cannan
Clare Watson
Bernard Dickerson
Richard Jackson
Ian Caley
c: Roderick Brydon
p: Anthony Besch
des: Peter Rice

Tchaikovsky
Mazeppa
Chelsea Opera Group
Eileen Hannan
Graham Clark
Michael Lewis
Willard White
Patricia Price
Edmund Barham
Rudolph Piernay
Hugh Hetherington
c: Mark Elder

1981
The Ricci brothers
Crispino
e la Comare
Phoenix Opera
Cost £28,849
Lynda Russell
Johanna Peters
Gordon Sandison
Michael Rippon
Donald Maxwell
Harry Coghill
Bonaventura
 Bottone
Delith Brook
Peter Robinson
c: James Judd
p: Tom Hawkes
d: Reginald
 Woolley/ Paul
 Hernon

Cimarosa
Gli Orazi
ed I Curiazi
Opera Rara
Cost £20,463
Nan Christie
Diana Montague
Sandra Dugdale
Patricia Cope
Kenneth Bowen
Eric Roberts
Paul Hudson
c: David Parry
p: Stephen Lawless
des: Steven
 Gregory

Sacchini
Renaud
Camden Festival/
BBC Radio 3
Cost £2864
Felicity Palmer
Yvonne Kenny
Richard Jackson
Anthony Roden
Michael Lewis
Marie Slorach
Patricia Conti
Julian Pike
Hugh Hetherington
Malcolm Arthur
Caroline Friend
Rosamund Illing
c: Richard Hickox

Puccini
Manon Lescaut
Chelsea Opera
 Group
Janice Cairns
Linda Strachan
Robert Dean
Laurence Dale
Tom McDonnell
Lanceford Roberts
Roger Carpenter
Hugh Hetherington
Simon Bainbridge
Keith Lockyer
c: Howard Williams

1982
Donizetti
Francesca di Foix;
La Romanziera
Opera Rara
Cost £27,500
Dinah Harris
Della Jones
Gillian Sullivan
Nuala Willis
Gordon Christie
John Hall
Kevin John
Donald Maxwell
Russell Smythe
Kevin West
c: David Parry
p: Sally Day
des: Steven
 Gregory

J C Bach
Adriano in Siria
Camden Festival/
Radio 3
(concert perf.)
Cost £3780
Maureen Lehane
(replaced Anne
 Murray)
Ryland Davies
Margaret Cable
Marie Slorach
Alan Woodrow
Eiddwen Harrhy
Marilyn Hill-Smith
c: Sir Charles
 MacKerras

Walton
Troilus and
Cressida
Chelsea Opera Group
Richard Angus
Charles Naylor
David Hillman
Bernard Dickerson
Jean Bailey
Linda Ormiston
Stephen
 Rhys-Williams
Christopher
 Booth-Jones
c: Roderick Brydon

Appendix 2 continued

c, conductor; p, producer (term used until c.1986); d = director; des = designer

Cavalli
Eritrea
Phoenix Opera
Sandra Browne
Sally Burgess
Ann Mackay
Linda Ormiston
Johanna Peters
James Bowman
John Michael
  Flanagan
Richard Jackson
Paul Parfitt
Christopher
  Robson
Adrian Thompson
c: Jane Glover
p: Tom Hawkes
des: Terence Emery

Barber
Antony and Cleopatra
Abbey Opera
(concert perf.)
Cost £750
David Wilson-
  Johnson
Alexander Gauld
Susan Bingeman
Donald Stephenson
Barnaby Mason
Sebastian Loew
Myrna Moreno
Maureen Lefevre
Christopher
  Bayston
Giles Dawson
Nicholas Greenbury
David Barrell
John Flower
c: Antony Shelley

1983
Wolf-Ferrari
The School for Fathers
Phoenix Opera
Yvonne Egan
Johanna Peters
William McCue
Laurence Richard
Ava June
Christine Bunning
Harry Nicol
Eric Shilling
Catherine Wilson
John Ayldon
Bernard Dickerson
c: Hilary Griffiths
p: Tom Hawkes
des: Terence Emery/
  Neville Currier

Pacini
Maria Tudor
Opera Rara
Penelope Walker
Marilyn Hill Smith
Christopher Blades
Keith Lewis
Timothy Oldroyd
Phillip O'Reilly
Assen Vassilev
c: David Parry
p: Nicholas Hytner
des: Robin Don/
  Paul Pyant

Stravinsky
Oedipus Rex
McCabe
Notturni ed Alba
Abbey Opera
(concert perf.)
Alberto Remedlos
Angela Hickey
Philip O'Reilly
Gerard Delrez
Christopher Gillett
David Barrell
Maurice Denham
  (narrator)
Philippa Dames-
  Longworth
c: Antony Shelley

Britten
Gloriana
Chelsea Opera
  Group
Geoffrey Dolton
Ian Caley
Robert Dean
Lois McDonall
Tom McDonnell
Henry Herford
John Dilhorne
David Fieldsend
Helen Walker
Jean Rigby
Eileen Hulse
Mark Richardson
Anna Steiger
c: Nicholas
  Cleobury

1984
Vivaldi
Juditha Triumphans
London Music
  Theatre Group
Cost £19,122
Robin Martin-Oliver
Helen Kucharek
Jean Bailey
Karen Shelby
Timothy Wilson
c: Timothy Dean
p/des: Paul Hernon

Lecocq
Doctor Miracle
Delius
Margot la Rouge
Park Lane Opera
Cost £37,005
Jill Washington
Nuala Willis
Adrian Thompson
John Ayldon
Stephen
  Richardson
Janine Roebuck
Maria Moll
Martin McEvoy
Stephen Rhys-
  Williams
Alan Watt
Fiona Dobie
Hilary Thomas
Jane Findlay
Anne Mason
Kim Begley
Keith Latham
Robert Dean
Rodney Macann
c: Clive Timms
p: Robert Carsen
des: Johan Engels/
  Tim Ball

Cilea
Adriana Lecouvreur
Abbey Opera
(concert perf.)
Alexander Gauld
Julia Dewhurst
Jennifer Higgins
Robert Bishop
Peter James
  Robinson
Gerard Delrez
Sebastian Loew
Amanda Thane
Warwick Dyer
Angela Hickey
c: Antony Shelley

Shostakovich
Lady Macbeth of Mtsensk
Chelsea Opera
  Group
Christine Bunning
Phyllis Cannan
Anne Conoley
Anne-Marie Owens
John Gibbs
Martyn Hill
John Milne
Donald Stephenson
Paul Wilson
Brian Bannatyne-
  Scott
Tom McDonnell
Roger Bryson
c: Howard Williams

1985
Caccini
L'Euridice
New London
  Consort
(concert perf.)
Cost £3900
Catherine Bott
Tessa Bonner
Lynne Dawson
Christopher
  Robson
Mark Tucker
Andrew King
Richard Lloyd
  Morgan
Gordon Jones
c: Phillip Picket/
  David Roblou

Boito
Nerone
Abbey Opera
(concert perf.)
Cost £6428
Alexander Gauld
Alastair Miles
Donald Pilley
Elizabeth Byrne
Sirry Ella Magnus
Louis Berkman
Patrick McCarthy
Mark Hoffman
Helen Watkins
Maureen LeFevre
c: Antony Shelley

Mozart
La Finta Semplice
Park Lane Opera
Cost £35,930
Glen Winslade
Phillip Guy-Bromley
Harry Nicoll,
Verona James
Janis Kelly
Hugh Mackey
c: Nicholas
  Cleobury
p: Robert Carsen
des: Richard
  Bullwinkle/Chris
  Cowell/Paul Pyant

Richard Strauss
Friedenstag
Chelsea Opera
  Group
Cost £3000
Marie Hayward
  Segal
Anna Steiger
Richard Angas
Donald Stephenson
John Treleaven
Steven Page
John Milne
Roger Bryson
Nigel Cliffe
Florian Cerny
c: Nicholas
  Cleobury

Appendix 2 continued

c, conductor; p, producer (term used until c.1986); d = director; des = designer

1986
Kurt Weill double bill
Abbey Opera
Cost £14,938
The Protagonist
Laurie Reed
Nigel Robson
Elizabeth Byrne
Martin Nelson
Leon Berger
Joy Robinson
John Morgan
David Skewes
The Czar has his photograph taken
Kathleen Summers
Adrian Scott
Elaine Padmore
Howard Milner
Stephanie Kulesza
Anthony Caplan
Helen Kucharek
Philip O'Reilly
Stephen Holloway
Arthur Coomber
Rodney Gibson
c: Antony Shelley
d: John Eaton
des: Lez Brotherston

Barker/Hawkins double bill
Modern Music Theatre Troupe
Paul Barker
Phantastes
John Oakley Tucker
Christine Barker
Robyna Houldsworth
Lucinda Broadbridge
Charles Kerry
Timothy Evans-Jones
Richard Hawkins
Other Voices
Sian Woodling
John Upperton
James Meek
c: Christopher Willis
d: Christopher Newell
des: Penny Brown

Mozart
La Finta Giardiniera
Park Lane Opera
Cost £40,998
Alison Hagley
Adrian Thompson
Glen Winslade
Louise Winter
Anne Mason
Janis Kelly
John Cashmore
c: Nicholas Cleobury
p: Robert Carsen
des: Paul Dart

Rimsky-Korsakov
The Snow Maiden
Chelsea Opera Group
Cost £3300
Jean Bailey
Anne Dawson
Eiddwen Harrhy
Fiona Kimm
Carole Rosen
Brian Bannatyne-Scott
Terry Jenkins
Justin Lavender
c: Howard Williams

1987
Kurt Weill
Silverlake
Abbey Opera
Cost £30,000
Christina Collier
Meriel Dickinson
Kate Flowers
Margaret Perry
Nigel Robson
Michael Heath
Johnny Worthy
Roger Bryson
c: Antony Shelley
d: John Eaton
des: Lez Brotherston/ John Waterhouse

Britten
Church Parables, Curlew River, The Prodigal Son
Volte Face
David Aldred
Christopher Blades
Simon Masterton-Smith
Robert Greenhill
Paul Parfitt
James Rainbird
musical d: Peter Crockford
p: Philippe Piffault, Antoine Fontaine

Kurt Weill
Happy End
St Donat's Music Theatre
Eric Roberts
Richard Morris
Johnny Worthy
Derek Barnes
Brendon Charleson
Diana Judd
Lisa Opie
Alison Truefitt
Kelvin Thomas
Rosamund Shelley
Amanda Douglas
Simon Baxter
c: Wyn Davies
d: Mike Ashman
des: Simon Banham, John Bishop

Robert Ashley
Atalanta (Acts of God)
Camden Festival/ Serious Productions
Cost £47,000 approx
Robert Ashley
Sam Ashley
Thomas Buckner
Jacqueline Humbert
d+des: Lawrence Lemak Brickman
Music d: 'Blue' Gene Tyranny
Sound des: Paul Schorr

Appendix 3 Musicians and dancers performing in the Festivals

Orchestras
Band of the Grenadier Guards
Bournemouth Symphony Orchestra
Camden Festival Orchestra/ Orchestra of St John's Smith Square
Chanticleer Orchestra
Hungarian State Symphony Orchestra
The Kensington Symphony Orchestra
London Bach Orchestra
London Philharmonic Orchestra
London Symphony Orchestra
London Mozart Players
Modern Symphony Orchestra
New Philharmonia Orchestra
Philomusica of London
Polyphonia Symphony Orchestra
Riddick Orchestra
Royal Philharmonic Orchestra
Schoenberg Symphony Orchestra
West Hampstead Symphony Orchestra

Chamber Orchestras
Ben Uri Orchestra
Camden Chamber Orchestra
Chamber Music Players of London
Divertimenti
English Chamber Orchestra
Morley College Chamber Orchestra
London Sinfonietta
Thames Chamber Orchestra

Orchestras amateur/ student
Crowndale Symphony Orchestra
ILEA Camden Schools Orchestra
Young Musicians Symphony Orchestra

Ensembles
Academy of Ancient Music
The Art of Minstralsye
Aeolian String Quartet
Alberni Quartet
Allegri String Quartet
Amadeus String Quartet
Amati Ensemble
The Amici String Quartet
Amphion String Quartet
Ars Antiqua di Milano
Ars Nova
Athena Ensemble
Austrian Woodwind Quintet
Bartok String Quartet
Camden Wind Quintet
Chilingirian String Quartet
The City Waites Circle
The Cohen Trio
Concentus Musicus of Denmark
Coull String Quartet
Dartington String Quartet
Debussy Trio
Delmé String Quartet
Dolmetsch Ensemble
Dreamtiger
Early Music Consort
Endymion Ensemble
Fitzwilliam String Quartet
Florilegium
Francis Chagrin Ensemble
Francis Ensemble
Gabrieli Ensemble/Consort
Gabrieli String Quartet
Georgian String quartet
Guildhall New Music Ensemble
Hampstead Wind Ensemble
Heutling String Quartet
Huggett-Cunningham-Woolley Trio
Jaye Consort
Landini Consort
La Salle String Quartet
London Brass Ensemble
London Brass Virtuosi
London Contemporary Chamber Players
London Gabrieli Brass Ensemble
London Pro Musica
London Ripieno Society
London Saxophone Quartet
London Soloists Ensemble
London Wind Soloists
Manson Ensemble of the Royal Academy of Music
Martin Best Consort
Matrix Ensemble
Macnaughten Quartet
Medici Quartet
Musica Antica e Nuova
Musica Nova of Stockholm
Music Projects London
Musica Reservata
Nash Ensemble
New London Consort
New London Ensemble
New London Wind Ensemble
New Music Group of the Guildhall School of Music
New Piano Quartet
New Viennna String Quartet
Omega Guitar Quartet
Orion Piano Trio
Orpheus Trio
Paganini Trio
Park Lane Ensemble
Peasants All
Pierrot Players
Purcell Quartet
Redcliffe Ensemble
Redcliffe Percussion Ensemble
The Sheba Sound
Stockholm Philharmonic Wind Quintet
Tatrai String Quartet
Tel-Aviv String Quartet
Twentieth Century Ensemble of the Royal College of Music
The Vesuvius Ensemble
Westminster Baroque Ensemble
Wind Music Society

Organisations
Youth and Music
Macnaughten Concerts
Park Lane Group
Society for the Promotion of New Music
Music in our Time
The Electro-Acoustic Music Association

Choirs
Ambrosian Singers
Board of Trade Choir 1960
Camden Choir
Camden Chamber Choir
The Chancery Singers
City of London Choir
Collegium Musicum of London
Dowland Chamber Choir
Finchley Choral Society
Finnish Radio Chamber Choir
Glasgow Phoenix Choir
Goldsmiths' College Choir
Hampstead Choral Society
Highgate Choral Society
Ickenham Male Voice Choir
Kensington Choir
London Bach Society
London Welsh Choir
London Welsh Male Voice Choir
London Oratory Choir
New London Singers
Mary Ward Cantata Choir
Morley College Choir
Orpington Junior Singers
Polish Chopin Choir
Scuola di Chiesa
Saltarello Choir
Stevenage Male Voice Choir
St Pancras Municipal Choir
St Pancras Vocal Ensemble
William Byrd Choir
Zemel Choir

Appendix 3 continued

Prize Winners' Concerts

1968
Donna-Faye Carr *soprano*
Patricia Purcell *mezzo*
William Elvin *baritone*
Thomas Allen *baritone*
Nerine Barrett *piano*

1969
Gwyneth Griffiths *soprano*
Christian Blackshaw *piano*
Laureen Livingstone *soprano*
Delia Wallis *mezzo*
Donald McVay *viola*
William Elvin *baritone*
Thomas Allen *baritone*
Nerine Barrett *piano*

1970
Imogen Cooper *piano*
Chilingirian-Benson Duo *violin/piano*
Brian Rayner Cook *baritone*
Nan Christie *soprano*
Paul Hudson *bass*

1971
Abigail Ryan *soprano*
Wendy Pashley *soprano*
Stuart Kale *tenor*
Felicity Palmer *soprano*

1972
Mitsuko Uchida *piano*
Stoika Milanova *violin*

Conductors
Harald Andersen
Richard Arnell
Malcolm Arnold
Moshe Atzmon
Alan Barlow
Steuart Bedford
Walter Bergman
Richard Bernas
James Blair
Harry Blech
Richard Bradshaw
Igor Buketoff
John Carewe
Donald Cashmore
Francis Chagrin
Dudley Cohen
Geoffrey Corbett
Ronald Corp
Colin Davis
Arthur Davidson
Edward Downes
Norman del Mar
Arthur Dennington
Bryan Fairfax
Sydney Fixman
Louis Frémaux
Ruth Gipps
Richard Gonski
Charles Groves
Vernon Handley
Geoffrey Hanson
Leslie Head
Laszlo Heltay
John Hoban
Elgar Howarth
Joseph Horovitz
George Hurst
Emanuel Hurwitz
Granville Jones
Rudolf Kempe
Nicholas Kraemer
Peter Lea Cox
Henry Lewis
David Littaur
James Loughran
John Lubbock
Charles Mackerras
Geoffrey Mitchell
Peter Mooney
David Munrow
Gyula Nemeth
Roger Norrington
Philip Pickett
John Pritchard
Simon Rattle
Hugo Rignold
Douglass Robinson
Gregory Rose
Martindale Sidwell
Paul Schmitz
Paul Steinitz
Gunnar Staern
Walter Susskind
Vilem Tausky
Graham Treacher
Julian Williamson
Barry Wordsworth
Brian Wright

Composers
Malcolm Williamson
Joseph Horovitz
Olivier Messiaen
Thea Musgrave
Malcolm Arnold
Nicholas Maw
Donald Swan

Pianists
Daniel Adni
Vladimir Ashkenazy
Nerine Barrett
Terence Beckles
Clifford Benson
Malcolm Binns
Susan Bradshaw
Benjamin Britten
Cornelius Cardew
Patricia Carroll
Nigel Cave
Phillip Challis
Shura Cherkassky
June Clark
John Constable
Nigel Coxe
Peter Croser
Christine Croshaw
Ivan Davis
Janette de Roet
Peter Element
Norma Fisher
Andar Foldes
Rhondda Gillespie
Alasdair Graham
Leslie Howard
Daphne Ibbott
Alexander Jenner
Graham Johnson
Peter Katin
Maria Kalogridou
Courtney Kenny
Stephen Kovacevich
Philip Levi
Harmon Lewis
Iris Loveridge
Moura Lympany
Hephzibah Menuhin
Dennis Matthews
Nina Milkina
Geoffrey Parsons
Peter Pettinger
Anthea Rael
Joan Ryall
Pnina Salzman
Craig Shepherd
Robert Sherlaw Johnson
Howard Shelley
Yonty Solomon
Kathryn Stott
Robert Sutherland
John Tilbury
Janis Vakarelis
Hazel Vivienne
Vronsky and Babin
Katharina Wolpe

Organists
Michael Austin
Jennifer Bate
Steuart Bedford
John Birch
Christopher Bowers-Broadbent
Daniel Chorzempa
John Constable
Nicholas Danby
Andrew Davis
Ralph Downes
Roger Firman
Christopher Herrick
Bedrich Janacek
Nicolas Kynaston
Susan Landale
Andre Marchal
John Morehen
Martin Neary
Simon Preston
Arnold Richardson
Barry Rose
Brian Runnett
David Sanger
Betty Stewart
Knud Vad
Gillian Weir
Karl-Erik Welin
Malcolm Williamson

Fortepiano
Virginia Pleasants

Violinists
Alfredo Campoli
Raymond Cohen
Anthony Howard
Ernst Kovacic
Manoug Parikian
Tessa Robbins
Sylvia Rosenberg

Guitar and Lute
Gilbert Biberian
Julian Bream
Desmond Dupré
Guitar Spectrum
Cy Grant
Charles Gregory
Philip John Lee
London Lute Ensemble
Ingolf Olsen
Paco Peña
Anthony Rooley
Turibio Santos
Segovia
Stephen Stubbs
James Tyler
Tim Walker
John Williams

Harpsichord
Valda Aveling
George Malcolm
Francis Monkman
Margaret Murray
Joseph Payne
Raphael Puyana
Lionel Salter
Viola Tunnard
Christopher Wood

Harp
Daphne Boden
Susan Drake
Osian Ellis
David Watkins
Sioned Williams

Appendix 3 continued

Percussion
Eric Allen
Patricia Brady
Tristran Fry
James Holland

Clarinet
Jack Brymer
Christopher Gradwell
Janet Hilton

Oboe
Evelyn Barbirolli
Neil Black
Leon Goossens

Harmonica
Larry Adler
Tommy Reilly

Trumpet
Denis Clift
Phillip Jones
John Wilbraham

Other wind instruments
Roger Bobo *tuba*
Martin Gatt *bassoon*
Ian Harper *horn*
Christopher Taylor *sopranino*
Denis Wick *trombone*

Cellists/double bass
Robert Cohen
Jacqueline du Pré
Olga Hegedus
Garry Karr

Vocal groups
Gothic Voices
Iverson Ensemble
The Parlour Quartet
King's Singers
The Scholars
Singers of London

Sopranos
Victoria de los Angeles
Norma Burrowes
Tracey Chadwell
Ann Dowdall
Barbara Elsy
Jill Gomez
Elizabeth Harwood
Linda Hirst
Lynne Hirst
Rita Hunter
Elizabeth Lane
Jane Manning
Morag Noble
Deirdre Pleydell
Eileen Poulter
Elisabeth Schwarzkopf
Irmgard Seefried
Elizabeth Simon
Rita Streich
Taru Valjakka
Penelope Walker

Mezzos/Contraltos
Janet Baker
Rachel Cooper
Ameral Gunson
Alfreda Hodgson
Anne Howells
Kerstin Meyer
Sybil Michelow
Jantina Noorman
Norma Proctor
Ethna Robinson

Tenors
Wilfred Brown
Edward Darling
Gerald English
Peter Hall
Gordon Honey
Peter Pears
Richard Johnston
David Johnston
Neil Mackenzie
John Mitchinson
Ronald Murdock
Andrew Murgatroyd
Ian Partridge
Duncan Robertson
Anthony Rolfe Johnson
Robert Tear
Robert Thomas
Philip Talfryn

Baritones/basses
Hervey Allen
Maurice Bevan
John Carol Case
Trevor Craddock
Bryan Drake
Dennis Dowling
Robert Hayward
Paul Hillier
Christopher Keyte
Matti Lehtinen
Marian Novakowski
John Shirley Quirk
Roger Stalman
Richard Suart
Stephen Roberts
David Wilson-Johnson

Countertenors
Charles Brett
Alfred Deller
Mark Deller
Paul Esswood

Dance companies
Astrakhan
Ballet Rambert
Contemporary Dance Experimental Group
Dance Umbrella
Dance for Everyone
Extemporary Dance Group
Festival Ballet
Green Candle Dance Company
Junction Dance Company
Contemporary Dance Trust
London Contemporary Dance Group
London Contemporary Dance Theatre
Lyra Ventura
Robert North and Dancers
Second Stride Dance Company
Janet Smith & Dancers
Sun Sum
Travelling Music Theatre
Contemporary Dance of Winnipeg
Welsh Dance Theatre

Dancers
Doreen Wells
Alexander Bennett
Kim Brandstrup
Terry Gilbert
Felicity Gray
Pamela Hart
Michael Hogan
Per Jonsson
Michael Kane
Kathryn Posin
Robert North
Selina Wylie

Appendix 4 Jazz, folk music and pop

**JAZZ
1954–1976**
Ken Baldock
Chris Barber
 and his band
Freddie Brinklow
 and his band
George Chisholm
 and the Gentlemen
 of Jazz
Graham Collier Sextet
John Dankworth
Michael Garrick
 Quintet
Joe Harriott
Laurie Holloway
Shake Keane
Tony Kinsey
Cleo Laine
Bobby Lamb
London Jazz
 Composer's Orchestra
Humphrey Lyttelton
 and his band
Marian Montgomery
National Youth Jazz
 Orchestra
New Jazz Orchestra
Buxton Orr
Ottilie Patterson
Ray Premru Orchestra
Rendell/Carr Quintet
Ron Rubin Quartet
Danny Thompson Trio
Stan Tracey Quartet
Mike Westbrook Jazz
 Band

**Jazz Weeks in the
Festival 1976–1987**
Muhal Richard Abrams
 Quartet
George Adams/Don
 Pullen Quartet
African Group
Art Ensemble of
 Chicago
Assum and
 Magnificent Force
Julian Bahula's Jazz
 Africa
Chet Baker
Gordon Beck

Art Blakey's Jazz
 Messengers
Carla Bley Sextet
Lester Bowie
Fontella & Martha Bass
The Breakfast Band
The Brighton Gang
Willem Breuker
 Kollektief
Rainer Bruninghaus
Gavin Bryars
Ian Carr's Nucleus
Ian Carr's Fusion Band
Ron Carter Quartet
Cayenne
Tommy Chase Quartet
John Chilton's
 Feetwarmers
Arnett Cobb
Billy Cobham's Glass
 Menagerie
Ornette Coleman
 and Primetime
Graham Collier
Larry Coryell Group
Lol Coxhill/Gerry
 FitzGerald duo
Crouch End All Stars
Ted Curson
Eddie Lockjaw Davis
The Decoding Society
District Six
Martin Drew Band
Dwarf Steps
Gil Evans Orchestra
John Etheridge –
 Ric Sanders Group
Farneji Warriors
Joe Farrell/Woody
 Shaw Quintet
Bud Freeman
Gailforce
Slim Gaillard
Michael Garrick
Mike Gibbs Orchestra
Dexter Gordon
Johnny Griffin Quintet
Barry Guy
Charlie Haden
Billy Harper Quintet
Beaver Harris French
 Horn Connection
Hi–Life International

Alan Holdsworth
Fred Hopkins
Freddie Hubbard
 Quintet
Chris Hunter Band
Ken Hyder's Big team
Abdullah Ibrahim/Max
 Roach Duo
Inversions
Jabula
Clifford Jarvis
Ronald Shannon
 Jackson
Jazz Defektors
Hugh John
Elvin Jones and the
 Jazz Machine
Duke Jordan
Melba Liston
London Jazz
 Composer's Orchestra
London Women's Big
 Band
Loose Tubes
Chris MacGregor's
 Bluenotes
Steve McCall
Dave Macrae's Current
 Event
John McCullough
Dianne McIntyre
Albert Mangelsdorf
 Quartet with SME
Charlie Mariano
John Marshall
George Melly
Midnite Follies
 Orchestra
Monk and More
Marian Montgomery
Alphonse Mouzon
Musicworks Choir
Amina Claudine Myers
 Trio
New Music Orchestra
James Newton & Strings
Keith Nichols
NicRa Quintet
Sal Nistico
Evan Parker/Orchestra
 of Lights
Hermeto Pascoal
 Group

David Peaston
John Picard Band
Courtney Pine
Dudu Pukwana's Zila
Enrico Rava Quintet
Danny Richmond
Howard Riley
Otis Rush
SOH (Alan Skidmore,
 Tony Oxley, Ali
 Haurand)
Wayne Shorter Quintet
El Sonido de Londras
Louis Stewart Trio
Steps Ahead
Sunwind
Bryan Spring Quartet
John Steven's Folkus
The Slickaphonics
Ian Stewart
John Surman Quartet
Buddy Tate
Cecil Taylor Unit
John Taylor Trio
Clark Terry Big Band
Gail Thompson's
 Approach
Henry Threadgill
Keith Tippett Duo /
 ARK
Stan Tracey
The Timeless All Stars
McCoy Tyner
Nana Vasconcelos
Bennie Wallace Trio
Bobby Watson
Charlie Watts
Trevor Watts Moiré
 Music
Randy Weston
Eberhard Weber's
 Colours
Bobby Wellins Quartet
Don Weller
Bob Wilber
Steve Williamson
 Quartet
Joe Lee Wilson with
 Peter Burden
Stinky Winkles Quintet
Working Week
World Saxophone
 Quartet

**Greater London
Arts Association
Young Jazz Musicians
of the Year 1978**
Lawrence Dundass
Brendan O'Neill
John Sanderson

**Jazz Band Ball
1976–85**
Humphrey Lyttelton
 and his band
The Crouch End
 All Stars
Wally Fawkes
Kathy Stobart
Bruce Turner
George Melly
John Chilton's
 Feetwarmers
Sheila Collier
Midnite Follies
 Orchestra
Victor Silvester
 Orchestra

**FOLK MUSIC
1954–1979**
Cecil Sharp House
Ram Gopal
Patrick Shuldham-Shaw
Nan Fleming-Williams
Bryan Fleming-Williams
Jean Forsyth
Elton Hayes
Victoria Kingsley
Bob Roberts
Pat Shaw
Nan & Brian
 Flemming-Williams
Denis Smith
Steve Benbow
Folk Four
Nadia Cattouse
John Foreman
Sydney Carter
Stan Kelly
The Seafarers
Joy Hyman
The Countryside
 Players
Maria Farandouri
Manesh Chandra (sitar)

Appendix 4 continued

INTERNATIONAL MUSIC & DANCE 1979–1987

Africa

Gambia
Dembo Konte
Malamini Jobarteh
The Kora and Mandinka Society
Ghana
Aklowa, Kabbala
Zaire
Les Quatre Étoiles
Tshala Muana

EUROPE

England
Maddy Prior Band
Mike Chapman
Greenwood Morris Men
The Albion Band
Bob Copper (Sussex)
Sam Sherry (Lancashire clog dancer)
Kathryn Tickell (Northumbrian piper and fiddle player)
John Kirkpatrick, melodeon
Martin Long
Adrian May
Colin Reece
Simon Rosser
Albion Morris
Greece
Andreas Markides Bouzouki Band
Theodorakis
Haroutune Bedelian
Maria Farandouri
Yannis Glezos
Mariza Koch
Yannis Makropoulos
Christos Pittas
St Andrews Greek Dancers
St Sophia Cathedral Choir

Hungary
Robert Mandel
East European Folk
Ireland
Bothy Band
Gasra na nGael
Jimmy Crowley
Mary O'Hara
John Faulkner
Dolores Keane
Terry Bowler Dancers
De Danan
Christy Moore
Scoraiocht
The Wild Geese
Lois Stewart and Band
Davy Spillane Band
Poland
Mazury folk dance and song
Portugal
Rao Kiao
Romania
Marama Music and Dance Ensemble
Spain
Paco Peña
Mari Carmen Ledesma
Paco Piñon
Los del Campo

THE AMERICAS

Afro-Caribbean
Alex Pascall
Eclipse
Grenada Shortney
The Henry Sisters
Volcanic Eruption
Deirdre Pascall
Odele Prince
Russ Henderson Steel Band
Sarah Cowrah
Ekome
Dagarti
Talisman
Orchestra Jazira
Bolivia
Los Awatinas
Ecuador
Peguche Band
Martinique
Ballet Martiniquais
Peru
Martina Portocarrero
South America
Los Olimarenos
Mayapi
Achalay
Daniel Viglietti
Carmen Maldonado Pueblo
Cesar Isell
USA
Sweet Honey in the Rock
Women of the Calabash a
West Indies /Caribbean
Bible Way Tabernacle Youth Orchestra
Groovers Steel
Clint Eastwood
General Saint Abacush Reggae Orchestra
Legba Singers and Dancers
Steel an' Skin

MIDDLE EAST & ASIA

China
The Guo Brothers
Jing Ying Soloists
Nancy Kuo
Li Wen
Lu Zhaoli
Moon Goddess
Cyprus
The Barnet Cypriot Dance Group,
London Turkish Theatre Folk Dancing Group
Group Diomedes Komnenos
Lefkosiatiki Kompania
Egypt
Les Musiciens du Nil
India
Hariprasad Chaurasia
Punita Gupta
Imrat Khan
India Music
Kathak Dance Ballet Company
Zakir Hussain Khan
Ashish Khan
Dhyanesh Khan
Birju Maharaj
Rita Mehta
Rajasthan Folk Theatre
Surnai
Esmail Sheik
Shiv Kumar Sharma
Israel
Zemel Choir
Oranim Israeli Dance Troupe
Japan
Demon Drummers of Sado
Java
Sasono Mulio Dance Company
Korea
Samulnori

POPULAR ENTERTAINERS

Abacush
Aba Daba Music Hall
Screaming Abdabs
Lord Eric's Agor MMBA
Kathy Acker and Gasrattle
Kurtis Blow
Brighton Zap Club
Chuck Brown and the Soul Searchers
Chloe and Wilma
Dirty Money
Echo City
Far 1 Upsetter Militant Rockers
Doug E Fresh and the Get Fresh Crew
Will Gaines, tap dancer and musicians
Benny Green
Jeremy Hardy
Hip Hop Alliance
Red herring Installation
Kassav
Kiosk Video
Alan Jay Lerner
Little Green Hondas
Lumière and Son in Panic
Shirley and Tony Menary
Ova
Pennywood
Players Theatre Company
Jacey Prince of Limbo
Elise Ross
Salt and Pepper
Ian Smith
Dougie Squires
Second Generation
Elaine Strich
Ra Ra Zoo

Appendix 5 Drama groups, plays, actors, players and writers

AMATEUR DRAMATIC SOCIETIES
Alexandra Repertory Company
Birkbeck Players
Conservative Amateur Dramatic Society of Holborn and St Pancras South
Coram Drama Guild
Court Drama Guild/Group
Camden Mission Dramatic Society
Festival Players
The Green Circle
Goldsmith & Haverstope Players
Holiday Players
Holly Lodge Dramatic Society
London University Drama Society
Maurice Hall Players
Mary Ward Players
Murray's Goode Companions
National Cash Register Dramatic Society
Parlysians Dramatic Society
Portland-Bradfield Players
Progressive Players
Shakespeare Festival Players
S K Amateur Players
Tavistock Repertory Company

Unity Theatre 1955–1972
Euripides *The Women of Troy*
Margaret Shaw *Mind the Baby*
Arthur Miller *The Crucible*
Sholom Aleichem *The big win*

Maxim Gorky *The Lower Depths*
Brecht *The Good Woman of Szechwan*
Raymond Cross (devised) *Burlesque, the original Bowery Show*

AMATEUR OPERATIC SOCIETIES
Baltic Operatic Society
Glebe Operatic Society
London University Opera Group

PROFESSIONAL COMPANIES

Hampstead Theatre 1965–1972
Euripides *Hippolytus*
Dylan Thomas *Adventures in the Skin Trade*
Patrick Garland *The Rebel*
John Bowen *Little Boxes*
John Hale *The Black Swan Winter*
Tom Jones & Harvey Schmidt *The Fantasticks*
W Gordon Smith *Vincent*
Raisins & Almonds (late night revue)
Nicholas Salaman *Mad Dog*

Open Space Theatre
Howard Brenton *How Beautiful with Badges*

International Theatre Company
Pirandello *Think it over, Giacomino*

London Traverse Company
Sandro Key-Aberg *Oh!*

Soho Theatre
John Grillo *Blubber*

In-Stage
William Saroyan *The Cave Dwellers*

RADA 1955–1961
Charles Morgan *The River Line*
Allan R Kenward *Cry Havoc*
G B Shaw *Candida*
G B Shaw *Heartbreak House*
Oscar Wilde *An Ideal Husband*
G B Shaw *Major Barbara*

Greek Arts Theatre Club
Aeschylus *Prometheus Unbound*

Round House Trust
Bettina Jonic & Charles Robinson *The Wheel*

Theatre Group Productions
Peter Albery *Anne Boleyn*

Centre Stage
Muriel Spark *The Ballad of Peckham Rye*

'Clap' Music Theatre Ensemble

Toucan Theatre Company

ACTORS
Peggy Ashcroft
Jill Balcon
Martin Browne
Greta Burke
John Carroll
Lewis Casson
Constance Cummings
Judy Dench
Richard Denning
Robert Eddison
Edith Evans
Marius Goring
Joan Greenwood
Christopher Hassall
David Hemmings
Michael Hordern
Barbara Jefford
Esmond Knight
John Laurie
Barbara Leigh Hunt
Cyril Luckham
Margery Mason
André Morell
Robert Morris
Stephen Murray
Siân Phillips
Guy Kingsley Poynter
Margaret Rawlings
Robert Rietti
Victor Rietti
Margaret Rutherford
George Rylands
Margareta Scott
Rosalind Shanks
David Spenser
William Squire
John Stuart
Eric Thompson
Sybil Thorndike
Sam Wanamaker
Gwen Watford
John Westbrook
Michael Williams
Donald Wolfit
Margaret Wolfit
Gabriel Woolf

GROUPS
Ambit
Apollo Society
The Barrow Poets
The Company of Nine
Highgate Poetry Circle
St Pancras Poets

POETS AND WRITERS
Dannie Abse
John Agard
J G Ballard
Martin Bax
Thomas Blackburn
Edwin Brock
Tony Connor
Gavin Ewart
Francis Fytton
Grace Hallworth
Douglas Hill
Anselm Hollo
Laurie Lee
Christopher Logue
George MacBeth
Tom McGrath
Jack Marriott
Eric Mathieson
Spike Milligan
Adrian Mitchell
Grace Nichols
Peter Porter
John Pudney
Jeremy Robson
Michael Rosen
Vernon Scannell
John Smith
Stevie Smith
Robert Sward
John Wain

Appendix 6 # Exhibitions and lectures

Exhibitions
Looking at London 1954
Creative Recreation 1955
Drama in Education 1957
Lost Theatres of St Pancras 1958
Jubilee Exhibition, English Folk Song
  and Dance Society 1961
Swedish Design 1962
The Artist at Work 1966
Exhibition of Finnish Books 1967
Helsinki, Capital of Finland 1967
De Stijl 1968
Exports: Detroit USA, Metalwork and Silver,
London at our feet, Hexagon – contemporary art
from Sweden 1969
Swedish Cinema 1969
Manufactured Art 1970
Hoffnung drawings 1971
Hampstead Heath: 100 years 1971
Covent Garden Workshop 1971
Delius and America 1972
Dalí through the Looking Glass 1972
Manifestations 1972
Camden Craftsmen 1972
Opera in Victorian London 1973
Designs for Kent Opera Productions 1977
A Man of our Time (Sir Michael Tippett) 1981
Igor Stravinsky at Work – drawings by
  Milein Cosman 1982
Stravinsky rehearsing Stravinsky –
  photographs by Laelia Goehr 1982
Benjamin Britten 1983
Song and Dance – theatre designs 1983
Frederick Delius 1984
Trogview 1984
The Camden Festival 1954–1985
Musicians (photographic exhibition) 1985
Musicians by Caroline Forbes 1987
Paul Robeson 1987

**One-man shows
in the St Pancras
Artists series**
Bruno Manini 1958
Doreen Roberts 1959
Peter Luther 1960
A E Dennis 1961
Arthur Quesnel 1962

Talks and lectures
Harold Rosenthal
Ida Cooke
Alan Blyth
Edward Greenfield
Charles Osborne
Henry Pleasants
Michael Scott
Felix Aprahamian
Lennox Berkeley
Wilfrid Mellers
Joseph Horovitz
Jonathan Miller
Imogen Holst
Joan Cross
Peter Pears
Lord Harewood

Appendix 7 **Annual gross and net expenditure on the Festival**

To give these figures a context, figures are also provided (for some years) of a) the total spend on cultural activities and b) the total departmental budget, which rose from £70,000 in 1955 to £19 million in 1987

1954
£650

1955
Concerts: £435
Book week: £163
Drama Festival: £301
Art Exhibition: £132
Lectures, recitals: £489
Department Budget: £70,732

1957
Concerts & operas: £856
Lectures, recitals: £415
Book Week: £268
Drama festival: £159
Art Exhibition: £180
General expenses: £587

1958
Concerts & operas: £913
Drama festival: £206
General expenses: £642

1959
Total expenditure on cultural activities: £7,664

1960[*]
Gross £9,634,
net £5,190
Department budget:
£106,205

1961
Gross £9,420,
net £7,882

1962
Gross £12,898,
net £8,605
Department budget:
£150,439

1963
Gross £12,939,
net n/a

1964
Gross £13,132,
net £11,354:

1965
Gross £25,506,
net £18,583
Total cultural activities:
£60,033
Department budget:
£619,750

1966
Gross £32,115,
net £16,992

1967
Gross £30,709,
net £18,469

1968
Gross £29,750,
net £17,963
Department budget:
£772,909

1969
Gross £28,496,
net £17,331
Department budget:
£844,084

1970
Gross £36,078,
net £18,992
Total cultural activities:
£85,594
Department budget:
£1,000,791

1971
Gross £37,680,
net £26,080
Total cultural activities:
£85,680
Department budget:
£2,302,151

1972
Gross £39,676,
net £26,896

1973
Gross £29,950,
net £20,915

1974
Gross £29,826,
net £15,245
Total cultural activities:
£234,000
Department budget:
£4,221.000

1975
Gross £32,750,
net £18,060

1976[**]
Estimated gross budget
£59,358
Estimated net budget
£33,328

1977
Gross £54,321,
net £22,525

1978
Gross £54,173,
net £22,778
Total cultural activities:
£316,000
Department budget:
£6,500,000

1979
Gross £100,419,
net £38,900

1980
Gross £108,605,
net £58,119
Total cultural activities:
£546,000
Department budget:
£10,023,000

1981
Gross £91,877,
net £45,633

1982
Gross £116,200,
net £59,000

1983
Estimated gross budget
£130,000
Estimated net budget
£59,500
Total cultural activities:
£845,000
Department budget:
£13,372,000

1984
Gross £139,579,
net £59,916

1985
Gross £131,730,
net £61,400

1986
Gross £222,460,
net £97,321
Total cultural activities:
£1,354,000
Department budget:
£18,129,000

1987
Gross £270,007,
 net £116,972
Total cultural activities:
£1,291,000
Department budget:
£19,286,000

[*] From 1960 it was decided to show the Festival costs in one lump sum to maintain better control of costs.

[**] In 1976 a new accounting procedure was introduced based on the net expenditure incurred by the Council. From now on the true gross costs and a true income figure were shown. The director of Libraries and Arts was free to incur whatever gross expenditure was necessary provided the net expenditure did not exceed the approved amount.

Index

Index to the text (Chapters 1-6) and, selectively, to Appendixes 1-7; * = illustration; (exhib.) = exhibition

A

Aarnio, Eero 47
Abbey Community Centre 87
Abbey Opera 82, 85, 102, 104, 105
Acacia Avenue 20
Acland Burghley Youth Centre 58
actors 124
Addison, John 29
Adler, Larry 47, 48
Adrian, Max 14
Adriana Lecouvreur 70, 85, 114, 117
Adriano in Siria 83, 116
African music & dance 123
Afro-Caribbean music & dance 123
Agnew, Jennifer 36
Alberni Quartet 92
Albery, Peter 29
Alcina 2*, 19, 19*, 24, 111
Alexander, Charles 96
Alexandra Repertory Co. 14, 14*
Aleko 71, 114
All Hallows, Gospel Oak 105
Allister, Jean 27
Alfandary, Michael 58, 62, 69
Allegri Quartet 47
Allen, Thomas 52
Almeida, Francisco A de 83, 115
Almeida Festival 101
Amadeus String Quartet 47, 79
amateur dramatic societies 124
amateur operatic societies 124
amateur *vs* professional 42-43
Amati Ensemble 102
Ambrosian Singers 36
American music & dance 123
American-themed events 81
Amici String Quartet 44
Andrew, Milla 48*
Anne, Princess 68
Anne Boleyn (Albery) 29
Ansdell Gallery 69
Antony & Cleopatra (Barber) 85, 117
Apartment House 1776 102
Apollo Children's Concerts 92
Apollo Society 16, 19, 26, 27, 29
Aprahamian, Felix 23, 43, 53, 68, 96, 106

Ark, Keith Tippett's 87
Arkwright Road, *see* Camden Arts Centre
Arne, Thomas 30, 112
Arnell, Richard 45
Arnold, Malcolm 29, 42, 43, 47, 48
Aroldo 34, 34*, 112;
Art Ensemble of Chicago 86, 86*
'Art Exhibitions' 12, 13, 14, 16, 17, 20; *see also* ' St Pancras Artists'; 'Camden Artists'
Art Unlimited 57
Artaxerxes 30, 30*, 112
Arthur, Maurice 60*
Artists' International Assoc. 40
Artists' Place Society 58
'Arts and Civic Week' 12, 53
Arts Council 10, 17, 18, 25, 26, 31, 42, 43, 44, 46, 66, 68, 75, 81, 84, 85, 93, 96, 100, 104, 105
Ashcroft, Michael 91
Ashcroft, Peggy 10, 14, 16, 58
Ashkenazy, Vladimir 44
Ashley, Robert 105, 106, 118
Asian music & dance 123
Asian Music Circle 25, 88
Aspinall, Michael 72, 73*, 76
Assembly Hall (*aka* Assembly Rooms; St Pancras Town Hall; *later* Camden Town Hall; *then* Camden Centre) 11, 12, 14, 18, 19, 22, 23, 27, 31, 32, 33, 45, 48, 50, 51-52, 56, 59, 66, 69, 76, 76, 79, 80, 81, 84, 85, 87, 88, 89, 94, 97
Association of Metropolitan Chief Librarians 22
Astrakan 106
Atalanta 106, 118
Atkins, Ronald 87
Audley, Maxine 76
Auerbach, Frank 52
Autumn Theme Festivals 72, 77, 79, 81
Awatinos, Los 88, 88*
Ayre, Leslie 31

B

Bach, J C 83, 116
Bach, J S 27, 29, 44, 87
Back, Sven-Erik 30, 31, 112
Baker, Chet 86
Baker, Janet 23, 27, 37, 44, 94
Balalaika Dance Group 63

Balcon, Jill 29
Ballad of Peckham Rye, The 32
ballet 10, 11, 24, 28, 65
Ballet Circle 11
Ballet Rambert 24, 65, 65*
Ballo dell' Ingrate, Il 43
balls, *see* 'Festival Balls'
Baltic Operatic Society 19
Bancroft family 15
'Band Festival' 57, 57*, 58
Barber, Chris 20
Barber, Samuel 85, 117
Barbirolli, Evelyn 90
baritones 121
Barker, Noelle 21
Barker, Paul 102, 118
Barnet Cypriot Dance Group 88
Barrow Poets 37
Barstow, Josephine 51
Bartlam, Bridget 82*
Basilica Opera 36, 45, 45*, 70
basses 121
bassists 121
Bastable, Roger 55
Baxter, John 77
BBC coverage 9, 10, 20, 21, 37, 52, 59, 65, 70, 71, 83, 103
Beatrice & Benedict 59, 114
Beaumont & Fletcher 20
Bedelian, Haroutune 89
Bedford Theatre 15
Bedford Way, *see* Logan Hall
Beecham, Sir Thomas 22, 43, 83, 94
Bennett, Alexander 28
Bennett, Richard Rodney 45, 65
Bergmann, Dr Walter 29, 34
Berkeley, Lennox 27, 36
Berlioz, Hector 59, 114
Besch, Anthony 20, 30
Bible Way Tabernacle Youth Orchestra 88
Binns, Malcolm 91
Birkbeck Players 20
Birtwhistle, Harrison 45, 91
Bishop, Stephen 37
Bizet, Georges 30, 80, 112, 115
Blacher, Boris 25, 111
Blakey, Art 86, 103*
Bley, Carla 106, 107*
Bliss, Sir Arthur 24, 29, 90
Bloomsbury Theatre, *see* Collegiate Theatre
Blubber 69
Blue Gene Tyranny 106

Blunt, Sir Anthony 45
Blyth, Alan 64, 66
Board of Trade Choir 18, 26
Bohan, Edmund 45*
Bohème, La (Leoncavallo) 64
Boito, Arrigo 85, 117
Bolivian music 88, 123
Bononcini, Antonio 90
'Book Weeks' 12, 13, 14, 16, 17
Boris Godunov (film) 21
Borough Youth Parliament 12
Bottone, Bonaventura 80*
Boundary Road 89
Bournemouth Symphony Orchestra 34
Bowen, John 52
Bowen, Kenneth 21, 35
Bowers-Broadbent, Christopher 44, 44*, 95, 103
Bowman, James 84
Bowyer, Peter 69, 71
Braden, Sue 96
Brahams, Michael 96
Brannigan, Owen 25, 33
Bream, Julian 19, 95
Brecht, Bertolt 34
Brewer, Bruce 78
Brian, Havergal 29
Briars, Gavin 87, 106
British Broadcasting Corporation, *see* BBC
British Drama League 9-10, 11, 14, 15, 27
British Museum 18, 64, 85, 85*, 89, 100
British Music Hall Society 42
Britten, Benjamin 44, 91, 95, 105;
Church Parables 118;
Curlew River 106, 118;
Gloriana 85, 95, 117;
Noye's Fludde 33, 33*, 36, 112;
Prodigal Son 106, 118;
The Rape of Lucretia 32
brochures 14*, 44, 58*, 71*
Brotherston, Lez 105
Broughton, Sandy 103, 107
Browne, E Martin 14, 15, 16, 41
Browne, Sandra 76, 77*, 84
Bruckner, Anton 31
Brymer, Jack 20, 95
Burgess, Sally 84
Burgh House 40, 63, 72, 89, 90
Burmese Harp, The 26

Index to the text (Chapters 1-6) and, selectively, to Appendixes 1-7; * = illustration; (exhib.) = exhibition

Bush, Alan 11
Busoni, Ferruccio 29
Butt, Dame Clara: tribute 76
Butterworths 96
Byron, Lord: anniversary 79

C
cabaret 87
Caccini, Francesca:
 L'Euridice 100, 117
Cage, John 102
Cairns, David 31, 32, 56, 106
Caley, Ian 77*
Calman: cartoon 104*
'Camden Artists' (exhib.)
 45, 47, 52, 58, 63, 69, 75
Camden Arts Centre 41,
 42, 45, 47, 52, 63, 71, 72, 91
Camden Borough Council
 36, 37, 39, 40, 50, 52, 66,
 67, 68, 72, 93, 98, 104, 108;
 Libraries & Arts C'ttee
 39, 42, 49, 50, 64;
 Libraries, Arts & Recreation
 Committee 70, 72, 73, 74;
 Leisure Services C'ttee 62,
 74, 75, 77, 96, 97, 99, 100;
 Libraries & Arts Sub-
 Committee 74;
 Arts Sub-C'ttees 41-42, 53,
 55, 61, 68, 70, 71, 77;
 Community Arts Working
 Party 75, 97;
 Advisory Panel on the
 Visual Arts 68;
 Music Advisory Panel
 49, 68, 95, 96;
 (Libraries &) Arts Dept. 41,
 42, 43, 55, 61, 67, 73-74;
 Leisure Services Department
 78, 100
Camden Centre, *see*
 Assembly Hall
Camden Chamber Orchestra
 65, 77, 79
Camden Committee for
 Community Relations 77
Camden Chamber Choir 90
Camden Choir 90
Camden Festival 43;
 (1967) 46-50; (1968) 50-
 52; 53, 55-62; (1970) 63-68;
 (1971) 68-71; (1972) 71-
 74; (1973) 75-78; (1974)
 78-80; (1975) 80-81; (1976)
 81-82; (1983-1987)
 94-108; Working Party 62,
 66, 68

Camden Festival Trust 96,
 97, 100, 103, 104
Camden Fringe Festival,
 see Fringe Festival
Camden History Society 69
Camden Jazz Festivals,
 see 'Jazz Weeks'
Camden Journal 56
Camden Junior Festival
 55, 72
Camden Library Journal
 42, 57, 75
Camden Library Service
 93, 98
Camden Lottery 88, 94
Camden Music Festival 75
Camden New Journal 49
'Camden Potters' (exhib.) 57
Camden Rock Festival 63
Camden School for Girls
 91; *(as venue)* 34, 48
Camden Town 97
Camden Town Group 15
Camden Town Hall,
 see Assembly Hall
Camden Wind Quintet 37
Cameron, Basil 9
Campbell, Leila 75
Candida 20
Cantata for Easter 90
Cantelo, April 20, 21*
Canti di Prigionia 34
Canticum Sacrum 36
Canyons des Etoiles, Des 106
Capon, Susanna 68
Capua, Marcello da 114
Caribbean music
 & dance 123
Carissimi, Giacomo 27, 111
Carline, Richard 40
carnival 70
Caro, Anthony 52
Carr, Ian 86, 86*
Carroll, John 90
Cassini, Leonard 11
Castello di Kenilworth, Il
 82, 82*, 115
Castle, Joyce 78
Casson, Lewis 27
Cavalli, Francesco 84, 117
Cave Dwellers, The 27
Cayford, George 63
Cecil Sharp House 27;
 see also English Folk Song...
'Celebrity Concerts' 37,
 44, 48, 52, 55, 71, 94
cellists 121
CEMA 10, 11, 43

Central Office of
 Information 52
Central School of Speech
 & Drama 45, 52, 58, 63
Centre "42" 40, 57
Centre Stage 32
Chabrier, Emmanuel
 27, 73, 111
Chagrin, Francis 29, 44, 45
Chalk Farm, *see* Round House
chamber ensembles 119
Chamber Music Players
 of London 87
Chandos Chorus 33
Chanticleer Orchestra 29
Chaplin, Charlie 24
Chappell, William 76
Chard, Geoffrey 45*
Charlesworth, Maurice 55
Charlotte Street 15, 19
Charrington Hall 9
Chasey, Katharine 55
Chelsea Opera Group 79,
 80, 82, 85, 94, 102
Cherkassky, Shura 52, 76
Cherubini, Luigi 35, 112
children's activities 12,
 55, 57, 91
Chilton, John 87
Chinese music
 & dance 11, 123
choirs 119
Christie, Nan 83*
'Christmas Pantomime' 98
Church Parables 118
Cilea, Francesco 70,
 85, 114, 117
Cimarosa, Domenico 24,
 82, 83, 111, 116
circus 24
City Literary Institute
 40, 53, 58
'Civic Exhibition' 31
Clap Music Theatre
 Ensemble 123
clarinettists 121
Clark Terry Big Band 87
Clark, Patricia 35
Classic Cinema,
 Hampstead 65
Clemenza di Tito, La 19, 111
'Club Nights' 79
Coates, Edith 33
Cochrane Theatre 47,
 49, 53, 65
Cohan, Robert 58
Cole, Frank 81
Coleman, Ornette
 87, 106, 107*

Coleridge-Taylor, Samuel 81
Collegiate Theatre 58, 59, 66,
 69, 71, 72, 73, 75, 76,
 78, 79, 80, 102
Collier, Sheila 87
Collins, Richard 50
Comedy of Errors, The
 (Storace) 78, 78*, 115
composers (appearing) 120
'Composers in Person' 48
'Concert Nights' 33
conductors 120
Congress House 47
Constanduros, Mabel
 & Denis 20
Contemporary Ballet
 Trust 58
contraltos 121
Conway Hall 52
Cook, Deborah 80*
Cooke, F Cromwell 42
Cooper, Imogen 65, 95
Cooper, Jack 50, 51,
 53, 98, 99
Copper, Bob 89
Coronation celebrations
 12, 13, 14
Corsaro, Il 45-46, 113
Cosman, Milein 85, 91
costs, *see* finance
Cortis, Marcello 26, 26*
Council for the
 Encouragement of Music
 & the Arts 10, 11, 43
Country Doctor, A (Henze)
 45, 113
Company of Nine, The 20
'Contemporary Music' 90
Convenienze Teatrali, Le 71-72
Coull String Quartet 95
countertenors 121
Covent Garden, *see*
 Royal Opera House
Cox, John 34
Crafts Centre of
 Great Britain 52, 69
Craig, Douglas 20
Crane Feathers 30, 31, 112
Cripps, Stafford 10
Crispino e la Comare 84, 116
Crosland, Anthony 47
Cross, Joan 79, 95
Crosse, Gordon 45
Crouch End All Stars
 81, 87, 92
Crucible, The (Miller) 20
Cry Havoc (Kenward) 20
Cumming, John 103
Cummings, Constance 16

Index to the text (Chapters 1-6) and, selectively, to Appendixes 1-7; * = illustration; (exhib.) = exhibition

Curlew River 106, 118
Cypriot community 63; music & dance 88, 123
Czar has his Photograph Taken, The 118

D
Dallapiccola, Luigi 34
dance 4*, 11, 25, 63, 65; *see also* ballet
dance companies; dancers 121
Dane, Clemence 16
Danish Chamber Orchestra 71
Danish-themed events 71
Dankworth, John 23, 44, 44*, 48, 52, 65, 79, 94
Dart, Thurston 24
Dartington String Quartet 44
Davenport, Jean 103
Davidson, Wild Bill 85
Davies, Ryland 76, 83
Day Lewis, Cecil 16, 29
De Peyer, Adrian 35
De Stijl Group (exhib.) 52
Dean, Peter 50
Debussy, Claude 36, 122
Deidamia 18
Del Mar, Norman 36, 95
Delius, Frederick 64, 71-72, 83, 114, 116, 117: anniversary 91
Delius Trust 71, 83
Deller, Alfred 29
Delmé String Quartet 47
Dench, Judi 90
Dent, Edward J 18
Denza, (Cllr) Luigi 61, 68, 70, 96
Deutsche Messe (Krenek) 90
Diaghilev, Serge: centenary 71
Dickens, Charles: centenary 65
Diorama, Regent's Park 102
Divertimenti 90, 106
Dobson, Frank 74, 75
Doctor Miracle 30, 112
Dogg's Troupe Jug Band 64
Dolmetsch, Carl 29
Dolmetsch Ensemble 19
Don Giovanni (film) 26
Don Quixote (Henze/Paisiello) 83, 116
Donizetti, Gaetano 45: *Il Castello di Kenilworth* 82, 115;

Le Convenienze Teatrali 71-72, 73*;
Francesca di Foix 82, 116;
Marino Faliero 48, 56, 113;
Maria Stuarda 45, 112;
The Prima Donna's Mother... 71-72, 73*, 115;
La Romanziera 82, 116;
Torquato Tasso 78, 79, 81, 115
donkey derby 58
Donkey's Shadow, The 64, 114
Donna del Lago, La 59, 60*, 113;
Dorow, Dorothy 45*
Downshire Hill 102
Drak Puppets 92
'Drama Festivals/Competitions' 12, 14, 14*, 16, 17, 20, 24, 25, 26
drama groups 124
drama productions 124
Dramateurs, The 63
Du Mont, Councillor 79
Du Plessis, Christian 79*
Du Pré, Jacqueline 37
Duenna, The (Linley) 81, 115
Dugdale, Sandra 77*
Dunlop, Lionel 27
Durrant, Colin 91
Dvorak, Antonin 85, 116

E
Eagleton, Terry 97
Earlham Street 52, 69
Ecce Homo (Stoker) 45
Ecuadorian music 123
Education Manquée, Une 27, 111
Edwards, Anne 34
Egerton, Francis 78*
Egyptian music 123
Elder, Mark 85
Electro-Acoustic Music Association 101
Elgar, Edward 29
Elisabetta, Regina d'Inghilterra 51, 113
élitism *vs* populism 15-16, 96-100 *passim*
Elizabeth, Queen Mother 44
Elkins, Margareta 78, 79*
Ellington, Duke 44
Ellis, Osian 29
Embassy Theatre 45, 63
EMI Records 71
End of a World, The 45, 45*, 113
Endymion Ensemble 91

England, Whose England? 77
English Chamber Orchestra 27, 36
English folk music & dance, *see* folk music
English Folk Song & Dance Society 20, 21, 28, 42
English National Opera 82, 85
ENSA (Entertainments National Service Association) 10, 11
ensembles 119
Epithalamion 90
Equity (union) 94
Eritrea (Cavalli) 84, 117
Ernani 32-33, 32*, 85, 112
Etoile du Nord, L' 80, 115
Euripides 37
European music & dance 123
Euston Road School 15
Euston Station 69
Evans, Dame Edith 16, 26
Evans, Geraint 20
Evans, Gil 86, 86*
Evans, Joy 49*
Evans, Nancy 20, 26
Everyman Cinema 47, 52, 58, 75, 95, 106
exhibitions 125
expenditure, *see* finance
'Exports: Detroit USA' (exhib.) 52
Extension Activities 12

F
Fairfax, Bryan 27, 29, 31
'Family Concerts' 91
Fantasticks 65
Far I Upsetter Militant Rockers 101
Farandouri, Maria 72, 89
Farncombe, Charles 18, 18*, 22, 24, 26
Fawkes, Wally 87, 92, 92*
Fedeltà Premiata, La 69, 114
Feetwarmers, John Chilton's 87
Fennimore & Gerda 4, 83, 114, 116
Fenton House 43, 58, 63, 68, 72, 89
'Festival Balls' 21, 24, 25, 87
Festival of Britain 12
'Festival of Leisure' 12
Feuersnot 85, 116
finance 93-94, 98, 100, 104, 126

Finchley Children's Music Group 33, 33*, 34, 36, 44
Finchley Choral Society 29
Finnish Radio Chamber Choir 48
Finnish-themed events 47-48
Finsberg, Geoffrey 99
Finta Giardiniera, La 17, 118
Finta Semplice, La 100, 117
Fire Raisers, The (Frisch) 45
First Commandment, The 51, 113
Fitzroy Square 10
flower shows 12, 13
folk music 20, 21, 28, 52, 123; *see also* International Music & Dance
'Folk Music Tour' 89
folk musicians 122
Folk Variety Theatre 28
Forbes, Elizabeth 59
Forgan, Liz 96
fortepianists 120
48 Club, Boundary Road 89
Foster, Arnold 21, 111
Fox, Ivor 15
Francesca di Foix 82, 82*, 116
Francis Chagrin Ensemble 29, 31, 34
Fredman, Myer 25
French operetta 87
Friendenstag 85, 117
Friends' House 27, 29, 34, 44
Fringe Festival 54, 55, 57, 57*, 58*, 60, 62, 63, 66, 67
Fringe Working Party 55, 56-57, 60
Frisch, Max 45
Fürtwängler, Kurt 26

G
Gabrieli Quartet 48
Gambian music & dance 123
Gardner, John 90
Garland, Ken 46
Garland, Patrick 49
Gatehouse Theatre 69
Geliot, Michael 36, 49
Gellhorn, Peter 27
Gershwin, George 44, 81, 115
Gerson, Mark 45
Ghanaian music & dance 123
Gibson, Patrick 75
Gilbert, Patrick 25, 68, 70, 71
Gillespie, Rhondda 44, 76
Giorno di Regno, Un 27, 28*, 111
Giovanna d'Arco 34

Index to the text (Chapters 1-6) and, selectively, to Appendixes 1-7; * = illustration; (exhib.) = exhibition

Gipps, Ruth 29
Glasgow Phoenix Choir 24
Glass House, Downshire Hill 102
Glenilla Arts Group 63, 69, 70
Gloriana (Britten) 85, 95, 117
Glover, Jane 84
Gluck, Christoph W von 34-35, 112
Gode, (Ald.) Miss W E C 11
Goehr, Alexander 91
Good Woman of Szechuan, The 34
Gopal, Ram 25, 88
Gordon, Christopher 55
Gordon, Dexter 86, 86*
Goring, Marius 90
Gospel Oak 57, 105
Gotch, Christopher 25, 43
Gover, Gerald 22, 34, 45, 48, 59, 62
Graham, Colin 21, 35, 64
'Grand Carnival Dance' 12
Grande Duchesse de Gerolstein, La 83, 115
Grandma's Footsteps 51
Grange Park, Kilburn 58
Grant, Keith 68
Graubert, Michael 57
Gray, Jack 19
Gray's Inn 89, 90, 103
Great Russell Street 47
Greater London Arts Association 42, 71
Greater London Council 42, 46, 64, 75, 93, 100, 102
Greek Arts Theatre Group 42, 63, 124
Greek Ministry of Culture 89
Greek music & dance 11, 123
Greek-themed events 89
Green, Benny 55, 95
Green, Charles Samuel 53
Greenfield, Edward 47
Greenwood, Joan 52, 76
Grétry, André 116
Greycoat London Estates 96
Grier, Christopher 38, 39
Griffin, Johnny 86, 86*
Griffiths, Paul 102
Grillo, John 69
Group Eight 25*, 27, 30, 33, 36, 43, 53
guitarists 120
Gulbenkian Foundation 26
Gurrelieder 27
Guy, Barry 69

H
Hackett, Bobby 85
Haden, Charlie 106, 107*
Halstead, Peter 63
Hamilton House 32
Hammond-Stroud, Derek 16, 21, 27
Hampstead 34, 42, 54, 55, 60, 62-63; pubs 57
Hampstead & Highgate Express 22, 25, 33, 41, 42, 43, 44, 48, 49, 50, 51, 52, 53, 58, 61-62, 63, 66, 70, 73, 76, 79, 95, 96, 99, 100, 106, 107
Hampstead Artists' Council 40-41, 42, 45, 61-62, 63, 91
Hampstead Borough Council 13, 40, 41, 43, 44
Hampstead Central Library 40; *see also* Swiss Cottage Library
Hampstead Chamber Orchestra 57
Hampstead Choral Society 40, 48, 53, 60-61, 76, 90
Hampstead Community Centre 87
Hampstead Drama Guild 40, 63, 69
Hampstead Festival 40, 42, 43, 50, 53, 60, 61, 63, 70
Hampstead Heath 40, 57, 58; acquisition centenary 69
Hampstead Music Club 40, 63, 72
Hampstead Parish Church (St John's) 58, 68,
Hampstead Photographic Society 40, 69
Hampstead Theatre 40, 49, 52, 58, 67, 69, 70, 90, 124
Hampstead Theatre Club 37, 40, 45, 61, 65, 70, 72, 99
Hampstead Town Hall 32, 45, 48, 87
Handel, G F 22, 23, 27, 33; *Alcina* 2*, 19, 19*, 24, 111; *Deidamia* 18; *Hercules* 17; *Theodora* 20, 21*, 111
Handel Opera Society 17-19, 20, 21*, 22, 24, 25, 27, 30, 33, 35, 35*, 36, 36*, 45, 48, 51
Happy End (Weill) 106, 118
Hardy, Jeremy 101
Harewood, Lord 17, 79
harmonica 47, 48, 96, 121
Harper, Heather 16, 23, 24, 30*, 37, 44, 44*, 46, 47

harpists 121
harpsichord 120
Harrhy, Eiddwen 83
Harwood, Peter 25
Hassall, Christopher 20, 26
Hawkes, Tom 23, 84
Hawkins, Richard 118
Haydn, Joseph 26; *L'Anima del Filosofo* 16; *La Fedeltà Premiata* 69, 114; *L'Incontro Improviso* 45, 112; *L'Infedeltà Delusa* 35, 35*, 112; *Il Mondo della Luna* 26, 26*, 111; *Orfeo ed Euridice* 111; *The Seasons* 26
Hayes, Tony 55
Head, Leslie 24, 27, 45
Heartbreak House 24
Heath & Old Hampstead Society 69
Heath Street 40, 58
Heininen, Paavo 46
Helicon Ensemble 69
Hemmings, Peter 21
Henderson, Jack 37, 38, 41, 43, 44, 45, 47, 55, 60, 68, 70, 73, 76, 81, 82, 90, 99, 100, 102
Henriques, Kevin 85
Henze, Hans Werner 84; *A Country Doctor* 45, 113; *Don Quixote* 116; *The End of the World* 45, 45*, 113; *The Miracle Theatre* 45, 113
Hercules (Handel) 17
Herrmann, Bernard 106
Hess, Myra 10
Hiawatha, Song of 81
Hicks, Miss W M 15, 42
Highgate 69, 105
Highgate Chamber Orchestra 57
Highgate Choral Society 90
Highgate Library 14, 37
Highgate Literary & Scientific Institute 11, 31, 52
Highgate New Town Community Centre 89
Highgate Poetry Circle 32
Hill, The 57
Hill, Mary 73*
Hindemith, Paul 36, 48-49, 79, 113, 115
Hippolytus (Euripides) 37
'Historic Buildings, Music in' 82, 85, 89, 102

Hitchcock, Alfred 106
Hoddinott, Alun 90
Holborn 42, 53, 65
Holborn Assembly Rooms 76
Holborn Borough Council 40, 41
Holborn Film Society 42, 58
Holborn Library 47, 52, 58, 65, 76, 95
Holborn Town Hall 45
Holland, Bill 108
Holst, Gustav 9, 48, 113
Holt, Thelma 83, 96
Holy Trinity, Kingsway 65, 68, 76, 95
Honegger, Arthur 29
Hope-Wallace, Philip 80
Hopkins, Michael 102
Hordern, Michael 19
Hornsey Borough Council 31
Horovitz, Joseph 35, 36, 37*, 44, 45, 48, 95
Howard, Robin 58
Howells, Anne 76
Howlett, Neil 49*
Hungarian music & dance 123
Hungarian State Puppet Theatre 92
Symphony Orchestra 31
Hunter, Rita 85
Hurwitz, Emmanuel 90

I
Ibsen, Henrik 45
Ichikawa, Kon 26
Ideal Husband, An 29
Idomeneo 20, 26, 111
ILEA Music Centre 91
Impresario, The (Mozart) 17
Impresario Society 16, 17, 19, 20, 24, 26, 27, 28*, 51
Incontro Improvviso, L' 45, 112
Indian music & dance 11, 25, 60*, 89, 123
Indian Queen, The 73, 76, 115
Infedeltà Delusa, L' 35, 35*, 112
Inner London Education Authority, *see* ILEA
Innes, Hammond 14
In-Stage 26
Institute of Education 84
Inter-Action 64
'International & Urban Trax' 105
'International Music & Dance' 82, 88, 88*, 98, 99, 101, 103, 105, 123

Index to the text (Chapters 1-6) and, selectively, to Appendixes 1-7; * = illustration; (exhib.) = exhibition

International Theatre Company 16
Iolanta 51, 113
Iphigenia in Aulis 34-35, 35*, 112
Irish Centre 89
Irish music & dance 123
Irwell Opera 48-49, 49*
Isaaman, Gerald 52, 61, 96
Islington Borough Council 99
Israeli music & dance 123
Italian Straw Hat 69, 84, 116
Italiana in Algeri, L' 27, 111

J
Jackson, Glenda 17*
Jackson, Jeanette 42, 63
Jacobin, The 85, 116
Jacobs, Arthur 29, 33, 48, 56, 64, 6, 72, 76
Jacobs, Gordon 37
Jan Hus (film) 20
Japanese music 123
Japanese-themed events 69
Jaques String Orchestra 11
Jarman, Derek 96
Javanese music & dance 123
jazz events 122; 'Jazz Band Ball' 81, 87, 89; 'Jazz Weeks' 80, 81, 82, 85, 87, 90, 99, 101, 103, 122
Jazz Centre Society 79, 81, 85, 96
jazz musicians 122
Jeannetta Cochrane Theatre 47, 49, 53, 65
Jefford, Barbara 20
Jenkins, Hugh 108
Jenkins, Simon 63
Jing Ying Soloists 90
Johnson, Julia 108
Jones, Della 83
Jones, Gwyneth 32
Jones, Philip 36
Jones, Tom (producer) 65
Josephs, Wilfred 45, 47, 68
Joubert, John 59, 67, 114
jousting 40
Joyce, Eileen 52
Judita Triumphans 117
'Jumbo May Day Carnival' 70
Junior Festivals 55, 72

K
Kalogridou, Maria 26
Keats, John: anniversary 69
Keats House 89, 90, 99
Keller, Hans 96

Kelly, Bernard 62, 63
Kemp, Tony 96
Kempe, Rudolph 44
Kenny, Yvonne 82*
Kensington Symphony Orchestra 24, 27, 45
Kent Opera 82
Kentish Town 97 police station 58
Kenward, Allan 20
Kenwood 58
Kenyon, Nicholas 94
Kerpel, Tony 96
Key-Aberg, Sandro: *Oh!* 49
Keynes, John Maynard 10
Khan, Imrat 89
Kilburn 58, 97
King and No King, A 20
King David (Honneger) 29
King's Singers 76
Kingsley-Poynter, Guy 16
Kingsway 65, 68, 76, 95
Kington, Miles 87
Kirkpatrick, John 89
Koanga 71-72, 72*, 114
Kokkonen, Joonas 48
Korean music 4*, 88, 88*, 123
Kossoff, David 34
Kovacevich, Stephen 37
Kraemer, Nicholas 90
Krenek, Ernst 90
Krishna Menon, *see* Menon...
Kubik, Gail 31

L
Lacey, Bruce 71
Laine, Cleo 23, 44, 44*, 48, 52, 65, 94
Lady & the Unicorn, The 90
Landini Consort 102
Langridge, Philip 83
Larrieu, Daniel 106
Lasdun, Sir Denys 84
Latin American music & dance 123
Lauderdale House 87, 89
Lawrence, Helen 78*
Lawrence, Martin 35*
Leaves of Grass 46-47
Lecocq, Charles 117
lectures 125
Lee, Mrs G F 15
Lee, Jennie 36, 39
Leeming, Peter 45*
Lees, Benjamin 51
Legal & General Assurance 96
Lehane, Maureen 35

Leigh, Adele 20
Lemare, Iris 36
Lennon/McCartney 87
Leoncavallo, Ruggiero 64
Lerner, Alan Jay 95
Lesson in Love, A 27, 111
Levin, Bernard 94
Levy, Roger 15, 42, 43
libraries & the arts 8-11, 15, 22, 41
Library Journal (St Pancras/Camden) 11, 15, 16, 20, 23, 26, 28, 42, 45, 57, 75
Lidholm, Ingvar 58
Lincoln's Inn 57, 89, 90, 103
Linley, Thomas 81, 115
Lipetz, John 75, 77, 97
Liszt, Franz 44
'Literary Evenings' 14, 16, 17
Littau, David 24, 57
Little Boxes (Bowen) 52
Littler, Emile 19
Litvin, Natasha 16
Lloyd-Jones, David 43, 70
Local Government Acts (1948) 12; (1963) 39, 41 93
Lodger, The (Tate) 36, 112
Logan Hall 84, 85, 87, 94
'London at Your Feet' (exhib.) 52
London Bach Society 27, 29, 31, 34, 37, 44
London Boy Singers 33
London Chamber Orchestra 58, 64
London Contemporary Dance 4*, 58, 59*, 65, 69, 76, 79, 81
London County Council 10, 25
London Jazz Composers Orchestra 69
London Lottery Club 94
London Mozart Players 20, 58
London Opera Centre 58
London Orchestral Concert Board 43, 75, 81
London Philharmonic Orchestra 11, 12, 13, 14, 16, 19, 92
London Pro Musica 103
London Ripieno Society 44
London Soloists Ensemble 44
London String Orchestra 11
London Symphony Orchestra 24, 29, 71, 81

London Traverse Theatre Company 49
London Turkish Theatre Folk Dancing Group 88
London Wind Soloists 44
'Looking at London' (exhib.) 14
Loppert, Max 82
Lord Bateman 21, 111
Lord Eric's Agor MMBA 101
Lott, Felicity 83
Loughran, James 34
Love from Judy (musical) 19
Lubbock, John 65, 79
Lucio Silla 48, 113
Luckham, Cyril 76
'Lunchtime Jazz' 47, 58
'Lunchtime Recitals' 47, 95
lutenists 120
Luther, Peter 25
Lutyens, Elisabeth 36
Luxon, Benjamin 87
'Lyricist as Poet' 95
Lyttelton, Humphrey 19, 20, 24, 81, 87

M
Macbeth (Shakespeare) 58
Macbeth of Mtsensk 85, 117
McCabe, John 85, 117
McCleary, Gwyneth 18
Macdonald, Ramsay 9
Mackerras, Charles 83
MacNaughton Concerts 36, 44 String Quartet 16
McNichol, Richard 92
Maconchy, Elizabeth 49, 113
MacOwan, Michael 16
Magee, Bryan 91
Mahler, Gustav 23, 27, 31, 33
Maidment, William R 41, 52, 53, 55, 67, 70, 81
Maire, Emily 25*
Major Barbara 26
Makropoulos, Yannis 89
Malcolm, George 24
Mamelles de Tiresias, Les 64, 114
Mann, Mabel 55
Mann, William 46, 78
Manning, Jane 76
Manon Lescaut (Puccini) 116
Manson Ensemble 106
Manton, Franz 30, 32
'Manufactured Art' (exhib.) 63
Maple's store 36
Marchal, André 31

Index to the text (Chapters 1-6) and, selectively, to Appendixes 1-7; * = illustration; (exhib.) = exhibition

Marchant, Graham 55
Marcus, Leonard 8*, 10, 11, 12, 13, 15, 17, 18, 21, 22, 23, 24, 25, 28, 33, 37-38, 39, 41, 46, 51, 53, 55, 62, 70
Margot la Rouge 117
Maria Golovin 81, 115
Maria Stuarda 45, 112
Maria Tudor 117
Marino Faliero 48, 48*, 56, 113
Marks & Spencer 96
Marowitz, Charles 27, 58
Martin, Hugh 19
Martinique: dance 123
Marttinen, Tauno 46
Mary Ward
  Cantata Choir 29
  Settlement 9, 24, 26
Maschwitz, Eric 19
Masnadieri, I 29, 30, 30*, 111
Massenet, Jules 48, 71, 113, 114
Mathis der Maler 79, 115
Maurel, Michael 34
Mavra 83, 84*, 116
Maw, Nicholas 31, 48
Maxwell Davies, Peter 36
'May Day Carnival' 70
Mayapi 88
Mayer, Sir Robert 33
Mazeppa 85, 116
Medcalf, Steven 102
Medici String Quartet 95
'Medieval Music Dramas' 51, 113
Medium, The (Menotti) 27, 111
Mellors, Dr Wilfred 95
Melly, George 87
'Melodramas' 76
Menary, Shirley & Tony 101
Menon, V K Krishna 8*, 8-9, 10-11, 53, 108
Menotti, Gian-Carlo 27, 81, 111, 115
Menuhin, Hephzibah 48
Menuhin, Yehudi 63
Merilainin, Usko 46
Messiaen, Olivier 106
'Metalwork & Silver' (exhib.) 52
Meyer, Kerstin 58
Meyerbeer, Giacomo 80, 115
mezzo-sopranos 121
Midland Grand Hotel 90
Miles, James 55, 82, 96, 104
Milhaud, Darius 26, 111
Milkina, Nina 14, 20

Miller, Arthur 20
Milnes, Rodney 82, 83, 84
Miracle Theatre, The 45, 113
Mitchell, Donald 35
Mitridate, Rè di Ponto 83, 116
Moiré Music 86
Mondo della Luna, Il 26, 26*, 111
Montague, Diana 83*
Monteverdi, Claudio 36, 43, 112, 115
Montgomery, Marian 58, 95
Moran, Angela 45*
Morgan, Charles 16
Morley College Chamber Orchestra 51
Mornington Music Club 9, 20
Morris dancers 40, 57, 89, 89*
Moscow State Opera Co. 21
Mozart, W A 23, 27, 31, 38, 102;
  Don Giovanni (film) 26;
  La Clemenza di Tito 19, 111;
  La Finta Giardiniera 17, 118;
  La Finta Semplice 100, 117;
  The First Commandment 51, 113;
  Idomeneo 20, 26, 111;
  The Impresario 17;
  Lucio Silla 48, 113;
  Mitridate... 83, 116;
  Il Rè Pastore 80, 115;
  Il Sogno di Scipione 51, 113
  Mozart & Salieri 51, 113
'Mozart Festival' 17
Murray, Ann 83
Murray, Stephen 14
Musgrave, Thea 48, 76
Music and Arts in Camden 42, 43, 50, 52, 53, 54, 57, 66, 67, 68, 69, 70, 71;
  in Hampstead 25, 40
'Music and Arts Weeks' 40, 70
'Music and Dance' 85, 103
'Music and Film' 103
music hall 15, 42, 58, 69, 87
'Music in Historic Buildings' 82, 85, 89, 102
'Music in our Time' 90
'Music in the Streets' 57
Musica Nova Group 58
musicians 119-123
Musicians' Union 20, 94
Mussorgsky, Modest 21

N
National Conference of Artists 45
National Council for Civil Liberties 77
National Gallery 10, 11, 45
National Jazz Centre 87, 101
National Portrait Gallery 45
National Youth Theatre 67, 68, 93
Navarraise, La 71, 114
Neighbourhood Festivals 77, 80, 81, 98, 99, 108
Nereid Gallery 85, 85*, 89, 100
Nerone (Boito) 85, 117
New Chamber Choir 89
New English Opera Workshop 21
New London Consort 100
New London Wind Ensemble 34, 37
New Opera Company 59, 82, 84
New Philharmonia Orchestra 36, 71, 81
Nono, Luigi 76
Norrington, Roger 64
North Camden Schools Orchestra 91
North London Music Festival 9
North London Press 49, 51, 60, 62, 63, 99
Notturni ed Alba 85, 117
Noye's Fludde 33, 33*, 36, 112
Nyman, Michael 106

O
oboists 121
Odeon, *see* Swiss Cottage Odeon
Oedipus Rex (Stravinsky) 5, 117
Offenbach, Jacques 76, 77, 83, 115
Ogden, John 32
'Old Time Music Hall' 58, 69, 87
Old Vic Company 10
Oliver, Alexander 80*
one-man shows 125
'Open Air Exhibitions' 40, 58
'Open Rehearsal' 76
Open Space Theatre 58, 124
'Open Studios' 57
Opera Concerts (company) 34, 34*, 36, 45, 48, 51, 59, 70, 71

Opera da Camera 73, 76
opera productions *(criticised)* 56; *(listed)* 110;
  casts 111-118
Opera Rara 71, 76, 77*, 82
Opera Viva 45, 48
Orangery, Kenwood 68
Orazi ed i Curiazi, Gli 82, 83*, 116;
Orchestra of St John's, Smith Square 79
orchestras 119
Orfeo (Monteverdi) 115
Orfeo ed Euridice 111
organ recitals 31, 34, 44, 47, 52, 58, 68, 103;
  organists 120
Other Voices 118
Ova 101
Overruled (Shaw) 14

P
Pacini, Giovanni 117
Paisiello, Giovanni 83, 116
Palmer, Felicity 83
pantomime 98
Park Lane Group 31, 48, 51, 59, 64, 70, 71, 76, 81, 82, 83, 90, 96
Parkin, Eric 91
Parliament Hill Fields 12, 13, 61, 70
Parlour Quartet 81
Parsons, Geoffrey 48, 71, 94
Pears, Peter 33
Pêcheurs de Perles, Les 80, 115
Pelléas et Mélisande 36, 112
Peña, Paco 58
Pepys, Samuel 90
percussionists 121
Peri, Peter 32
Peruvian music 123
Peters, Johanna 30*, 84
Phantastes 102, 118
Phillips, Sian 20, 44
Phillips Records 47
Philomusica of London 24, 44, 79
Philopera Circle 29-30, 32, 32*, 34, 35*
Phoenix Opera 82, 83, 84, 96
pianists 120
Pietra del Paragone, La 33, 112
Pinches, J 24
Pine, Courtney 86
Pirandello, Luigi 16, 17
Pittas, Christos 89
Place, The 58, 65, 69, 81, 91, 102

Index to the text (Chapters 1-6) and, selectively, to Appendixes 1-7; * = illustration; (exhib.) = exhibition

plays 124
Pleasants, Henry 95
Plowright, Rosalind 83
poetry 16, 20, 26, 29, 32, 34, 37, 52, 57, 63
'Poetry & Jazz' 32, 34, 47, 52, 58, 75, 80
'Poetry & Music' 14, 26, 29, 37, 52, 69, 90
'Poetry Competition' 52
poetry groups 124
'Poetry Marathon' 57
poets 124
Polish music & dance 123
Polyphonia Symphony Orchestra 27, 29
pop concerts 58, 61, 63, 64*, 69, 71, 76
pop musicians 123
popular entertainers 123
populism vs élitism 96-100 passim
Porgy & Bess 81, 115
Porter, Andrew 17, 19, 56
Portuguese music & dance 123
Positive Movement 70
pottery 57
Poulenc, Francis 64, 65, 114
Pretenders, The (Ibsen) 45
Price, Janet 78, 80*
Prima Donna's Mother..., *The* 71-72, 73*, 115
Primrose Hill Community Centre 87
Prince of Wales Road Baths 11
Prince of Wales Theatre 15
'Prize-winners Concerts/ Recitals' 52, 58, 65, 68, 75, 120
'Procession of Industry' 12
Prodigal Son (Britten) 106, 118
'Progressive Pop' 76
Prokofiev, Sergei 24
The Protagonist (Weill) 118
Psycho (Hitchcock) 106
public houses 11
public libraries, *see* libraries
Puccini, Giacomo 116
puppet theatre 92
Purcell, Henry 31, 73, 76, 115
Pygmalion (Cherubini) 35, 112
Pygmalion (Shaw) 14, 17*

Q
Quem Quaritis Singers 51

R
Rachmaninov, Sergei 71, 114
racism 77
RADA 16, 17*, 20, 24, 26, 29, 124
Rank Organisation 43
Rape of Lucretia, The (Britten) 32
Ratchford, Charles 42
Rate capping 93, 100
Rattle, Simon 81
Rautavaara, Aulikki 47
Rawlings, Margaret 14
Rawsthorne, Alan 91
Rè Pastore, Il 80, 115
Read, Sylvia 29
Rebel, The (Garland) 49
Regent Theatre 15
Regent's Canal 58
Regent's Park Estate Tenants' Association 51
Regent's Park Open Air Theatre 67
Reid, Norman 52
Reilly, Tommy 95
Relapse, The (Vanbrugh) 24
Remedios, Alberto 85
Renaud (Sacchini) 83, 116
Ricci, Luigi & Federico 84, 116
Rice, Peter 72
Richard Cobden School 15
Richards, Denby 33, 43, 46, 47, 48, 51, 60, 62, 66, 102
Richardson, John 13, 22, 33, 38, 39, 41, 42, 43, 46, 49, 55, 62, 70, 98, 109
Richardson, Sir Ralph 12
Rietti, Victor 16
Rignold, Hugo 16
Rimsky-Korsakov, Nikolai 20, 51, 102, 112, 118
Ritorno d'Ulisse in Patria, Il 36, 112
River Line 16
Robbins, Tessa 34, 44
Robertson, Anne 96
Robeson, Paul 106
Robinson, Stanford 43, 68
Robinson Crusoe (Offenbach) 76, 77*, 115
'Romance and the Romantic' 57
'Romance to Rhythm' 76
Romanian music & dance 123
Romanziera, La 82, 116
Romeo and Juliet (film) 24
Roose-Evan, James 37
Rosa, Carl 22

Rose, Gregory 102
Rosenthal, Harold 34, 35, 36, 55
Rossini, Gioacchino 23, 33, 36;
   La Donna del Lago 59, 60*, 113;
   Elisabetta, Regina... 51, 113;
   L'Italiana in Algeri 27, 111;
   La Pietra del Paragone 33, 112;
   Tancredi 70, 114;
   Il Turco in Italia 36, 36*, 112
Rosslyn Hill Chapel 91
Rostand, Edmond 65
Rota, Nino 84, 116
Round House, The 40, 57, 63, 64*, 67, 69, 71, 72, 80, 81, 83, 87, 88
Round House Trust 123
Routh, Francis 91
Routledge, Patricia 83
Royal Academy of Dramatic Art, *see* RADA
Royal Academy of Music 106
Royal Ballet 24, 28
Royal Opera House 18, 19, 33, 56, 82, 85
Royal Philharmonic Orchestra 43, 44, 46, 47, 51, 52, 58, 64, 75, 81
Russell, Tom 11
Russell Square 69
Russian dance 63

S
Sacchini, Antonio 83, 116
Sadie, Dr Stanley 56
Sadler's Wells Ballet 10
Sadler's Wells Theatre 19, 56, 71, 72, 73
St Dominic's Priory 76
St Donat's Music Theatre 106
St George the Martyr Church 95
St John's, Church Row, *see* Hampstead Parish Church
St Mary's, Primrose Hill 51
St Michael's, Highgate 90
St Pancras 13, 62-63
'St Pancras Artists' (exhib.) 20, 24, 25, 31, 32, 34, 36
St Pancras Arts & Civic Council 10-12, 15, 40, 42, 53
St Pancras Arts Festival 37, 39, 42, 43, 51, 53, 71, 88;
   (1954) 14; (1955) 15-17;
   (1957) 19- 20; (1958) 20-24;
   (1959) 24; (1960) 24-26;
   (1961) 26-28; (1962) 28-31;
   (1963) 31-33; (1964) 33-35;
   (1965) 35-37; (1966) 43-46
St Pancras Assembly Hall, *see* Assembly Hall
St Pancras Borough Council 8, 9, 11, 12, 16, 17, 18, 23, 24, 25, 31, 37, 40, 41, 68;
   Public Libraries C'ttee 8, 12, 15, 19, 22, 24, 28, 20, 31, 33;
   Arts Sub-C'ttee 15, 27;
   Arts & Libraries Dept 18
St Pancras Chronicle 49, 52
St Pancras Church, Upper WoburnPlace 20, 29, 31, 33, 34, 44, 47, 52, 95, 103, 106
St Pancras Library 67, 68, 93*
St Pancras Library Service 8, 9, 10, 11, 15, 21, 24, 37
St Pancras Municipal Choir 24
   Collection 25
St Pancras Old Church 83, 89
St Pancras People's Theatre 9
St Pancras Players 9
St Pancras Schools Music Assoc. 9
St Pancras Town Hall, *see* Assembly Hall
Saint-Saëns, Camille 29
St Sophia Cathedral Choir 89
Sallinen, Aulis 106
Saltarello Choir 76
Salvation Army 11
Samulnori 4*, 88, 88*
Sand Kitchen, The 69
Sapho (Massenet) 48, 48*, 113
Saroyan, William 27
Sarti, Laura 26*
Sassoon, Philip 31
Scala Theatre 15, 19
Scarlatti, Alessandro 64, 114
Schmid, Patric 56, 71, 73, 78
Schmidt, Harvey 65
Schönberg, Arnold 27
Schoenberg Wind Quartet 34
School for Fathers, The 84, 84*, 117
Schubert, Franz 44
Schwarzkopf, Elisabeth 55, 71, 79, 81, 94, 95*
Scott, Margretta 19
Screaming Abdabs 101
Seasons, The (Haydn) 26
Secret, The (Smetana) 71, 114

Index to the text (Chapters 1-6) and, selectively, to Appendixes 1-7; * = illustration; (exhib.) = exhibition

Secret Marriage, The 24, 111
Seefried, Irmgard 48
Segerstam, Lief 46
Segovia, Andrés 68, 70
Serge, John 60*
Sessions, Roger 51
Shaftesbury Theatre 66
Shakespeare, William 58
Sharp, Cecil 21, 111
Sharp, Joan 21
Shaw, Dan 55
Shaw, George Bernard 15;
  Candida 20;
  Heartbreak House 24;
  Major Barbara 26;
  Overruled 14;
  Pygmalion 14, 17*
Shaw, Roy 96
Shaw Theatre 23, 28, 67, 68, 70, 72, 75, 79, 81, 87, 88, 90, 91, 92, 93, 93*, 95, 100, 101
Shawe-Taylor, Desmond 19, 76
Shelley, Antony 105
Shelton, Anne 79
Sherry, Sam 89
Shields of Faith (Bliss) 90
Shilling, Eric 35
Shostakovich, Dmitrii 85, 117
Sickert, Walter 15
Sidwell, Martindale 48, 62, 90
Sigurd Leeder School of Drama 24
Silveri, Paulo 48, 48*
Silverlake 105, 105*, 106, 118
Sinclair, Andrew 45
Sinclair, Frederick 8, 11, 13
Sinclair, Jeanette 46
Sinclair, Monica 20, 21*, 25, 27
singers (classical) 121;
  (jazz) 122; (popular) 123
SK Amateur Players 20
Slade School of Fine Art 15, 20
Smetana, Bedřich 71, 114
Smith, Cyril (pianist) 13
Smith, Donald 46
Smith, John Christopher:
  Ulysses 33, 112
Snow Maiden, The 102, 118
Society for the Promotion of New Music 29, 76, 90, 101
Sofa, The (Maconchy) 49, 49*, 113
Sogno di Scipione, Il 51, 113
Soho Theatre 69

Solomon, Yonty 46, 47, 62
Solomos, Dionysios 89
Somers Town 77
Sommerich, Philip 95
Songmakers' Almanac 90
Songs of Death & Immortality 45
sopranos 121
Sorrows of Orpheus, The 26, 111
South American music & dance 123
South Place Ethical Society 9
Spanish music & dance 11, 123
Spark, Muriel 32
Spence, Basil 39
Spender, Stephen 16
Spinalba, La 83, 115
Stabat Mater (Berkeley) 36
Stadlen, Peter 84
Staern, Gunnar 58
Standard Telephones & Cables 96
Stanhope Institute 14, 20
Staples Hall 89
Statira, La 64, 114
Steinitz, Paul 27
Sterling Trust 96
Stewart-Munro, Christine 53, 55, 60, 62, 70, 73
Stilgoe, Richard 65
Stockholm Philharmonic Wind Quintet 58
Stoker, Richard 45
Storace, Stephen 78, 115
Strauss, Johann 87
Strauss, Richard 64, 85, 114, 116, 117
Stravinsky, Igor 34, 83, 84, 91*, 116, 117
'Street Level' 103
Streich, Rita 81
Strich, Elaine 95
string players 120-121
string quartets 119
Studholme, Marion 18, 52
Sumray, Richard 100
Susskind, Walter 46, 47
Sutherland, Joan 2*, 19, 19*, 23, 24
Swann, Donald 52
Swedish Cultural Institute 31
Swedish-themed events 58, 64
Sweet Honey in the Rock 89
Swiss Cottage Baths 28, 106
Swiss Cottage Civic Centre 28, 67, 68, 99

Swiss Cottage Community Centre 89
Swiss Cottage Library 28, 39, 40, 45, 47, 52, 58, 63, 69, 72, 76, 106
Swiss Cottage Odeon 43, 44, 47, 51, 58, 62, 64, 65, 71, 75
Sykes, Eric 77
Sylvester, Victor, Orchestra 87

T
tabla player 60*
talks 125
Tam O'Shanter (Arnold) 48
Tancredi 70, 114
Tate, Phyllis 36, 112
Tate Gallery 45
Tatrai String Quartet 47
'Tattoo' 13
Tavener, John 51
Tavistock Place 9, 24, 26
Tavistock Repertory Company 24
Taylor, William 8, 11, 13, 15, 21, 41
Tchaikovsky, Pyotr 51, 85, 113, 116
te Kanawa, Kiri 59, 60*
Tear, Robert 87
Tel-Aviv String Quartet 47
Telemann, Georg P 44
tenors 121
Terry, Clark, Big Band 87
Thanet Street 11
theatre, *see* drama
Theatre Group Productions 29
Theodora 20, 21*, 111
Theodorakis, Mikis 89
There & Back (Hindemith) 48-49, 113
Think it Over, Giacomino 16
Thomas, Dylan 45
Thomas, Robert 27
Thomas Coram Foundation 90, 103
Thompson, Barbara 86
Thompson, J Walter 38
Thorndyke, Dame Sybil 11, 27
Tickell, Kathryn 89
Tide, The (Blacher) 25*, 111
Tinsley, Pauline 29, 30, 30*, 46
Tippett, Keith 87, 87*
Tippett, Michael 91
Tollefsen, Toralf 11
Tomisson, I D 62, 100
Tomlinson, A 15

Tomlinson, John 76, 85
Torquato Tasso 78, 79*, 81, 115
Torrance, Sydney 55, 62
Toucan Theatre Co. 123
'Towards a Theatre of Sound' 100
Town & City Properties 96
Town & Country Club 105
Tracey, Stan, Quartet 58, 80
Trades Union Congress 39-40
Tree, Herbert Beerbohm 19
Troilus & Cressida (Walton) 85, 116
trumpeters 121
Turco in Italia, Il 36, 36*, 112
Turkish music 88

U
Ucko, Dr Hans 16, 22, 24, 51
Ulysses 33
Under Western Eyes 59, 67, 114
United States Embassy 81
Unity Theatre 11, 20, 24, 34, 42, 58, 67, 124
University Collegiate Theatre, *see* Collegiate Theatre

V
Valjakka, Taru 48
Van Barthold, Kenneth 52
Vanbrugh, Sir John 24
'Variety Show' 76
Vaughan-Thomas, Wynford 14
Vaughan Williams, Ralph 37, 90
Les Vêpres Siciliennes 85, 115
Verdi, Giuseppe 23, 29, 32, 39, 56;
  Aroldo 34, 34*, 112;
  Il Corsaro 45-46, 113;
  Ernani 32-33, 32*, 85, 112;
  Un Giorno di Regno 27, 28*, 111;
  Giovanna d'Arco 34;
  I Masnadieri 29, 30, 30*, 111;
Victoria & Albert Museum 45
Vienna State Opera 26
Viggo-Bentzon, Niels 29
violinists 120
Vivaldi, Antonio 29, 44, 87, 117
vocal groups (classical) 121
'Voices and Verses' 76
Voix Humaine, La 64, 65, 114

Index to the text (Chapters 1-6) and, selectively, to Appendixes 1-7; * = illustration; (exhib.) = exhibition

W
Walker, Ivor 55, 75, 96, 98, 101
Walker, Norman 18
Wall, Richard 69
Walsh, Stephen 49
Walton, Sir William 25, 85, 116
Wanamaker, Sam 16
Wandering Scholar The 48, 113
Ward, Joseph 49*
Wares, Christine 81
water polo 57
Waterproof (Larrieu) 106
Watford, Gwen 90
Watney Mann Ltd 59, 67
Watts, Trevor 86, 86*
Webster, Jean 19
Weill, Kurt 44, 51, 102, 105, 106, 107
Weir, Gillian 44
Welch, Elizabeth 88
Welfare State, The 71
Welin, Karl Erik 58
Wellcome Foundation 91
Wells, Doreen 28

Wesker, Arnold 32, 40
West Hampstead Community Centre 89
West Indian music & dance 123
West Square Electronic Music Ensemble 100
Westbrook, John 90
Westbrook, Mike 37, 52, 80, 86
Wheldon, Huw 14
Whettam, Graham 46
White, Don 71, 76
White, Willard 81
Whitestone Pond 40, 57
Whitman, Walt 46-47
Wicks, Denis 25*
Wilde, Oscar 29
William Ellis School 91
Williams, John 23, 37, 37*, 44, 52, 58, 65, 72, 95
Williams, Michael 90
Williamson, Julian 90, 90*
Williamson, Malcolm 48
Willis, Chris: *Other Voices* 102
Wilson, Harold 50

Wilson, Rowland Holt 25
Wind Music Society 20
wind players 121
Wirkkala, Tapio 47
Wistrich, Enid 42, 70
Witts, Dick 99, 101-102, 104, 106, 107
Wolf, Hugo 44, 81
Wolf, Ilse 26, 29
Wolf, Mary 55
Wolf-Ferrari, Ermanno 73, 84, 117
Wolfit, Sir Donald 29
Wood, Anne 96
Woolf, John 96
Woolf, Noel 40, 42, 43, 50, 53, 55, 57, 61, 62, 66, 67, 68
Workers' Educational Association 58
Workers' Music Association 11
Working Class Dramatic Club 9
Working Men's College 9, 15, 19, 20, 26, 36, 42, 97

world music, *see* 'International …'
World Saxophone Quartet 86
World War Two 9-10
Wright, Brian 90, 90*
writers 124
Wynn, Sandy 97

Y
'Yesterday and Today' (exhib.) 13
Young Musicians' Symphony Orchestra 81
Young, Alexander 20
'Young Festival' 103, 105
'Your Concert Nights' 33
'Your Discussion Nights' 33
Youth and Music 33, 34, 37, 44, 48, 51, 105
youth parliaments 10, 12

Z
Zairean music & dance 123
Zemel Choir 48
Zemire & Azor 116

The Camden History Society

was formed in 1965, soon after the amalgamation of three metropolitan boroughs into the London Borough of Camden, to explore and portray aspects of the history of all parts of the new borough. Its publications result from research into Camden's buildings, institutions, former residents, artistic endeavour (as in this book), modes of transport, political change, family history, popular entertainment, or working and living conditions of the poor and unsung as well as the rich and powerful. The range of length as well as subject matter is wide, from articles of 1000–5000 words in the annual *Camden History Review* through the longer, separate publications called Occasional Papers on subjects such as the railways of Camden, magistrates' courts, or an inner-London mission in the 19th century, to full-length books which include nine historical street surveys in different parts of the Borough. Monthly talks are held in different parts of the Borough. Outings and walks are arranged in the summer. Members of the Society receive a bi-monthly illustrated Newsletter gratis.

To join the Society, write to the Hon. Secretary, c/o Camden Local Studies and Archives Centre, Holborn Library, 32–38 Theobalds Road, London WC1X 8PA

For a list of the Society's publications, write to the Publications Manager Flat 13, 13 Tavistock Place, London WC1H 9SH

Printed by Witley Press Hunstanton Norfolk